# WOMEN AS SCRIBES

*Book Production and Monastic Reform in Twelfth-Century Bavaria*

Professor Beach's book on female scribes in twelfth-century Bavaria – the first full-length study of the role of women copyists in the Middle Ages – is underpinned by the notion that the scriptorium was central to the intellectual revival of the Middle Ages and that women played a role in this renaissance. The author examines the exceptional quantity of evidence of female scribal activity in three different religious communities, pointing out the various ways in which the women worked – alone, with other women, and even alongside men – to produce books for monastic libraries, and discussing why their work should have been made visible, whereas that of other female scribes remains invisible. Beach's focus on manuscript production, and the religious, intellectual, social, and economic factors which shaped that production, enables her to draw wide-ranging conclusions of interest not only to paleographers but also to those interested in reading, literacy, religious and gender history.

ALISON I. BEACH is Assistant Professor of Religion, College of William and Mary, Williamsburg, Virginia.

*Cambridge Studies in Palaeography and Codicology*



This series has been established to further the study of manuscripts from the Middle Ages to the Renaissance. It includes books devoted to particular types of manuscripts, their production and circulation, to individual codices of outstanding importance, and to regions, periods, and scripts of especial interest to scholars. The series will be of interest not only to scholars and students of medieval literature and history, but also to theologians, art historians, and others working with manuscript sources.

ALREADY PUBLISHED

Bernhard Bischoff, translated by Michael Gorman *Manuscripts and Libraries in the Age of Charlemagne*

Richard Gameson *The Early Medieval Bible: Its Production, Decoration and Use*

Nancy Netzer *Cultural Interplay in the Eighth Century: The Trier Gospels and the Making of a Scriptorium at Echternach*

William Noel *The Harley Psalter*

Charles F. Briggs *Giles of Rome's* De regimine principum: *Reading and Writing Politics at Court and University, c. 1275–c. 1525*

Leslie Brubaker *Vision and Meaning in Ninth-Century Byzantium: Image as Exegesis in the Homilies of Gregory of Nazianzus*

Francis Newton *The Scriptorium and Library at Monte Cassino, 1058–1105*

Lisa Fagin Davis *The Gottschalk Antiphonary: Music and Liturgy in Twelfth-Century Lambach*

Albert Derolez *The Palaeography of Gothic Manuscript Books: From the Twelfth to the Early Sixteenth Century*

# WOMEN AS SCRIBES

*Book Production and Monastic Reform in Twelfth-Century Bavaria*

ALISON I. BEACH

CAMBRIDGE
UNIVERSITY PRESS

**CAMBRIDGE**
**UNIVERSITY PRESS**

University Printing House, Cambridge CB2 8BS, United Kingdom

Published in the United States of America by Cambridge University Press, New York

Cambridge University Press is part of the University of Cambridge.

It furthers the University's mission by disseminating knowledge in the pursuit of education, learning and research at the highest international levels of excellence.

www.cambridge.org
Information on this title: www.cambridge.org/9780521792431



First published 2004

*A catalogue record for this publication is available from the British Library*

*Library of Congress Cataloguing in Publication data*
Beach, Alison I.
Women as scribes: book production and monastic reform in twelfth-century Bavaria / Alison I. Beach.
p. cm. – (Cambridge studies in palaeography and codicology; 10)
Originally presented as author's thesis (doctoral) – Columbia University
Includes bibliographical references (p. 173) and index.
ISBN 0 521 79243 6
1. Scriptoria – Germany – Bavaria – History – To 1500.
2. Scribes – Germany – Bavaria – History– To 1500. 3. Women in Christianity – History – Middle Ages, 600–1500. 4. Books – Germany – History – 400–1400.
5. Manuscripts, Medieval – Germany – Bavaria – History. 6. Monasticism and religious orders – Germany – Bavaria – History– To 1500. 7. Wessobrunn (Monastery) – History – To 1500. 8. Stift Admont – History – To 1500. 9. Schèftlarn (Monastery: Schèftlarn, Germany) – History – To 1500. 10. Civilization, Medieval – 12th century. I. Title. II. Series.
Z801.B3B43 2003
745.6′1 – dc21 2003048559

ISBN 978-0-521-79243-1 Hardback
ISBN 978-0-521-12694-6 Paperback

For David

# *Contents*

# *Illustrations*

COLOPHONS



PALAEOGRAPHICAL FIGURES

These will be found between pp. 149 and 173.

# *Tables*

# *Acknowledgments*

This book began as a question – a question posed to me in 1992 by Maria Grandinette (then head of the Conservation Unit at the University of Michigan Libraries, now head of Conservation Treatment at Stanford University), a fellow participant in one of the early online discussion groups at the University of Michigan. Her question was a simple one: "Did women copy books in the Middle Ages?" What follows here is the beginning of an answer to her question.

I could not have undertaken and completed this project without the encouragement and support of many people. My greatest thanks are due to Robert Somerville, my doctoral advisor at Columbia University, who encouraged me to pursue this project and has remained supportive throughout. Special thanks are also due to Caroline W. Bynum, Consuelo Dutschke, Joan Ferrante, Elisabeth Klemm, Raymund Kottje, Milton McC. Gatch, and Johann Tomaschek, who provided useful comments and criticism when the book was still a dissertation, and to Giles Constable, Barbara Rosenwein, and Rodney Thomson, who generously read the typescript and provided a wealth of helpful suggestions. Many other friends and colleagues also provided support and advice along the way, especially Michael Blum, Katrinette Bodarwé, Stephan Borgehammar, Adam Cohen, Rachel Fulton, and Stefanie Seeberg. I would also like to thank Rosamond McKitterick and Teresa Webber, my series editors at Cambridge University Press, through whose patience and criticism this has become a much better book.

I would also like to acknowledge the support and hospitality of a number of institutions: the Bayerische Staatsbibliothek, the Department of Religion at Columbia University, Hill Monastic Manuscript Library, the Institute for Advanced Study, Stift Admont, Stift Vorau, and the Universitätsbibliothek Würzburg.

Finally, I would like to thank my family: my parents, who have accepted my calling beyond our family business with grace, love, and even heartfelt enthusiasm; my children, Andrew and Eliza, who always remind me of what is most important in life; and my husband David, whose love and support are beyond measure.

# *Abbreviations*

| | |
|---|---|
| AASS | Acta sanctorum . . . editio novissima |
| CLA | Lowe, Elias Avery, ed. *Codices latini antiquiores: A Palaeographical Guide to Latin Manuscripts prior to the Ninth Century.* Oxford, 1934–1966 |
| Clm | *Codex latinus monacensis* |
| CSEL | Corpus scriptorum ecclesiasticorum Latinorum |
| JL | Jaffé, Philipp, *Regesta pontificum romanorum ab condita ecclesia ad annum post Christum natum MCXCVIII.* Second edition, corrected and supplemented by Samuel Loewenfeld, Ferdinand Kaltenbrunner, and Paul Ewald. 2 vols. Graz, 1956. |
| *LThK* | *Lexikon für Theologie und Kirche* |
| MBKg | *Mittelalterliche Bibliothekskataloge Deutschlands und der Schweiz,* vol. IV/2. ed. Günther Glauche and Hermann Knaus |
| MBKr | *Mittelalterliche Bibliothekskataloge Deutschlands und der Schweiz,* vol. III/1. ed. Paul Ruf |
| MGH | *Monumenta Germaniae Historica* |
| ÖMBK | *Mittelalterliche Bibliothekskataloge Österreichs*, vol. III, ed. G. Möser-Mersky |
| PL | *Patrologiae cursus completus: series latina*, ed. J. P. Migne, 221 vols., Paris, 1841–1864 |
| RB 1980 | *RB 1980: The Rule of Saint Benedict in Latin and English*, ed. Timothy Fry. Collegeville, MN, 1981 |
| *StM* | *Studien und Mitteilungen zur Geschichte des Benediktiner-Ordens und seiner Zweige* |

# 1

## *Introduction*

In the last quarter of the twelfth century, a scribe at a newly founded Premonstratensian monastery near Munich put the finishing touches to a manuscript containing homilies on the Epistles and Gospels. She then took an unusual step. At the bottom of the final folio she drew a cross, and within it wrote: "This book, which sister Irmingart wrote with the permission of Prior Henry, belongs to the monastery of Saint Dionysius, Schäftlarn."[1] Irmingart thus became one of a small number of twelfth-century scribes – female or male – to record her own name.[2]

It would be easy to assume that Irmingart was exceptional in her role as a scribe since hers are among the very few surviving twelfth-century manuscripts that bear a female name.[3] But most of the surviving manuscripts from the early and central Middle Ages are unsigned, a fact that may in part be attributed to the monastic quest for humility. The exacting work of copying manuscripts was seen as a pious labor, and at many monastic communities, taking credit for scribal work with a signature might have been interpreted as an expression of pride. But some monastic scribes – male and female – did record their names, reminding us that the decision

1 "Iste liber pertinet ad sanctum dyonisium sceftlaren quem scripsit soror Irmengart obtentu domni. Hainrici prepositi." Munich, Bayerische Staatsbibliothek Clm 17087, f. 223v. See Figure A.

2 The names of scribes – both female and male – were seldom recorded before the fifteenth century, at least so far as surviving evidence suggests. For a systematic listing, see Bénédictins du Bouveret in *Colophons de manuscrits occidentaux des origines au XVIe siècle*, Spicilegii Friburgensis Subsidia 2–7 (Fribourg, 1979). Later manuscripts have survived in greater numbers, partially accounting for the higher numbers of signed manuscripts from the fourteenth and fifteenth centuries. For a discussion of the factors that led to the increase in the use of scribal colophons after the fourteenth century, see the introduction to P. R. Robinson, *Catalogue of Dated and Datable Manuscripts c. 737–1600 in Cambridge Libraries* (Cambridge, 1988), pp. 5–12, and Bernard Bischoff, *Latin Palaeography: Antiquity and the Middle Ages*, trans. Dáibhí Ó Cróinín and David Ganz (Cambridge, 1990), pp. 42–44.

3 Of the approximately 1,615 pre-twelfth-century scribal subscriptions listed in Bénédictins du Bouveret, *Colophons*, only roughly 1 percent (16) are female.

to sign or not to sign a manuscript was informed by more than interest, or lack thereof, in humility.[4]

In spite of their propensity to anonymity – whatever its motivations – female copyists emerge also from other monastic houses in Bavaria. The names of female scribes from Benedictine Admont and Wessobrunn survive in a variety of written sources: necrologies, charters, booklists, and in the prefaces of exegetical works. While these women did not identify themselves, their contemporaries celebrated their achievements and recorded their names. The shadowy presence of female scribes at other monastic centers, in Bavaria as well as in other parts of Europe, suggests that Admont, Schäftlarn, and Wessobrunn were exceptional, not in their employment of women in the scriptorium, but in the degree to which their female scribes are now visible to us. This fact has important implications for the study of the role of medieval women in the production of books and the transmission of texts. Rather than ask why the names of so few have survived, we must explore the process by which the names that are known have been preserved. How did these scribes escape anonymity? What elements of their monastic life permitted them to record their names, or prompted others to commemorate their activity in written form? And most importantly, what do these women and their books have to say about female participation in, and contributions to, the monastic reformation of the twelfth century – particularly in Germanic lands, which have often been neglected in studies of medieval intellectual development and religious reform?

## SETTING THE STAGE

The record of a medieval scribe's name and the copy to which it was added first had to win the fight for physical survival. The carefully repaired tear extending diagonally across the cruciform colophon in Irmingart's book of homilies (see Figure A) reflects the fragility of the evidence. Charred folios in several volumes attributed to the twelfth century's most prolific known female scribe, Diemut of Wessobrunn, also remind us of how easily manuscripts can be damaged and destroyed. In fact, when her monastery's library was cataloged in 1803, only fourteen of Diemut's original corpus of forty-five books were still extant in the collection. The preservation of the bulk of the evidence of female scribal activity, it seems, is the result of chance.

[4] See Albert Derolez, "Pourquoi les copistes signaient-ils leurs manuscrits?" in *Scribi e colofoni: le sottoscrizioni di copisti dalle origini all'avvento della stampa*, ed. Emma Condello and Giuseppe de Gregoria, Atti del seminario di Erice 10. Colloquio del Comité international de paléographie latine. 23–28 October 1993 (Spoleto, 1995), pp. 37–56.

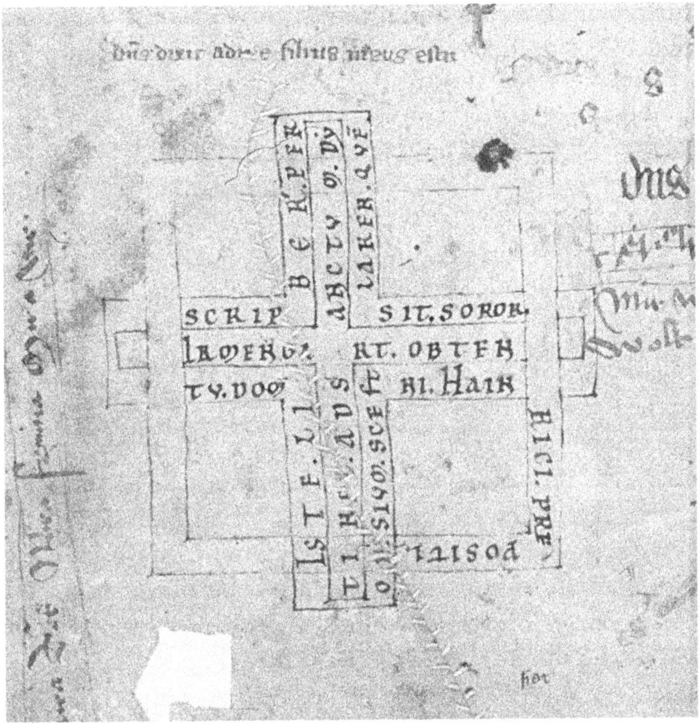

Figure A Cruciform colophon in Irmingart's book of homilies which reads: *Iste liber pertinet ad sanctum dyonisium sceftlaren quem scripsit soror Irmengart obtentu domni. Hainrici prepositi.* (This book, which sister Irmingart wrote with the permission of Prior Henry, belongs to the monastery of Saint Dionysius, Schäftlarn.)

A second critical factor was the success in Germany of the double monastery.[5] Dual-sex monasticism, wherever it was present and whatever form it took, could prove a favorable climate for female scribes throughout the Middle Ages.[6]

5 Recent scholars have called into question the use of this term, which has traditionally been used to describe a variety of institutional arrangements at religious communities with both female and male members. See Penelope D. Johnson, *Equal in Monastic Profession: Religious Women in Medieval France* (Chicago, 1991), p. 7; Penny Schine Gold, *The Lady and the Virgin: Image, Attitude and Experience in Twelfth-Century France* (Chicago, 1985), pp. 101–102; Sharon Elkins, *Holy Women of Twelfth-Century England* (Chapel Hill, 1988), pp. xvii–xviii. While the term may, in fact, obscure the diversity of types of dual-sex communities, it is a convenient description that can be supplemented and refined with a discussion of the precise institutional relationship between male and female members. I use it in this study to indicate a community of both male and female religious organized under one superior and sharing a common endowment. The details of the individual structure and the relationship between the sexes (as far as these are known) will be provided for each community. On early medieval dual-sex religious communities, see Catherine Peyroux, *The Governance of Women: Double Monasteries in the Early Medieval West* (Ithaca, NY, forthcoming).

6 Rosamond McKitterick, "Nuns' Scriptoria in England and Francia in the Eighth Century," in her *Books, Scribes and Learning in the Frankish Kingdoms, 6th–9th Centuries* (Aldershot, 1994), article VII,

Twelfth-century dual-sex monasteries tended to receive the support of wealthy aristocratic and royal families, and wealth brought freedom from the daily manual tasks required for subsistence in poorly endowed communities, leaving monks and nuns more time for intellectual pursuits.[7] Operating a scriptorium was expensive, in terms of both materials and human capital, putting book production out of the reach of many small women's monasteries. At some double communities, nuns had access to a larger library for books to read or copy than they had at small, isolated, all-female houses. Greater financial resources, combined with the lively intellectual life that characterized many twelfth-century dual-sex monasteries, encouraged the production of books by both men and women.

The post-medieval politics of centralization also played a role in the preservation of the names and work of twelfth-century female scribes. The transfer of many Bavarian manuscripts to a central library in Munich under Napoleon in 1803 may partially explain why most of the surviving examples of the work of known named and namable female scribes are from Bavaria.[8] Consolidation within a secular institutional context helped to ensure the survival of numerous monastic libraries – including those of Wessobrunn and Schäftlarn – by preventing the further scattering and destruction of books through sale, theft, and war. Admont, which was not secularized in the nineteenth century, has remained in continuous operation since the eleventh century, and still houses its medieval library almost intact.[9]

The survival of a scribe's work is not sufficient, however, to ensure recognition of his or her activity. Preserving the identity of those named – and discovering still others whose names are lost – depends even now on attracting the attention of scholars. The prevailing assumption that monks but not nuns produced books in the Middle Ages is a formidable obstacle. While scholars have long been aware

pp. 29–30 notes the importance of double monasteries as a context in which female scribes are found. Not all double monasteries, however, provided such a favorable climate. The Gilbertines did not encourage female participation in book production. See Brian Golding, *Gilbert of Sempringham and the Gilbertine Order c. 1130–1300* (Oxford, 1995), pp. 183–184. The Premonstratensians likewise restricted female reading. See p. 115 below.

7 Jean Leclercq, "Otium Monasticum as a Context for Artistic Creativity," in *Monasticism and the Arts*, ed. Timothy Gregory Verdon (Syracuse, 1984), pp. 63–80.

8 Elisabeth Klemm, *Die romanischen Handschriften der Bayerischen Staatsbibliothek*, 3 vols. (Wiesbaden, 1980–). Annemarie Weyl Carr, "Women as Artists in the Middle Ages," *The Feminist Art Journal* 5 (1976): 5, notes that the majority of known female artists from the twelfth century were German.

9 The most recent catalog was compiled in the nineteenth century by librarian Jakob Wichner. Copies of his *Catalogus codicum manu scriptorum Admontensis* (Admont, 1888) are available from University Microfilm International (UMI) through their Books on Demand program. Not all of Admont's surviving twelfth-century manuscripts remain at the monastery. The house experienced serious financial difficulties during the 1930s and sold seventy-five of its medieval manuscripts. A large collection of Bohemian manuscripts once owned by Admont is now in Prague, and there are twelfth-century manuscripts from Admont in Chicago at the Newberry Library, in New York at the Pierpont Morgan Library, and at Princeton University. See ÖMBK III, pp. 8–12 for a list of manuscripts sold and their destinations.

that women copied books in some medieval monasteries, they have tended not to consider women's houses or double communities when investigating the origin of a book.[10] As medieval manuscripts are cataloged and localized, the presumption of male scribal identity deflects attention from women's houses. Recent scholarship has taken note of a few extraordinary women and the books that they helped to create, particularly Hildegard of Bingen and the Wiesbaden codex of her *Scivias*, and Herrad of Hohenbourg's *Hortus deliciarum*. But the more ordinary women who did more ordinary work have largely escaped notice.[11]

## LOOKING FOR FEMALE SCRIBES

In this book, I propose a systematic approach to identifying the work of female copyists. I begin with the conviction that it is impossible to determine the sex of a scribe based on any supposed inherent difference in the handwriting of men and women. Female hands have been described variously as delicate, irregular, nervous, and light – judgments based on attitudes toward women rather than on sound paleographical evidence.[12] Women at a particular scribal center may have been trained to write a highly distinctive book hand, but only its demonstrated use by female copyists marks that hand as feminine.[13] I propose a more critical approach to identifying female hands that draws on a variety of sources including manuscript colophons, paleographical analysis, and references to female copyists in literary works and monastery records.

10 Rosamond McKitterick, for example, has criticized the absence of any reference to women's houses in Hartmut Hoffmann's survey of Ottonian and early Salian manuscripts in his *Buchkunst und Königtum im ottonischen und frühsalischen Reich*, MGH, Schriften 30 (Stuttgart, 1986). See Rosamond McKitterick, "Continuity and Innovation in Tenth-Century Ottonian Culture," in *Intellectual Life in the Middle Ages*, ed. Lesley Smith and Benedicta Ward (London, 1992), pp. 17–21.

11 One exception is P. R. Robinson, "A Twelfth-Century *Scriptrix* from Nunnaminster," in *Of the Making of Books: Medieval Manuscripts, their Scribes and Readers: Essays Presented to M. B. Parkes*, ed. P. R. Robinson and Rivkah Zim (Aldershot, 1997), pp. 77–93.

12 According to Meta Harrsen, "The Manuscripts," in *Hroswitha of Gandersheim: Her Life, Times, and Works, and a Comprehensive Bibliography*, ed. Anne Lyon Haight (New York, 1965), Conrad Celtes made one of the earliest known attempts to identify a "female" hand, reporting his findings in the first printed edition of Hrotsvita von Gandersheim's *Opera* (Nuremberg, 1501). Celtes came upon a manuscript of Hrotsvita's complete works at Regensburg, effectively rediscovering the work of the poet after centuries of obscurity, and identified the manuscript (Clm 14485) as the work of a nun. For a summary of Celtes' assessment of the "female" hand found in the manuscript, see Harrsen, "The Manuscripts," p. 43.

13 The ninth-century nun-scribes of Chelles, for example, wrote a distinctive script, the so-called b-type. See Bernard Bischoff, "Die Kölner Nonnenhandschriften und das Skriptorium von Chelles," *Mittelalterliche Studien* 1 (Stuttgart, 1966): 16–34 and Bischoff, *Latin Palaeography*, pp. 106–107. There is nothing identifiably feminine about the formation of the letters or their execution by the nuns.

The only definitive evidence of a scribe's sex is a self-identification in a contemporary colophon, a written notice containing any combination of date, manuscript origin, or scribe's name, but these are uncommon before the fifteenth century, and even then the increase is confined to certain regions.[14] When a copyist's name appears in a manuscript produced by a team, it is usually found at the beginning or end of the last gathering in the hand of that quire or group of quires and allows the positive identification of only that one hand as female. Slightly more common is a contemporary record of a scribe's name written at the bottom of a folio at the beginning or end of a quire by a hand other than the text hand, sometimes in combination with the word *scripsit.* Since identification thus depends on a second party's knowledge of the manuscript's production, some element of doubt as to the copyist's identity is introduced.[15] A scribal identification written by a later hand is less secure still, especially if the writer relied on a traditional attribution to a particular scribe rather than on first-hand knowledge. Additional corroborating information, either paleographical or external, is needed before an attribution based on the later addition of a scribe's name can be accepted.[16]

Anonymous female scribes can sometimes be identified by their intimate collaboration with a named female scribe when hand changes occur within a quire. Scribes from a community of strictly enclosed canonesses or nuns must have had their own scriptorium, even if their work was subsequently supervised and corrected by one or more of the men.[17] Cloistered women would not have worked side by side with monks or canons, and it is difficult, in this context, to imagine the collaboration of male and female copyists within quires. For this degree of collaboration to work in a cloistered setting, a gathering would have passed from the nuns' enclosure into the monks' scriptorium and back again, and in cases where hands alternate, this scenario would have been repeated several times. It is much more likely that cloistered nuns or canonesses worked together within quires with

[14] For a collection of recent studies on scribes and colophons, see *Scribi e colofoni*, ed. Condello and de Gregoria.

[15] The process of binding, which generally included trimming to produce uniform margins, may account for the absence of names, commonly recorded at the bottom of the folios, in most manuscripts. Some names could be retained and others lost when the manuscript was prepared for successive bindings.

[16] In monastic scriptoria of the Carolingian age where scribes worked in teams, it was not uncommon for individual gatherings to be marked with the name of the copyist to whom each section was assigned. David Ganz, "The Preconditions for Caroline Minuscule," *Viator* 18 (1987): 35–36. On the difficulties with and issues surrounding the identification of named and namable scribes, see James J. John, "The Named (and Namable) Scribes in *Codices Latini Antiquiores*," in *Scribi e colofoni*, ed. Condello and de Gregoria, pp. 107–121.

[17] I use the term scriptorium throughout the book to signify not only a particular room within the monastery, but any place or places (such as a recluse's cell or cloister walk) where writing was done as part of the organized activity of two or more scribes.

other women. This assumption allows for the provisional recognition of the work of a number of previously unidentified female collaborators.

Once the hand of a named scribe or an unnamed female collaborator has been identified, it is sometimes possible to identify additional examples of her work. But a scribe was a person whose mood and pace of work, level of skill and age changed, preventing her from using uniform letter forms, abbreviations, and duct throughout her career. She might also adapt her writing to reflect changing stylistic concerns. To reflect the inherent uncertainty in scribal identifications, I have adopted the following terminology to describe the likelihood of a scribal match: very likely not identical, possibly identical, probably identical, very likely identical.[18]

Non-manuscript evidence of the scribal skills of women can come in a variety of forms, and can help to document the existence of scriptoria at individual communities. A few necrologies from the twelfth and early thirteenth centuries record the names of female copyists. These death records consist simply of the woman's name and the title *scriba* or *scriptrix*. Although it is seldom possible to isolate the work of these women among the surviving manuscripts produced at their communities, evidence from necrologies alerts us to the presence there of female scribes. Occasionally an author credits a religious woman with recording or transcribing his or her work, opening up the possibility of finding examples of the hands of women in the earliest copy of the text and in any subsequent authorial recensions. In several instances surviving correspondence to and from women's communities contains a request that books be sent or copies be made, or a discussion of procuring materials needed for copying and illuminating. And in the unique case of Diemut of Wessobrunn, there is a contemporary list of the books she copied.

Once a female scribe and, where possible, her books have been identified, the next step is to situate these in their institutional context. Here, her community provides insight into the training and employment of women in the scriptorium, the local importance of books, and the status of those who could help to produce them. The books, in turn, extend our knowledge of the community that made them. What can a manuscript copied by a woman tell us about her community? The archaeology of the book – its parchment, handwriting, construction, and other physical features – can yield information unavailable elsewhere about the community that created it. Did the monastery operate a school in which women were taught to write? Did they copy books for their own use, the use of their male counterparts, or for sale or exchange beyond the immediate community? Were women given inferior materials with which to work? What were the intellectual interests of the community? The working practices of individual

18 This is an adaptation of the terminology used by Christine Elizabeth Eder, *Die Schule des Klosters Tegernsee in frühen Mittelalter im Spiegel der Tegernseer Handschriften*, Münchener Beiträge zur Mediävistik und Renaissance-Forschung (Munich, 1972), p. 54, n. 3.

scribes – speed of execution (as indicated by, for example, the degree of attention paid to calligraphic detail and consistency of form), level of productivity, type of texts copied, and patterns of collaboration with other scribes– tell us about the needs and circumstances of each community. Some manuscripts even provide clues as to the strictness of claustration and the extent of interaction between the sexes.

## FROM EIGHTH-CENTURY ENGLAND TO TWELFTH-CENTURY BAVARIA

The female scribes of twelfth-century Bavaria were part of a long tradition of female involvement in monastic book production in Germany, beginning with the arrival of the Anglo-Saxon nuns involved with the missions of Saints Boniface and Lul. The evidence of the book-related activity of these early medieval women is a composite of brief moments of visibility pieced together from saints' lives, monastic rules, correspondence, and manuscripts that bear witness to their interest in literary pursuits and in the production of books. The communities in which early medieval female scribes lived and worked were linked to their twelfth-century counterparts by a common interest in literary pursuits, and consequently, in assembling book collections.

### *A shared tradition of women's education*

Boniface's German mission depended heavily upon a network of newly established religious houses to promote Christianity in recently evangelized rural areas, and English double monasteries were a primary source of people to colonize these outposts. The nuns who traveled to Germany to populate the new monastic centers are links in a strong tradition of education for religious women that can be traced at least as far back as the early fifth century, when St. Jerome wrote a letter to Laeta in response to her inquiry about the proper way to educate her daughter, Paula, who was destined for life as a virgin.[19] He instructed Laeta to make Paula a set of letters of boxwood or ivory so that she might learn their order and sounds, and to guide her hand as she learned to write using a stylus and wax tablet.[20] As she grew

[19] Letter 107, dated 403. Isidorus Hilberg, ed., CSEL 55, pp. 290–305; F. A. Wright, ed. and trans., *Select Letters of Saint Jerome* (London, 1933), pp. 338–370.

[20] "Fiant ei litterae vel buxae vel eburneae et suis nominibus appellentur. Ludat in eis, ut et lusus eius eruditio sit, et non teneat litterarum, ut memoria nominum in canticum transeat, sed ipse inter se crebro ordo turbetur et mediis ultima, primis media misceantur, ut eas non sonu tantum, sed et visu noverit. Cum vero trementi manu stilum in cera ducere, vel alterius superposita manu teneri regantur articuli vel in tabella sculpantur elementa, ut per eosdem sulcos inclusa marginibus trahantur vestigia et foras non queant evagari." (Get her a set of letters made of boxwood or ivory

older, Paula was to be instructed in both Greek and Latin to facilitate her study of Scripture.[21]

Expectations for female literacy in some religious houses in Merovingian Gaul were similarly high. The nuns of St. John at Arles, a women's community founded in 512 by Bishop Caesarius (d. 543), followed a rule that included a precise schedule for devotional reading and that stipulated that girls were not to be admitted to the community until they were old enough to learn their letters. Most of the nuns at Arles were from either aristocratic or royal families – families that tended to value education, and Caesarius himself was a product of this milieu. His aristocratic views of literacy likely contributed to his insistence that his nuns learn to read and write.[22] Caesarius' hagiographer confirmed that these were critical activities at Arles, adding that the nuns copied sacred texts, a skill that they learned from their abbess.[23]

Contemporary Irish monastic and cultural traditions also influenced the education and activities of nuns in Gaul. Monks from Luxeuil, St. Columbanus' monastery in Gaul, supported the expansion of women's monasticism in the seventh century and were involved directly with several important foundations.[24] A network of Frankish double monasteries, including Jouarre, Faremoutiers, Chelles, Notre-Dame de Soissons, and Notre-Dame de Laon began to grow under the influence of Luxeuil.[25] The hagiographers of nun- and abbess-saints from these communities also considered intellectual gifts to be evidence of female sanctity,

and call each by its proper name. Let her play with these, so that even her play may teach her something, and let her not only learn the correct order of the letters and remember their names in a simple song, but also frequently upset their order and mix the last letters with the middle ones, the middle with the first. Thus she will know them all by sight and sound. Also, as soon as she begins to use a stylus upon wax and her hand is still unsteady, either guide her soft fingers with your hand laid upon hers, or else have simple copies cut upon a tablet so that her writing may follow their outlines and keep to their limits without straying away.) CSEL 55, p. 294; Wright, *Letters*, pp. 345–347.

21 "Reddat tibi pensum cotidie scripturarum certum. Ediscat Graecorum versuum numerum. Sequatur statim et Latina eruditio." (Let her repeat to you a portion of the Scriptures every day as her fixed task. She should learn a good number of Greek verses by heart, but knowledge of the Latin should follow soon after.) CSEL 55, p. 300; Wright, *Letters*, pp. 358–359. Large portions of this letter were incorporated into the Aachen legislation for canonesses promulgated during 816–819 under Emperor Louis the Pious. See below, p. 20.

22 See Pierre Riché, *Education and Culture in the Barbarian West*, trans. John J. Contreni (Columbia, SC, 1976), p. 293, and Suzanne Fonay Wemple, *Women in Frankish Society: Marriage and the Cloister, 500–900* (Philadelphia, 1985), pp. 175–187.

23 "inter psalmos atque ieiunia, vigilias quoque et lectiones, libros divinos pulchre scriptitent virgines Christi, ipsam matrem magistram habentes." (between the psalms and fasts, vigils and readings, the virgins of Christ copied divine books beautifully, having the mother herself for a teacher.) *Sancti Caesarii vita*, Sancti Caesarii Episcopi Arelatensis Opera Omnia 2, ed. D. Germanus Morin (Maretioli, 1942), p. 320.

24 Riché, *Education and Culture*, p. 377; Wemple, *Women in Frankish Society*, p. 159.

25 For a discussion of female scribal activity at these houses, see McKitterick, "Nuns' Scriptoria," article VII, pp. 1–35.

and education generally was thought to encourage spiritual growth by facilitating devotional reading and scriptural study. This connection between learning and sanctity, which tells us as much about hagiographer as about saint, is consistently made from the sixth through the ninth century. Literacy could provide religious women with an outlet for good works as teachers and scribes, even from within the confines of the cloister. Among the books produced at these centers are a number that bear the name of a female scribe or scribes.

The positive evaluation of the spiritual benefits of reading common to both the Caesarian and Columbanian monastic traditions was transmitted also through absorption into several seventh-century rules for women. Aurelian of Arles and two monks from Luxeuil, Donatus and Waldebert, wrote rules for nuns that combined educational elements of both traditions.[26]

By the end of the century, a growing number of double houses followed the Rule of Saint Benedict, which also mandated both private and communal reading.[27] In his commentary on Benedict's Rule, written around the middle of the ninth century, Hildemar stated that literate adults were to gather in the cloister where they were to sit apart during the periods of *lectio*. They were expected not only to read, but to demonstrate some degree of comprehension before receiving a new book.[28] Children were expected to read in a supervised group in which, presumably, instruction might be offered.[29]

The monasteries adhering to these rules provided a favorable climate for the intellectual activities of nuns in Gaul. According to Bede, many daughters of the English aristocracy entered the monasteries of Merovingian Gaul in the seventh century, and the king of Kent, Earconberht (d. 664), sent his daughter Earcongota to Brie to become a nun at Faremoutiers.[30] Before she became abbess of Hartlepool in Northumbria and later first abbess of Whitby, Hild had planned to travel to Gaul to join her sister Hereswitha at Chelles.[31]

26 For a translation (with commentary) of the Rules of Donatus and Waldebert, see Jo Ann McNamara, *The Ordeal of Community* (Toronto, 1993). See also Hope Mayo, "Three Merovingian Rules for Women," Ph.D. diss. (Harvard University, 1974).

27 RB 1980 38: 1–12 (mealtime readers and reading), 48: 4–5 and 13 (private devotional reading), 48: 16–23 (Lenten reading).

28 Mary Alfred Schroll, *Benedictine Monasticism as Reflected in the Warnefrid-Hildemar Commentaries on the Rule* (New York, 1941), pp. 120–121.

29 Mayke de Jong, "Growing up in a Carolingian Monastery: Magister Hildemar and his Oblates," *Journal of Medieval History* 9 (1983): 115.

30 Bede, *Ecclesiastical History of the English People*, ed. and trans. Bertram Colgrave and R. A. B. Mynors (Oxford, 1969), pp. 236, 238. See also Dagmar Beate Baltrusch-Schnieder, "Klosterleben als Alternative Lebensform zur Ehe?" in *Weibliche Lebensgestaltung im frühen Mittelalter*, ed. Hans-Werner Goetz (Cologne, 1991), pp. 45–64.

31 See Sarah Foot, *Veiled Women I. The Disappearance of Nuns from Anglo-Saxon England* (Aldershot, 2000), pp. 22, 25, 37, 40, and 44–45. See also Lina Eckenstein, *Woman Under Monasticism: Chapters on Saint-lore and Convent Life between A.D. 500 and A.D. 1500* (Cambridge, 1896), p. 82.

Women's education flourished similarly in England when double monasteries, under the strong influence of Continental models, began to appear there in the seventh century. Like many similar institutions in Gaul, Anglo-Saxon double houses could provide an environment in which women's education and intellectual activity flourished. Aldhelm, abbot of Malmesbury and bishop of Sherborne, noted the scholarly leanings of the nuns of Barking (f. 657) in his prose treatise, *De virginitate*, a work that he wrote in response to inquiries from a group of the monastery's nuns.[32] In his introduction, Aldhelm praised the nuns for the rhetorical skill that they demonstrated in their letters,[33] and compared their intellectual activities both to the exercise of skilled athletes,[34] and to the work of bees who roamed "widely through the flowers of scripture, [traversing them] with thirsty curiosity."[35] According to Aldhelm, the women did not limit their reading to religious texts – they also read ancient histories and chronicles, and studied the rules of grammar and meter.

There were also educated nuns at the double communities of Wimborne and Minster-in-Thanet. The nun Lioba began her monastic career at Minster, where she had Eadburga as her teacher. Lioba exchanged letters with her kinsman, St. Boniface, in which she demonstrated that she could write eloquent Latin prose and compose poetry. Her request for Boniface's assistance with the latter shows that letters could provide a medium of intellectual exchange between cloistered women and male teachers beyond the immediate community.[36] Strict claustration was not an insurmountable barrier to intellectual interaction between the sexes.[37]

32 Stephanie Hollis, *Anglo-Saxon Women and the Church* (Woodbridge, 1992), pp. 75–77.

33 "Cumque singulos epistolarum textus recitans pernicibus pupillarum obtutibus specularer . . . verborum facundiam ac virginalem urbanitatis disertitudinem magnopere admirarer" (And when, reading aloud the individual texts of your letters, I had scanned [them] with the keen gaze of [my] eyes . . . and had very much admired the extremely rich verbal eloquence and the pure expression of sophistication). Aldhelmus, *De virginitate: Prosa*, ed. Rudolph Ehwald, MGH, Auctores antiquissimi 15/1, pp. 229–230; trans. Lapidge and Herren, p. 59.

34 "Et quamvis gimnicorum exempla qui agilitate corporis theatrales populi pompas et praeconia circensium adpiscuntur, rite congruant ad comparationem eorum, qui per ampla scripturarum stadia decurrentes sagacissimam animorum industriam et vivacis ingenii qualitatem assidua lectionis instantia exercere noscuntur." (And however much the examples of athletes who with [their] bodily agility win popular honors in the theater and the applause of the circus, might properly pertain to a comparison of those who, traversing the spacious recourses of the Scriptures, are known to exercise the most subtle industry of their minds and the quality of their lively intelligence through assiduous perseverance in reading.) Aldhelmus, *De virginitate*, p. 231; trans. Lapidge and Herren, p. 61.

35 ". . . per florulenta scripturarum arva late vagans bibula curiositate . . ." Aldhelmus, *De virginitate*, p. 232.

36 Boniface, *Briefe des Bonifatius, Willibalds Leben des Bonifatius*, ed. M. Tangl, Ph. H. Kälb, and Reinhold Rau (Darmstadt, 1968), pp. 102, 104; Patrick Sims-Williams discusses this letter in *Religion and Literature in Western England, 600–800* (Cambridge, 1990), pp. 211–212.

37 See Alison I. Beach, "Claustration and Collaboration between the Sexes in the Twelfth-Century Scriptorium," in *Monks and Nuns, Saints and Outcasts: Religion in Medieval Society*, ed. Sharon Farmer and Barbara Rosenwein (Ithaca, 2000), pp. 57–75.

Her biographer, Rudolph, a ninth-century monk of Fulda, praised Lioba for her intellect and her deep devotion to sacred study:

> Trained in the liberal arts from her early youth, she sought the perfection of her spiritual knowledge with such intensity that through her reading and natural intelligence, that is by the double good of industry and nature, she became most learned. For poring over codices of the old and new Testament with keen mind, she memorized the divine precepts.[38]

The monastic *lectio divina* was a "three-way conversation – between the biblical text, the 'ruminating reader' . . . , and the author of a patristic commentary," in which the student read each verse in conjunction with the commentary and considered each exegetical problem carefully enough to make the patristic train of thought and conclusion a personal discovery.[39] Her training in the liberal arts enabled Lioba, among other things, to use patristic exegetical texts as an aid to pondering the layers of meaning thought to comprise the Bible.

In *c.* 748 Lioba moved from the relative comfort of convent life in England to the perilous life of the frontier – a dramatic step that symbolizes the bridge between the intellectual worlds of the Anglo-Saxon and the German cloister. Boniface, impressed by the intellectual talent that Lioba had demonstrated in her letters, wrote to Abbess Tetta requesting that the young nun be sent to help with his mission.[40] Tetta consented, Lioba acquiesced, and upon her arrival in Germany she was made abbess of Bischofsheim, a Benedictine monastery for women. As her reputation for learning and holiness spread throughout the dioceses of Würzburg and Eichstätt, many monasteries in the area chose their abbesses from among her followers.[41] Rudolph tells us that "these [nuns] were trained according to [her] principles in the discipline of monastic life and made such progress in her teaching that many of them afterwards became superiors of others, so that there

[38] "Lectionis studio tanta diligentia incubuit, ut, nisi orationi vacaret aut alimento vel somno corpusculum reficeret, numquam divina pagina de manibus eius abscederet. Nam, cum ab ipsis infantiae rudimentis grammatica et reliquis liberalium litterarum studiis esset instituta, tanta meditationis instantia spiritualis scientiae perfectionem conabatur assequi, ut, consentiente cum ingenio lectione, duplicato naturae et industriae bono eruditissima redderetur. Veteris enim novi Testimenti codices sagaci mente perlustrans, divina praecepta memoriae commendabat": *Vita Leobae abbatissae biscofesheimensis auctore Rudolpho*, ed. Georg Waitz, MGH, Scriptores 15, p. 126. Author Rudolph, a monk of Fulda, wrote the *Vita Leobae* in 837 or 838, some fifty years after her death, using earlier written accounts, and especially that of the priest Mago, who gathered his information from four nuns who had known her personally.

[39] The language used by Sims-Williams to describe Anglo-Saxon exegesis can also be applied more generally. Patrick Sims-Williams, *Religion and Literature*, p. 180. For an overview of the monastic *lectio*, see Beryl Smalley, *The Study of the Bible in the Middle Ages* (Notre Dame, IN, 1964), pp. 26–36 and 37–46.

[40] See *Vita Leobae*, p. 122.

[41] Mary Pia Heinrich, *The Canonesses and Education in the Early Middle Ages* (Washington, DC, 1924), pp. 96–97.

was hardly a convent of nuns in those parts which had not one of her disciples as abbess."[42]

But female education on the German frontier was not limited to Lioba's monastic circle. At Heidenheim, which was the only double monastery known to have existed in eighth-century Germany, Abbess Hugeburc, a self-described "unworthy sister of Saxon origin," wrote an account of the pilgrimage to the Holy Land made by her kinsman, Bishop Willibald.[43] This text, the first known travel narrative written by an Anglo-Saxon author, gives a detailed account of Willibald's life, travels, and virtues, as well as of the mission to convert the Germans and the Franks to Christianity.[44] Hugeburc, who was clearly able to write grammatically correct Latin, seems to have modeled her work upon both heroic poetry and Willibald's own Life of St. Boniface.[45] The selection of a nun as Willibald's biographer is an indication of the high esteem in which the community held the intellectual abilities of its women.

German monasteries continued to operate internal schools for women during the following century. The contemporary biography of Liutbirga (d. *c.* 865), a Saxon nun and recluse, states that there was a school for women at the community of Wendhausen in the diocese of Halberstadt. It was at Wendhausen that Liutbirga learned to study Scripture before leaving the convent to become the companion of the widowed Countess Gisla, who was impressed, among other things, by the young woman's intelligence.[46] Abbess Hathumoda of Gandersheim (d. 874) was educated in the school at Herford where, according to her brother and biographer Agius, she devoted herself to sacred studies and encouraged her nuns to follow her example.[47]

42 "quae ad exemplum beatae magistrae caelestis disciplinae studiis instituebantur et in tantum doctrina eius proficiebant, ut plures ex illis postmodum magistrae fierent aliarum, ita ut aut nulla aut etiam rara in illis regionibus essent monasteria feminarum, quae non discipularum eius magisteria desiderarent." *Vita Liobae*, p. 126; trans. C. H. Talbot, *The Anglo-Saxon Missionaries in Germany* (London, 1954), p. 214.

43 *Vita Willibaldi episcopi Eichstetensis et Vita Wynnebaldi abbatis Heidenheimensis auctore sanctimoniali Heidenheimensi*, ed. O. Holder-Egger, MGH, Scriptores 15, pp. 80–117; Heidenheim was founded in 751, probably as a male community. Women appear to have entered the community only after the death of its founder, Wynnebald, in 761. From this time, Heidenheim was patterned after Anglo-Saxon double monasteries. In 761 Wynnebald's sister Walburga was made abbess; on Hugeburc, see Eva Gottschaller, "Hugeburc von Heidenheim: philologische Untersuchungen zu den Heiligenbiographien einer Nonne des achten jahrhunderts," *Münchener Beiträge zur Mediävistic und Renaissance-Forschung* 12 (1973): 9–115, and Elizabeth Alvilda Petroff, ed., *Medieval Women's Visionary Literature* (New York and Oxford, 1986), pp. 86–88 and 92–106. Hugeburc's name was not known until the twentieth century when Bernhard Bischoff deciphered the cryptogram that concealed it. See Bernhard Bischoff, "Wer ist die Nonne von Heidenheim?" *StM* 49 (1931): 387–388.

44 Petroff, *Visionary Literature*, p. 87.

45 Gottschaller, "Hugeburc," pp. 75–81 and Petroff, *Visionary Literature*, p. 88.

46 *Vita sanctae Liutbirgae*, ed. Georg Pertz, MGH, Scriptores 4, p. 159. On Liutbirga, see Wemple, *Women in Frankish Society*, pp. 173–174.

47 *Agii Vita et obitus Hathumodae*, ed. Georg Pertz, MGH, Scriptores 4, p. 167; Heinrich, *Canonesses and Education*, p. 98; for a brief historical sketch of the monastery, see p. 19 below.

### *Women's books and Christian missionaries*

Books were a valuable commodity in short supply on the German missionary frontier. All who were able to copy or to decorate could be called on to help produce them, and there is no reason to think that women were excluded from this effort. On the contrary, there is abundant evidence that nuns, even before Boniface's time, participated actively in the production and procurement of books. One of the earliest examples is Bertila (d. *c.* 700), first abbess of Chelles, who sent manuscripts to missionaries and newly established abbeys in England.[48] Her access to books and her willingness to give them away reflects not only Bertila's sanctity – at least in the view of her eighth-century hagiographer – but also the possibility that Chelles, known to have been an active center of book production during the ninth century, was already turning out books in the eighth century.[49]

It was thus not unprecedented when Eadburga, abbess of Minster-in-Thanet, sent books to support St. Boniface's mission.[50] Her contributions are documented in letters in which Boniface both thanked her for sending books critical to his mission:

> May the eternal one who rewards all righteous acts cause the dearest sister to rejoice in the choir of angels above because she has consoled with spiritual light by gifts of sacred books an exile in Germany who has to enlighten the dark corners of the Germanic peoples and would fall into the snare of death if he had not the Word of God as a lamp unto his feet and a light upon his path.[51]

and requested that she make a copy of the Epistle of Peter:

> And I beg you further to add to what you have done already by making a copy written in gold of the Epistles of my master, Saint Peter the Apostle, to impress honor and reverence for the Sacred Scriptures visibly upon the carnally minded to whom I preach. . . . I am sending by the priest Eoban the materials for your writing.[52]

This letter also provides a glimpse of the processes involved in the procurement of books in the eighth century: making manuscripts was expensive, especially when lettering was to be done in gold, and here the supplicant provided the costly raw materials by means of a trusted messenger-priest. The books that Eadburga had

48 *Vita Bertilae abbatissae calensis*, ed. W. Levison, MGH, Script. rer. mer. 6, pp. 106–107. See Sarah Foot, *Veiled Women*, vol. I, p. 37, and Sims-Williams, *Religion and Literature*, pp. 110, 204.

49 On the nuns' scriptorium at Chelles, see Bernhard Bischoff, "Die Kölner Nonnenhandschriften," pp. 16–34 and Rosamond McKitterick, "Nuns' Scriptoria," article VII, pp. 1– 35.

50 On Eadburga's identity and the identification of her community in England, see Patrick Sims-Williams, "An Unpublished Seventh- or Eighth-Century Anglo-Latin Letter in Boulogne-sur-mer MS 74 (82)," *Medium Ævum* 48 (1979): 22. See also Sims-Williams, *Religion and Literature*, p. 212. Ephraim Emerton had previously identified Eadburga as abbess of Minster-in-Thanet in his translation, *The Letters of Saint Boniface* (New York, 1940), p. 121.

51 Boniface, *Briefe des Bonifatius*, p. 104; trans. Emerton, *Letters*, pp. 60–61.

52 *Briefe des Bonifatius*, p. 114; trans. Emerton, *Letters*, pp. 64–65.

previously copied for Boniface must have been of a very high quality indeed for him to entrust her with such precious supplies.

There were probably many others who produced or procured books. A copy of Jerome's commentary on Ecclesiastes (Würzburg, M.p.th.q. 2), produced in Italy during the fifth century and bearing an ex-libris in the name of Cuthswitha (probably Abbess Cuthswitha of Inkberrow, who died in 709), traveled from England to the German frontier during the last three-quarters of the eighth century.[53] Did the nuns of Inkberrow send this book to Germany in the hands of a messenger? Did a woman from the community carry it herself as she made the journey? While the manuscript yields no answers, its travels remind us that Bertila and Eadburga were exceptional, not because they were able to produce or procure books, but because their efforts found a place in the written historical record.

## *Female scribes of the missionary period*

The names Guntza and Abirhilt appear in the margins of two manuscripts produced in the vicinity of Würzburg during the late eighth century, signaling that women worked as scribes or illuminators in some of the earliest religious houses in Germany.[54] Their Germanic names place them among the growing number of local converts to the religious life who joined communities of Anglo-Saxon nuns in monastic outposts on the frontier. There, like the many anonymous others who must have worked both alongside them and in other houses, they were trained by Anglo-Saxon teachers to copy books.

These women may have been nuns at Bischofsheim, Heidenheim, or another of the frontier communities, all of which required a variety of books for internal use. The local missionaries, whose efforts the women were there, in part, to support, also needed books for teaching, devotional reading, and liturgical use beyond the monastery. On-site production was certainly faster, and probably less costly, than procurement from England, and local workshops, some staffed by nuns, may have helped to meet at least a portion of their needs. The locally produced books that have survived from this period show an amalgamation of Anglo-Saxon and German codicological, paleographical, and ornamental elements that reflect not only the

[53] See *Die Bibliothek des Würzburger Domstifts: 742–1803*, ed. Gottfried Mälzer and Hans Thurn (Würzburg, 1988), pp. 46–47; Patrick Sims-Williams, "Cuthswith, Seventh-Century Abbess of Inkberrow, near Worcester, and the Würzburg Manuscript of Jerome on Ecclesiastes," *Anglo-Saxon England* 5 (1976): 1–21; Rosamond McKitterick, "Anglo-Saxon Missionaries in Germany: Reflections on the Manuscript Evidence," in *Books, Scribes and Learning*, article IV, pp. 313, 318; McKitterick, "Nuns' Scriptoria," in *Books, Scribes and Learning*, article VII, p. 27.

[54] These manuscripts, Würzburg, Universitätsbibliothek, M.p.th.f. 13 and 45, are treated in detail in the section beginning on p. 16 below.

encounter between imported teachers and native students, but also the difficult material circumstances of the frontier.

Guntza's name appears twice in contemporary notations in Würzburg, Universitätsbibliothek, M.p.th.f. 13, a copy of Defensor's *Liber Scintillarum* which was the work of at least three scribes writing inexpert insular script on parchment prepared in the insular manner.[55] Many of the manuscript's folios are irregular in size, defective, or made up of two pieces of parchment sewn together, and the simple ornamentation is limited to bold black or red and yellow initials surrounded in places by black dots. The scribes used insular abbreviation marks, and the common insular "confusion" between *s* and *ss* appears throughout the manuscript. These characteristics indicate that the manuscript was written at a center under strong insular influence. The text was copied by at least three scribes. Guntza may have been a German scribe who worked alongside two fellow scribes, perhaps under the tutelage of an Irish or Anglo-Saxon teacher.

Both E. A. Lowe and Bernhard Bischoff linked this manuscript to three others preserved in Würzburg: M.p.th.f 17 (Augustine's commentary on the Psalms), M.p.th.q. 28a (Isidore of Seville's *Synonyma*, the Life of Saint Eugenia, and a fragment of the Life of Saint Potius), and M.p.th.f. 78 (the Passions of the Apostles). One hand in M.p.th.f. 78 can be identified with the main hand of the Guntza manuscript, and M.p.th.f. 17 contains a second hand found also in M.p.th.f. 13.[56] The third manuscript, M.p.th.q. 28a, also shares one hand with M.p.th.f. 13.[57] All four books have in common the use of insular abbreviations and omission marks and insular-style parchment. Their paleographical and codicological similarities and the presence of common scribes suggest that the books were produced at the same place. If Guntza was in fact a female scribe who worked on the book, the other scribes, including those who worked on M.p.th.f. 17, M.p.th.f. 78, and M.th.q. 28a may have also been women. Because the Guntza manuscript could have been copied in a double monastery where there may have been scribes of both sexes, it impossible to know whether it was the work of nuns alone or the combined work of nuns and monks.[58]

The main scribe of Würzburg, Universitätsbibliothek M.p.th.f. 45, Gregory the Great's homilies on the Gospels, wrote the name Abirhilt in the top margin of folio

[55] Guntza's name appears first on folio 8r and again on folio 57v. Bernhard Bischoff and Josef Hofmann, *Libri Sancti Kyliani. Die Würzburger Schreibschule und die Dombibliothek im 8. und 9. Jahrhundert*, Quellen und Forschungen zur Geschichte des Bistums und Hochstifts Würzburg 6 (1952), pp. 50–51; CLA 1404.

[56] Bischoff and Hofmann, *Libri Sancti Kyliani*, p. 101; CLA 1405.

[57] Bischoff and Hofmann, *Libri Sancti Kyliani*, p. 103; CLA 1435.

[58] Bischoff makes this observation for Chelles in "Die Kölner Nonnenhandschriften," p. 32.

71v.[59] Like the manuscripts of the Guntza group, this book was written in a variety of hands writing insular minuscule on poor-quality parchment, and appears to have been the work of inexperienced scribes. It is linked to two other Würzburg manuscripts by what E. A. Lowe termed their "diluted insular" initials, which were done in red and black with interlacing and animal motifs, most in black outline. Similar initials are found in M.p.th.f. 69, a copy of the Pauline Epistles, although this is a higher quality manuscript (i.e. better quality parchment, more careful script, and several miniatures), probably because it contained a sacred text. The other related book is M.p.th.f. 28b, which combines two originally independent books, the first containing patristic homilies, the Lives of Saints Cecilia, Juliana, Agnes, and Agatha, and an allegorical interpretation of the Passion, and the second pseudonymous works of Augustine, Caesarius of Arles, Isidore's *Synonyma*, and interestingly, the plan of a Roman military encampment.

Guntza and Abirhilt were certainly not the only women on the eighth-century German frontier who helped to produce books. Many frontier nuns were active book users and producers whose identities and accomplishments are, unfortunately, lost to us. The rarity of colophons and other direct evidence of manuscript production by women makes it difficult to determine how significant and widespread their participation was.

### *Female scribes in the tenth and eleventh centuries*

Despite the political instability that punctuated the period, there was an overall increase between 750 and 1025 in the number of religious communities for women, especially in the areas of Saxony and Lotharingia.[60] While there were only forty-four monasteries for women in German territories in 750 (nineteen in Lotharingia, nine in Franconia, eight in Swabia, and eight in Bavaria), thirty-two new houses were founded between 750 and 900, twenty-two of which were in Saxony alone.[61]

[59] CLA 1412. For a study of the content and context of this and related manuscripts, see Felice Lifshitz, "Gender and Exemplarity East of the Rhine: Jesus, Mary, and the Saints in Manuscript Context," *Early Medieval Europe* 9 (2000): 325–343.

[60] In Bavaria, where the devastation had been particularly extensive, Wolfgang, bishop of Regensburg, was instrumental in restoring organized religious life. He installed as abbot of St. Emmeram, Ramwold, a monk of St. Maximin in Trier, which itself had been reformed with the help of the monastery of Gorze. See Joachim Wollasch, "Monasticism: The First Wave," in *The New Cambridge Medieval History*, ed. Timothy Reuter (Cambridge, 1999), vol. III, pp. 171–172. See also Gerd Tellenbach, *The Church in Western Europe from the Tenth to the Early Twelfth Century*, trans. Timothy Reuter (Cambridge, 1993), pp. 109–110, where he challenges the notion of the existence of a formal monastic *ordo* emanating from Gorze.

[61] Michel Parisse, "Les chanoinesses dans l'empire germanique (IXe–XIe siècles)," *Francia* 6 (1978): 118.

During the period between 900 and 1025, an additional fifty-four houses were established, with twenty-six in Saxony and seventeen in Lotharingia.[62] Between 936 and 1025, new foundations for women in the Saxon diocese of Halberstadt outnumbered new foundations for men by at least two to one.[63] Founded, endowed, and populated by the highest nobility, these houses generally prospered financially, especially in Saxony where, after 936 and beginning with the establishment of Quedlinburg, wealth from operations in Slavic lands provided resources for lavish endowments.[64]

Many of the new houses were communities of canonesses, either lay or regular, who were expected to follow the regulations for canonesses set down at the Council of Aachen in 816.[65] Canonesses differed from professed nuns in several important ways. A canoness took no formal vows, and was permitted to retain personal property. Because she took no vow of stability, a woman could spend a portion of her life at a religious institution – perhaps to receive an education – and later leave to marry.[66] Regular canonesses usually shared a common dormitory and refectory, and their daily life was similar to that of a community of nuns. Some houses, such as Gandersheim and Quedlinburg, were affiliated with neighboring Benedictine nunneries, where a more rigorous life was expected and formal profession required.[67] The synods of Orange (441), Epaon (517), and Orleans (533) had abolished communities of this type, and in the ninth century, French and Belgian church authorities continued to press for their suppression. Houses of canonesses fared better in Germany, where many thrived essentially unopposed until the second decade of the eleventh century.[68] At that time, wealthy noble benefactors again

62 Parisse, "Les chanoinesses," p. 118.

63 For a discussion of the social needs that provided the impetus for this profusion of women's religious houses, see Karl J. Leyser, *Rule and Conflict in an Early Medieval Society: Ottonian Saxony* (Oxford, 1979), pp. 63–73.

64 Leyser, *Rule and Conflict*, p. 63 and p. 71.

65 *Institutio sanctimonialium Aquisgranensis*, ed. A. Werminghoff, MGH, Concilia 2, pp. 421–456. See also Thomas Schilp, *Norm und Wirklichkeit religiöser Frauengemeinschaften im Frühmittelalter: die Institutio sanctimonialium Aquisgranensis des Jahres 816 und die Problematik der Verfassung von Frauenkommunitäten*, Veröffentlichungen des Max-Planck-Instituts für Geschichte 137 (Göttingen, 1998). The classic study of canonesses in the Middle Ages is Karl Heinrich Schäfer, *Die Kanonissenstifter im deutschen Mittelalter; ihre Entwicklung und innere Einrichtung im Zusammenhang mit dem altchristlichen Sanktimonialentum*, Kirchenrechtliche Abhandlungen 43–44 (Stuttgart, 1907). See also Franz J. Felten, "Wie adelig waren Kanonissenstifte (und andere weibliche Konvente) im (frühen und hohen) Mittelalter?" in *Studien zum Kanonissenstift*, ed. Irene Crusius, Veröffentlichungen des Max-Planck-Instituts für Geschichte 167 (Göttingen, 2001), pp. 39–128.

66 Parisse, "Les chanoinesses," p. 109.

67 Leyser, *Rule and Conflict*, p. 71.

68 Leyser, *Rule and Conflict*, p. 71, suggests that this decline may reflect the fact that existing institutions were meeting the need for a place of deposit for unmarried daughters of the nobility, and that Saxon princes were growing increasingly impatient with the outflow of the wealth of widows, who might otherwise remarry, into religious houses. See also Heinrich, *Canonesses and Education*, pp. 10–11.

focused their energies on establishing new communities of monks and canons, and many converted existing houses for women into houses for men.[69]

In the area of education, the women's houses of tenth- and eleventh-century Germany carried on the legacy of Lioba and the other nuns who had helped to establish monastic life on the frontier during the preceding centuries. Many of the new religious houses in Germany, including Essen, Herford, Gandersheim, and Quedlinburg, supported schools that enjoyed strong reputations, and noble girls were accepted as students at these centers. Having received training in reading, composition, handwriting, the study of Scripture, and various manual arts, a young woman could leave the community to marry.

There were two types of female religious at Gandersheim: nuns who took permanent monastic vows and followed the Benedictine Rule, and canonesses who took no irrevocable vows and maintained the right to own private property, to keep servants, and to come and go freely.[70] This second type of arrangement is reflected in the life of Matilda of Saxony (d. 968), who would later be married to Henry the Fowler. Matilda was sent to be educated at Herford where her grandmother served as abbess. There she demonstrated her virtue through a rigorous daily routine: on feast days she devoted herself to reading or to listening to the Scriptures read aloud, while on other days she prayed, sang the psalms, and engaged in manual labor.[71] Education was a hallmark of noble piety, the stamp of which Matilda carried even after she left the community in 913. Other women stayed on permanently. For example, Sophie, the daughter of Otto II, received her education at Gandersheim under Abbess Gerberga, took monastic vows, and later became abbess herself. Under the direction of Gerberga II, who had been educated at St. Emmeram in Regensburg, Gandersheim became a prominent religious and intellectual center.[72] The school's most famous pupil was the canoness Hrotsvit, the first known author of Christian dramas, poet, and the first woman historian of Germany.[73]

69 Leyser, *Rule and Conflict*, p. 65.

70 Margrave Liudolf of Saxony (d. 866) founded Gandersheim as a free imperial community of religious women in 852 in the diocese of Hildesheim. At least five of Liudolf's daughters joined the house, and three, Hathumoda (d. 874), Gerberga (d. 896), and Christina (d. 919), served as abbess. In 947, Otto I exempted Gandersheim from royal authority, thus granting the abbess the authority to establish legal courts, maintain an army, mint coins, and claim a seat in the imperial diet. Other daughters of the high nobility, including Abbess Gerberga II (959–1001), niece of Otto I and daughter of Duke Henry I of Bavaria, lived in and ruled over Gandersheim during the ninth and tenth centuries.

71 *Vita Mahthildis reginae antiquior*, ed. Rudolf Koepke, MGH, Scriptores 10, p. 579; *Vita Mahthildis reginae posterior*, ed. Georg Pertz, MGH, Scriptores 4, p. 285. On Mathilda's education and intellectual pursuits, see Heinrich, *Canonesses and Education*, pp. 98–99.

72 Peter Dronke, *Women Writers of the Middle Ages* (Cambridge, 1984), p. 56.

73 Katharina M. Wilson, "The Saxon Canoness: Hrotsvit of Gandersheim," in *Medieval Women Writers*, ed. Katharina M. Wilson (Athens, GA, 1984), pp. 30–63.

Quedlinburg, founded in 936 by Matilda of Saxony, was likewise a center for the education of the daughters of the nobility. The first nuns were brought in from Wendhausen, the monastery in which Liutbirga was educated in the ninth century. Another Matilda, the daughter of Otto I and Adelheid, was educated at Quedlinburg and ruled as abbess from the age of eleven until her death in 999.[74] Under Abbess Matilda, a number of important women were trained at Quedlinburg, including Adelheid, the daughter of Otto II and Theophanu.[75] Young boys, too, were admitted to the school: Thietmar of Merseburg (975–1018) is said to have studied at Quedlinburg until the age of twelve.[76]

What did an education at these schools comprise? Chapter twenty-two of the Aachen legislation for canonesses, which many communities followed, contains extensive excerpts of Jerome's letter to Laeta, one of which specified the biblical texts that a young girl should study and the order in which they were to be introduced:

> Let her treasures not be silks or gems, but manuscripts of the holy scriptures . . . Let her first study the Psalter. Then let her gather wisdom for life in the proverbs of Solomon. Let her learn in Ecclesiastes to despise the vanities of the world. Let her follow in Job the examples of virtue and patience. Then let her pass on to the gospels, never to be put aside once taken in hand. Let her also drink in the Acts of the Apostles and the Epistles with a totally willing heart, and then the rest of the New and Old Testament in their proper order.[77]

Ideally, canonesses were to receive – or to arrive at the monastery having already received at home – a basic education. The Aachen legislation seems to have established a minimum standard, while not restricting materials for those who were inclined to go on to more advanced study.

As in Lioba's communities in the eighth century, the curriculum at some tenth-century women's communities was organized around the study of the liberal arts – especially those branches like grammar and rhetoric, which were useful preparation for monastic *lectio*.[78] The author of the Life of John of Gorze (d. 976), for example, detailed the course of study that the women of Saint Peter in Metz followed. As

[74] Heinrich, *Canonesses and Education*, p. 100.

[75] On the debate over Theophanu's identity, see Gunther Wolf, "Die 'Große Frage': Wer war Theophanu?" in *Kaiserin Theophanu: Prinzessin aus der Fremde – des Westreichs Große Kaiserin.*, ed. Gunther Wolf (Cologne, 1991), pp. 223–236.

[76] Thietmar was a chronicler and bishop of Merseburg (1009–1018); Heinrich, *Canonesses and Education*, p. 103.

[77] "Pro gemmis et serico divinos codices amet. Discat primo psalterium. Erudiatur in proverbiis Salomonis ad vitam. Consuescat in Ecclesiasten calcare quae mundi sunt. Sectetur in Iob virtutis et patientiae exempla. Ad evangelia transeat, numquam ea positura de manibus. Apostolorum acta et epistolas tota cordis inbuat voluntate; et sic per ordinem seriem novi veterisque testamenti." *Institutio Sanctimonialium*, pp. 453–454. The letter to Laeta next calls for reading the works of Cyprian, Hilary, and Athanasius, but the authors of the Aachen Rule for Canonesses did not include this section.

[78] Logic may have been excluded. John of Gorze was reprimanded by his abbot for devoting too much attention to understanding Porphyry's *Isagoge*. See pp. 39, 43–44, and 45 below.

priest to the nuns there, John was impressed by their intellectual strength. In fact, so inspired was he by the intellect of one of the school's students, the nun Geisa, that he entered into a course of study with them to expand his own education. Together, John and the nuns of Metz studied a broad range of texts, including books of both the Old and New Testament, the homilies and sermons of the Church Fathers, the canons of councils, secular law, and music.[79]

If Hrotsvit's early education was at all typical, the curriculum at Gandersheim also focused on the liberal arts.[80] Hrotsvit seems to have received her early education within an established school at Gandersheim, suggesting that, at least at first, her education followed a common course. Once her individual intellectual talent was recognized, however, she may have been encouraged to pursue a more rigorous program of study. In any event, Hrotsvit claimed that all of her reading material and the sources for her literary works were found in the monastery's library, which tells us something important about both the range of books and the range of potential intellectual opportunity they provided. Because no contemporary booklist or inventory has survived, scholars have traced the literary influences in Hrotsvit's writings to identify the authors and texts with whom she was familiar. There seems to have been keen interest at Gandersheim in the works of antiquity, notably the classical poets Horace, Lucan, Ovid, Statius, Terence, and Virgil, as well as in patristic and medieval authors, including Jerome, Prudentius, Boethius, Avitus, Aldhelm, Bede, Alcuin, Ekkehard, and Notker, and a variety of other biblical, liturgical, hagiographical, and grammatical texts.[81] One can imagine even from this sketchy list a course of study organized around the intellectual tools provided by the trivium: grammar, rhetoric, and possibly even logic.

### *Book production and female patronage in south Germany*

After the defeat of the Magyars began the painstaking work of rebuilding lost libraries, both secular and monastic. Emperor Otto III (983–1002) assembled a palace library, rekindling the Carolingian tradition of the imperial library exemplified by the collections established in the eighth century by Charlemagne and his grandson Charles the Bald.[82] In the monastic sphere, many communities worked together, with houses that had been relatively unscathed by the violence of the preceding years taking the lead in the rebuilding by providing books

79 John of St. Arnulf, *Vita Iohannis abbatis Gorziensis auctore Iohanne abbate S. Arnulfi*, MGH, Scriptores 4, pp. 341–342; Heinrich, *Canonesses and Education*, p. 103.

80 On Hrotsvit's early teachers at Gandersheim, see Wilson, "The Saxon Canoness," p. 31. See also Dronke, *Women Writers*, pp. 56–57.

81 Wilson, "The Saxon Canoness," pp. 31–32.

82 F. Mütherich, "The Library of Otto III," in *The Role of the Book in Medieval Culture*, ed. Peter Ganz, Bibliologia 4 (Turnhout, 1986), pp. 11–26.

as exemplars to centers whose libraries had been decimated. At newly refounded Tegernsee, for example, monks copied texts borrowed from less-damaged libraries in Freising, Regensburg, and possibly Augsburg.[83] Manuscripts from Tegernsee then served as exemplars for Benediktbeuren, where religious life was restored slightly later.[84] The influence of even a single scribe could be significant in such a context: Otloh, a prolific scribe based at St. Emmeram in Regensburg, worked both within and beyond his own community. The hand of such a scribe could be widely imitated and play an important role in the development of a regional style.[85] During the eleventh century, a regional tradition of Caroline minuscule emerged within South Germany and Austria, presumably through the exchange of scribal labor and perhaps also exemplars.

Donor attributions and portraits in several surviving tenth-century manuscripts reveal that many of the larger communities of women used a portion of their great wealth to commission books. A portrait of Abbess Hadwig of Essen shows her as the donor of a deluxe manuscript containing the Lives of Saints Cosmas and Damian, Essen's patron saints.[86] This volume may have been produced at Fulda, or possibly at a scriptorium within Essen itself. At the end of the century, the canonesses of Niedermünster in Regensburg commissioned an illuminated copy of the Rule of Caesarius of Arles and a feminized (*Asculta o filia*, etc.) version of the Rule of Saint Benedict.[87] This manuscript contains a donor portrait of Abbess Uta, who also commissioned an early-eleventh-century evangelistary, the so-called Uta-Codex.[88] After the beginning of the eleventh century, Hitda, abbess of Meschede, commissioned a lavishly illuminated copy of the Gospels, which was produced in the vicinity of Cologne.[89]

[83] Eder, *Die Schule des Klosters Tegernsee*, p. 24. Hartmut Hoffmann challenges Eder's conclusions in his *Bamberger Handschriften des 10. und 11. Jahrhunderts* (Hanover, 1995).

[84] Eder, *Die Schule des Klosters Tegernsee*, p. 52.

[85] On Otloh and his influence on Bavarian handwriting, see Helga Schauwecker, "Otloh von St. Emmeram. Ein Beitrag zur Bildungs- und Frömmigkeitsgeschichte des 11. Jahrhunderts," *StM* 74 (1963): 3–240; Eder, *Die Schule des Klosters Tegernsee*, pp. 56–63 and 82–85; Hartmut Hoffmann, *Buchkunst und Königtum*, esp. at pp. 53 and 81.

[86] Bösensell bei Münster, Haus Ruhr, Archiv von un zur Mühlen, Nachlaß Iodokus Hermann Nünning. Essen was a religious community in Westfalia (diocese of Hildesheim), founded in *c.* 845 by Altfrid, who was bishop of Hildesheim from 851 to 874. The monastery began as a Benedictine community of nuns, and soon became a religious and cultural center for women. Its proximity to and affiliation with the male community of Werden (founded in 800) may suggest a relationship between the two similar to that found in a double monastery. Both Essen and Werden remained in existence until the secularization of the nineteenth century.

[87] Bamberg, Staatsbibliothek, Misc. Lit. 142. For a study of this manuscript in the context of eleventh-century monastic reform, see Adam Cohen, "The Art of Reform in a Bavarian Nunnery around 1000," *Speculum* 74 (1999): 990–1020.

[88] Munich, Bayerische Staatsbibliothek Clm 13601. On this evangelistary, see Adam Cohen, *The Uta Codex: Art, Philosophy, and Reform in Eleventh-Century Germany* (University Park, PA, 2000).

[89] Darmstadt, Hessische Landesbibliothek, MS 1640.

At Essen, as well as at Gandersheim, Nordhausen, and Quedlinburg, women maintained written necrologies, suggesting both a strong interest in the keeping of written records and the materials and skills with which to do so. These writings point also to the possibility that there were female scribes within these communities – a possibility that Katrinette Bodarwé has recently explored using evidence from charters, necrologies, book annotations, and manuscripts from Gandersheim, Essen, and Quedlinburg. She argues that these centers all had internal scriptoria, particularly in the tenth century, but also in the eleventh. Especially interesting is her paleographical analysis of the famous tenth-century copy of Hrotsvit's complete works.[90] The origin of this manuscript, long assumed to have been Gandersheim itself, had recently been called into question by scholars who argued that paleographical evidence pointed rather to production at an unidentified center in the vicinity of Regensburg.[91] Bodarwé demonstrates convincingly, however, that the manuscript did, in fact, originate at Gandersheim by linking one of the hands to the hand of a *magistra* from Gandersheim – the annotator and corrector of the Gandersheim Evangeliary.[92]

The evidence is still clearer for Essen.[93] A list of non-liturgical books in the nuns' library at Essen in *c.* 900 suggests that the community's women were literate and interested in patristic and Carolingian theological and exegetical texts.[94] An examination of surviving books from ninth- and tenth-century Essen confirms the impression of the nuns' literacy: women there annotated their books with numerous Old Saxon glosses.[95] While the monastery's ninth-century books seem to have been produced at various centers outside Essen,[96] in the tenth and eleventh centuries

[90] Elisabeth van Houts, "Women and the Writing of History in the Early Middle Ages: The Case of Abbess Matilda of Essen and Aethelweard," *Early Medieval Europe* 1 (1992): 53–68; for a study of female scribal activity, including the writing of necrologies, calendars, and charters at Essen, Gandersheim, and Quedlinburg, see Katrinette Bodarwé, "Sanctimoniales litteratae – Schriftlichkeit und Bildung in den ottonischen Frauenstiften Gandersheim, Essen und Quedlinburg," Ph.D. diss. (Bonn, 2001), pp. 112–194.

[91] Munich, Bayerische Staatsbibliothek Clm 14485. See Bischoff, *Latin Palaeography*, p. 213 and Walter Berschin, "Konrad Weiss über Hrotsvit von Gandersheim," *Literaturwissenschaftliches Jahrbuch*, NS 24 (1983): 240. Both assume an origin at Gandersheim. Raymund Kottje and Hartmut Hoffmann shared the hypothesis of an origin in Regensburg rather than Gandersheim with me during personal conversations in Bonn in October of 1992, and in Munich, in February of 1994, respectively.

[92] Coburg, Veste, Ms 1. See Bodarwé, "Sanctimoniales litteratae," pp. 102–105.

[93] Bodarwé, "Sanctimoniales litteratae," pp. 112–164; Hartmut Hoffmann, "Das Skriptorium von Essen in ottonischer und frühsalischer Zeit," in *Kunst im Zeitalter der Kaiserin Theophanu*, Akten des Internationalen Colloquiums veranstaltet vom Schnütgen-Museum Köln. 13.–15. Juni 1991, ed. Anton von Euw and Peter Schreiner (Cologne, 1993), pp. 113–153.

[94] Düsseldorf, Universitätsbibliothek, MS B4. See Gerhard Karpp, "Bemerkungen zu den mittelalterlichen Handschriften des adeligen Damenstifts in Essen (9.–19. Jahrhundert)," *Scriptorium* 45 (1991): 163–204, and McKitterick, "Continuity and Innovation," p. 20.

[95] Karpp, "Bemerkungen," p. 164.

[96] The monastery's ninth-century books may have originated in scriptoria at or near St. Amand (Düsseldorf, Universitätsbibliothek, MS A6, Old Testament), Laon (MS A14, New Testament),

women produced books at Essen itself. Female scribes were particularly productive during the second half of the tenth century as they rebuilt the library following a devastating fire in 947.[97] Having met their needs in the ninth century with books copied elsewhere, it seems that the women of Essen began to produce their own manuscripts in the tenth century.[98] Paleographical similarities between these books and books copied by monks at the neighboring monastery of Werden reveal the latter as a source of exemplars, teachers, or both, for the nuns' community. The presence in the library of as many as five manuscripts ascribed by Gerhard Karpp to Werden – including two that are paleographically so similar to the volumes tentatively ascribed to Essen that it is difficult to determine which of the two centers produced them – suggests that the two centers shared books and possibly teachers.[99]

There may also have been female scribes at Niedermünster, one of several religious houses for women restored in the tenth century by Wolfgang, bishop of Regensburg.[100] The first abbess of the new community of canonesses was Uta, the mother of Duke Henry the Quarrelsome of Bavaria.[101] It was from within this community that Uta commissioned a manuscript containing both the Rule of Caesarius of Arles for nuns and the Rule of Saint Benedict transcribed using

Corbie (MS B3, Alcuin's *Questions and Answers on Genesis*), and Werden, as well as unidentified centers in the Rhineland (MS B4, Alcuin's Commentary on the Gospel of John; MS B113, Rhabanus' *De institutione clericorum*), northwest Germany (MS D1, Sacramentary), Rome (MS E1, *Collectio Dionysio-Hadriana*) and northeast France (Essen, Domschatzkammer MS 1, Gospels). See Karpp, "Bermerkungen," pp. 172–182.

97 Bodarwé, "Sanctimoniales litteratae," pp. 117–121. Hartmut Hoffmann did not locate any of his *Schreibschulen* at any of the newly founded monasteries, many of which, as noted above, were for women. See Rosamond McKitterick, "Continuity and Innovation," pp. 17–18.

98 McKitterick, "Continuity and Innovation," p. 20.

99 Düsseldorf, Universitätsbibliothek, MS B 79 (1st half 10th c., Werden or another northwestern German center, Gregory the Great's Letters), MS B 80 (1st half 10th c., Werden?, Gregory the Great's Homilies), Ms. F1 (10th c., Werden or Essen, Prudentius' *Psychomachia*); Essen, Domschatzkammer MS 4 (2nd half 11th c., Werden or Essen, Quadruplex Psalter, 3 Latin and 1 Greek text in four columns); Hannover, Niedersächsisches Staatsarchiv, Ms. Z 01 (10th c., Werden or Essen), fragment of Isidore of Seville's *Etymologiae*).

100 Wolfgang (d. 994) had been master of the cathedral school at Trier before becoming a monk at Einsiedeln, and later undertaking a mission to Hungary. He became bishop of Regensburg in 972, where, influenced by the reform ideas of the monasteries of Gorze and St. Maximin, he set out to restore the observance of the Benedictine Rule in several Bavarian monasteries including St. Emmeram in Regensburg. Reforming ideas then passed from St. Emmeram to Tegernsee, Niederaltaich, Hersfeld, and others. Bishop Wolfgang also reestablished two houses of canonesses, Niedermünster and Obermünster, in his diocese of Regensburg. See Otloh, *Vita sancti Wolfkangi*, ed. Georg Waitz, MGH, Scriptores 4, pp. 533–534, and Kassius Hallinger, *Gorze-Kluny: Studien zu den monastischen Lebensformen und Gegensätzen im Hochmittelalter*, Studia Anselmiana 22–25 (Rome, 1950), pp. 136–137.

101 Uta was formerly a nun of Einsiedeln, a community that had recently been reformed with help from St. Emmeram. Hallinger, *Gorze-Kluny*, p. 137.

feminine forms.[102] Based on the verse written on folio 59 recto, Karin Dengler-Schreiber has argued that scribes at Niedermünster copied this Rule.[103] There was certainly a scriptorium of women at the house in the twelfth century, when Idung of Prüfening sent his *Dialogus duorum monachorum* to Niedermünster to be copied.[104] This scriptorium, which was well enough developed by the twelfth century to attract Idung's interest, may have been established already in the late tenth century. While the verse in question clearly identifies Abbess Uta as the patron of the manuscript, it does not state where or under whose supervision it was produced.[105] The style of decoration does suggest the influence of the school of illumination associated with Trier, but this may simply reflect an ongoing connection between individual artists within Wolfgang's reform circle and his former home.[106] Further, scribes from one center and illuminators from another (with connections to the artists of Trier) may have worked together to produce the manuscript. The choice of texts, the alteration of Benedict's Rule, and the naming of Uta as donor clearly indicate that the volume was intended for use by the women of Niedermünster. Charters recorded in the blank spaces left by the tenth-century scribes place the manuscript at the monastery of Michelsburg in Bamberg by the twelfth century, where scribes "corrected" the Rule for use by monks, replacing some of the female forms with male ones in the chapter headings, particularly at the beginning of the text.

## DEVELOPMENTS IN BAVARIA AT THE OPENING OF THE TWELFTH CENTURY

It is not until the beginning of the twelfth century that evidence of female participation in monastic book production begins to mount. This may be a simple statistical phenomenon: more books survive from the twelfth century than from the preceding centuries and thus more evidence of women's scribal work is visible to us. It may be that the output of existing monastic scriptoria increased during the twelfth century, or that new scriptoria emerged as new communities were founded and developed book collections, partly in response to religious reform and various aspects of the intellectual revival that scholars know as the renaissance of the twelfth century. But with the increase in the evidence of the activity of female scribes – whether this increase reflects increased production, higher rates

102 See p. 22 above.
103 Karin Dengler-Schreiber, *Scriptorium und Bibliothek des Klosters Michelsberg in Bamberg*, Studien zur Bibliotheksgeschichte, second edition (Graz, 1979), p. 294.
104 See p. 129 below.
105 Georg Swarzenski, *Die Regensburger Buchmalerei des X. und XI. Jahrhunderts* (Leipzig, 1901), p. 48.
106 Swarzenski, *Regensburger Buchmalerei*, p. 54.

of survival, or both – come important questions about the material, spiritual, and intellectual circumstances of their involvement in book production.[107] Were more women active as scribes during the twelfth century than they had been in earlier centuries? How were female scribes trained and with whom did they collaborate? And perhaps most importantly, what can their ability to produce books tell us about women's contributions to their local religious and intellectual setting and to the larger movements of monastic reform? A key to these questions is both the nature of the reform movements and of the roles women played within them.

The number of religious houses for women, and men's houses with affiliated female communities, grew steadily in the eleventh and twelfth centuries as zeal for monastic reform spread across Germany. At the beginning of the twelfth century, the reform ideas associated with the Lotharingian monastery of Gorze spread to both Lorraine and Germany. These reformers sought to reassert the boundaries between the monastery and the outside world by reclaiming estates and reducing the dues and services owed to lay lords.[108] They focused also on life within the monastery, calling for more exacting adherence to the Rule of Saint Benedict and greater focus on the liturgy.[109] The reformers intended their communities to function within the framework of episcopal jurisdiction and oversight, and never sought wide-scale exemption from this authority. Each newly converted community retained its autonomy, entering into a filiation centered upon the monastery from which it had received its customary. John of Gorze took over the operation of the newly restored monastery of Gorze in 933 and the influence of the monastery soon began to spread. Monks from Saint Maximin, reformed under influence from Gorze, went on to reform the imperial state church and several imperial abbeys at the request of Emperor Otto I (936–973).[110]

A second monastic reform movement, this one with eleventh-century origins, began at the monastery of Hirsau in the Black Forest.[111] The Hirsau reformers, like many others, called for a return to a strict observance of the Rule of Saint Benedict,

[107] Large book collections, such as those at Gorze and Cluny, certainly did exist prior to the twelfth century, but the number of houses with large collections grew, partly accounting for the greater overall book survival rate. On the size and scope of the library at Cluny during the tenth and eleventh century, see Veronika von Büren, "Le grand catalogue de la bibliothèque de Cluny," in *Le gouvernement d'Hugues de Semur à Cluny. Actes du colloque scientifique international. Cluny, September 1988* (Cluny, 1990), pp. 245–261.

[108] John Nightingale, *Monasteries and Patrons in the Gorze Reform: Lotharingia c. 850–1000* (Oxford, 2001), p. 14.

[109] Nightingale, *Monasteries and Patrons*, pp. 14–15.

[110] See Hallinger, *Gorze-Kluny*, pp. 132–160; C. Wolff, "Die Gorzer Reform in den Verhältnis zu deutschen Klöstern," *Elsass-lothringisches Jahrbuch* 9 (1930): 95–111; Uta-Renate Blumenthal, *The Investiture Controversy: Church and Monarchy from the Ninth to the Twelfth Century* (Philadelphia, 1988), pp. 8–11.

[111] For a history of the movement, see Klaus Schreiner, ed. *Hirsau St. Peter und St. Paul 1091–1991*, Forschungen und Berichte der Archäologie des Mittelalters in Baden-Württemberg 10. 3 vols. (Stuttgart, 1991).

but they also opposed all outside interference, either lay or episcopal, in the operation of monasteries.[112] This second characteristic marked a fundamental change for German monasticism, which had been dominated by a long, strong tradition of imperial and episcopal proprietorship. Hirsau rapidly became a powerful center of reform throughout Germany.

Many of the monasteries associated with Hirsau's program housed both male and female communities, and women were involved with the movement at many levels – as founders, nuns, and benefactors. In some cases, women who had been living in less formal connection with a particular house, were gathered and regularized.[113] In others, entirely new female communities were started. Unlike the double monasteries of the Merovingian period, Hirsau's dual-sex communities reflect a very different attitude toward women and their role in monastic government. An abbot, not an abbess, governed these double houses.

The head of the female community was normally called *magistra*, not abbess, emphasizing the reduced status of the office.[114] She was not fully the abbot's counterpart (i.e., a female abbot), but teacher and obedient leader of the nuns. The use of *magistra*, with its clear reference to teaching, may also reflect the movement's emphasis on education.[115] In the context of female religious education, the term *magistra* can be traced to Saint Jerome, who used it to describe the mother Laeta's role as her daughter Paula's moral model and teacher of letters.[116] The 816 Aachen legislation for regular canonesses, which contains the earliest known use of *magistra* to refer to the female head of a religious community, contains extensive excerpts from this letter to Laeta, picking up the connotations of a *magistra* as both

112 Hans-Josef Wollasch, *Die Anfänge des Klosters St. Georgen im Schwarzwald*, Forschungen zur oberrheinischen Landesgeschichte 14 (Freiburg im Breisgau, 1967), p. 115; Hallinger, *Gorze-Kluny*, p. 388.

113 Giles Constable, *The Reformation of the Twelfth Century* (Cambridge, 1996), p. 69.

114 Urban Küsters, *Der verschlossene Garten: volkssprachliche Hohelied-Auslegung und monastische Lebensform im 12. Jahrhundert*, Studia Humaniora 2 (Düsseldorf, 1985), pp. 69 and 165; the title is used to signify the head of two other women's communities, Urspring and Friedenweiler, affiliated with Hirsau, although these examples date from the thirteenth century. See Karl Sigfried Bader, *Das Benediktinerinnenkloster Friedenweiler und die Erschließung des südöstlichen Schwarzwaldes*, Veröffentlichungen aus den fürstlich Fürstenbergischen Archiv 2 (1938), p. 21; Immo Eberl, *Geschichte des Benediktinerinnenklosters Urspring bei Schelklingen, 1127–1806: Außenbeziehungen, Konventsleben, Grundbesitz*, Schriften zur südwestdeutschen Landeskunde 13 (Tübingen, 1978), p. 147; at Admont, the title *abbatissa* was still used on occasion. The *Annales Admuntenses* referred to Regilind as "*domina Regillinde abbatissa*" in an entry recording her departure to reform Bergen in 1156: *Annales Admuntenses*, ed. Wilhelm Wattenbach, MGH, Scriptores 9, p. 582; on the use of *magistra* and *priorissa* in some Premonstratensian houses in the twelfth century: see pp. 109–110 below.

115 The primary use of the title in antiquity was to denote a woman in charge, i.e. a female chief or superintendent, a high priestess, or female expert. *Oxford Latin Dictionary*, ed. P. G. W. Glare (Oxford, 1982).

116 PL 22, col. 875.

educator and supervisor.[117] Many houses of Augustinian canonesses followed both the Aachen rule and a version of the so-called Augustinian Rule, and this may have been the conduit for the title's later use by canonesses.[118] The basis for the term's use in the twelfth century is still less clear, but the Hirsau reformers may have encountered it in these same texts, or through contact with regular canons and canonesses.

A third magnet for female vocations was the Premonstratensian Order, which also expanded rapidly in German lands in the twelfth century. Founder Norbert of Xanten (1080–1136) had dreamed of an order that comprised communities of wandering preachers living a life of poverty on the model of the apostles.[119] Although this core ideal excluded women, many women were drawn to the movement, and many Premonstratensian monasteries were double houses. Norbert himself had established Prémontré as a house for both men and women to accommodate the many women who were attracted to the order.[120] Unlike their male counterparts, Premonstratensian women were restricted to their cloister, and they were always marginal and limited to a supporting role within both the order and the local community. They were expected to produce and wash clothes, and to cook both for themselves and for the men. In spite of this marginality, women were drawn to the

[117] *Institutio sanctimonialium Aquisgranensis*, p. 452. For a recent study, see Schilp, *Norm und Wirklichkeit.*

[118] C. H. Lawrence, *Medieval Monasticism: Forms of Religious Life in the Middle Ages*, second edition (London and New York, 1989), p. 166; Augustine used the term *praeposita* rather than *magistra* to identify the female head of community. See George Lawless, ed., *Augustine of Hippo and his Monastic Rule* (Oxford, 1987), pp. 110–118. For the various versions of Augustine's "Rule" and the relationship between them, see Luc Verheijen, *La règle de saint Augustin*, 2 vols. (Paris, 1967). For the earliest version, which is thought to have been written for women, see vol. II, pp. 19–21.

[119] The founding of the monastery of Prémontré in 1121 is generally regarded as the birth of the Premonstratensian order. For a concise historical sketch of the Premonstratensians, see Bernard Ardura, *Abbayes, prieurés et monastères de l'ordre de Prémontré en France des origines à nos jours* (Nancy, 1993), pp. 19–49; Lawrence, *Medieval Monasticism*, pp. 169–172; and Herbert Grundmann, *Religious Movements in the Middle Ages*, trans. Steven Rowan (Notre Dame, IN, 1995), pp. 19 and 21. For a more complete survey, see Norbert Backmund, *Geschichte des Prämonstratenserordens* (Grafenau, 1986). The Premonstratensian statutes were influenced both by the *Carta Caritatis* of the Cistercian order and by the customs of Cluny.

[120] A. Erens, "Les soeurs dans l'Ordre de Prémontré," *Analecta Praemonstratensia* 5 (1929): 13; Micheline de Fontette, *Les religieuses à l'âge classique du droit canon* (Paris, 1967), pp. 13–25; several studies that focus on a particular community also contain more general material relating to the role of women and double monasteries within the wider order. Most useful is Hugues Lamy, *L'Abbaye de Tongerloo depuis sa fondation jusqu'en 1263*, Recueil de travaux publiés par les membres des conférences d'histoire et de philologie 44 (Louvain and Paris, 1914), pp. 92–103; see also Pl. Lefèvre, "Le problème des sœurs aux origines de l'abbaye d'Averbode," *Analecta Praemonstratensia* 52 (1976): 38–43; Maur. de Meulemeester, "Les soeurs norbertines de Tusschenbeek," *Analecta Praemonstratensia* 4 (1928): 30–44; Joseph Zeller, "Das Prämonstratenserstift Adelberg, das letzte schwäbische Doppelkloster, 1178 (1188) bis 1476. Ein Beitrag zur Geschichte der Doppelkloster, besonders im Prämonstratenserorden," *Württembergische Vierteljahrshefte für Landesgeschichte* 25 (1916): 107–162, esp. at pp. 107–118.

movement in great numbers. The chronicler Herman of Tournai (d. 1147), writing in the middle of the twelfth century, claimed that there were by then 1,000 women at Prémontré and its dependent houses, and 10,000 women in the entire order.[121] Although historians must deflate these figures to allow for Herman's enthusiastic exaggeration, they suggest that the movement was popular with women, despite their exclusion from its most important activities. A more plausible report from the Swabian monastery of Roth (f. 1140) noted a modest community of approximately forty canonesses (and two hundred canons) under the first prior.[122]

One common element of monastic reform in eleventh- and twelfth-century German lands was the formation of double communities, motivated in part by a desire to make the *cura monialium*, the pastoral care of religious women, a part of the men's spiritual life. Cloistered nuns provided neighboring monks with an outlet for the pastoral duties of the active life (*vita activa*), which in turn allowed the women to live the contemplative life (*vita contemplativa*), an arrangement that contemporary writers attempted to legitimize by drawing parallels with the apostolic age.[123] Pressure to admit women may have come also from prospective female recruits or their families, responding to a shortage of suitable religious establishments. There were only approximately 70 convents for women in Germany in 900, and the number had risen only to 150 by 1100. Between 1100 and 1250, 350 new communities were founded.[124] And expansion could have economic benefits, with more professions bringing more donations, and more nuns doing more work in the service of the men. Whatever the motivation, women were recruited and entered reformed monasteries in significant numbers, and the men with whom they were affiliated were expected to tend to both their spiritual needs (through the administration of the sacraments and the hearing of confession) and their material well-being (by providing food, materials for clothing, etc.).[125]

121 Herman of Tournai, *De miraculis S. Mariae Laudunensis*, PL 156, cols. 996–997.

122 Romuald Bauerreiss, *Kirchengeschichte Bayerns*, vol. III (Munich, 1958), p. 41.

123 Grundmann, *Religious Movements*, p. 225; Küsters, *Der Verschlossene Garten*, pp. 143–145; *Acta Murensia*, ed P. Martin Keim, Quellen zur Schweizer Geschichte 3 (Basel, 1883), p. 60; *Casus monasterii Petrishusensis*, ed. Otto Feger, Schwäbische Chroniken der Stauferzeit 3 (Lindau and Konstanz, 1956), p. 24.

124 Edith Ennen, *The Medieval Woman*, trans. Edmund Jephcott (Oxford, 1989), pp. 122–125; Marc Frederick Stein, "The Religious Women of Cologne: 1120–1320," Ph.D. diss. (Yale University, 1977), pp. 37–38. Judging by the omission of any mention of women, double monasteries, or the *cura monialium* in the *Constitutiones Hirsaugiensis*, it seems likely that these were not important to the reform as originally conceived by founder William (d. 1091). See *Constitutiones Hirsaugienses*, PL 150, cols. 927–1146. The degree to which William's ideas about the role of women (as he expressed them in this text) changed over time is unclear; the organizers of each of the major eleventh- and twelfth-century monastic reform movements were faced with the question of what to do with the many women who flocked to join. See Lawrence, *Medieval Monasticism*, pp. 157–158.

125 Stephanus Hilpisch, *Die Doppelklöster: Entstehung und Organisation.* Beiträge zur Geschichte des alten Mönchtums und des Benediktinerordens 15 (1928), pp. 61 and 69; Küsters, *Der verschlossene Garten*, pp. 142–155.

Also associated with the monastic reform movements, as well as with the movements for clerical reform that characterized this period, was an increase in various kinds of intellectual activity. The eleventh-century papal reform movement brought as much as a fivefold increase over the previous century in the number of historical works written.[126] Treatises on matters of concern to the reformers such as clerical celibacy, simony, and lay investiture multiplied, and religious controversy stimulated interest in canon law and patristic authorities. In the reformed monasteries, as elsewhere, there was an increased interest in the monastic *lectio*, which focused on scriptural study, and called for the reading both of patristic and earlier medieval exegetical writing. The reformation of religious life thus encouraged increased intellectual activity, which both required and generated books, and surviving monastic libraries and contemporary book lists reflect this outpouring of spiritual and intellectual energy.

While women were generally excluded from the discourse of eleventh-century papal reform, many participated actively in the religious and intellectual revival taking place within the monastic sphere, some working as scribes, helping to copy biblical and liturgical texts, patristic sermons and commentaries, saints' lives, histories, grammars, and canon law texts, and others by writing their own works. Nowhere was interest in book copying and the formation of libraries more pronounced than in the monasteries affiliated with Hirsau, where a surge in book production often paralleled an increase in the composing of original texts.[127] At Michelsberg, a community that joined the Hirsau reform in 1112, there was a marked increase in the output of the scriptorium in the twelfth century, especially under the librarian Burchard. Burchard demonstrated his interest in the library and the work of scribes by compiling a number of booklists, including a record of scribal activity at Michelsberg between approximately 1112 and 1140.[128] Many Premonstratensian monasteries, in which the education of clerics was central, also had active scriptoria. Premonstratensians, for their part, were motivated to produce books because they needed libraries for training priests. Many other communities, too, pushed toward more intensive study by their respective reform traditions, had an urgent need to acquire books. Where there was a need for books, there was also a need for scribes. If women were on hand who could share the work, as must have been the case in many double monasteries, their services could be enlisted.

[126] See Horst Fuhrmann, *Germany in the High Middle Ages c.1050–1200* (Cambridge, 1986), pp. 69–72, on this increase in intellectual activity within the context of the conflicts over investiture and church reform.

[127] Raymund Kottje, "Klosterbibliotheken und monastische Kultur in der zweiten Hälfte des 11. Jahrhunderts," *Zeitschrift für Kirchengeschichte* 80 (1969): 145–162. See also Bauerreiss, *Kirchengeschichte* vol. III, pp. 132–174, for an excellent survey of the blossoming of interest in theology, historical writing, poetry, and drama.

[128] Dengler-Schreiber, *Scriptorium und Bibliothek des Klosters Michelsberg*.

From within the monastic scriptoria of southern Germany, as elsewhere, came an increased number of books during the eleventh and twelfth centuries. The steady exchange of exemplars for copying, and perhaps of scribal instructors, well developed already in the region as early as the tenth century, encouraged the continued development of a regional book hand – a variation of Caroline minuscule known as Slanting or Tilting Oval from the characteristic shape of the **o**. This script, and the cultural influences behind it, were strong enough to insulate the scribal schools of the region from the development of the "Gothic" styles of handwriting that were rapidly increasing in popularity elsewhere in Western Europe.[129] This south German and Austrian "monastic school" hand persisted in many Bavarian communities until the close of the twelfth century.[130]

It is within this context of monastic reform and intellectual revival that we must place the women and books that are the focus of this study. Each scribe and her books have stories to tell about the local spiritual and intellectual community – stories with significance beyond the immediate circumstances of individual book, copyist, and monastery. In the pages that follow I consider three very different religious houses, each telling its own stories, both local (as they shed light on the intellectual and institutional lives of religious women within a particular community) and regional (as they provide insight into the place of women in the religious and intellectual world of twelfth-century Germany). Our developing understanding of medieval book production compels us to reconsider the role of women in the spiritual and intellectual revival that was so central to the monastic reformation of twelfth-century Europe.

[129] Bischoff, *Latin Palaeography*, pp. 120–121.
[130] Karin Schneider, *Gotische Schriften in deutscher Sprache*, 2 vols. (Wiesbaden, 1987), vol. I, p. 24.

# 2

## *Diemut and the nun-scribes of Wessobrunn*

On 5 April 1707, in the presence of Abbot Boelzl and a crowd of onlooking monks, workers at the monastery of Wessobrunn broke ground for the construction of a new, grand chapel that would replace a more modest structure that had stood on that site for nearly a thousand years. As soon as the digging began, a large tomb was unearthed. The abbot ordered the vault opened, and a beautiful odor is said to have filled the air as the remains of seven tenth-century monks and one twelfth-century nun were discovered within. The seven were identified as the monks who had died in 955 attempting unsuccessfully to defend the monastery from the Magyars. Above the nun's grave, workers found two plaques – one of stone and one of lead – which read: "Diemut, a recluse of pious memory who with her own hands created a library for St. Peter's, died on 30 April."[1] In a festive procession, the monks carried all of the newly excavated relics into the main church and placed them beside the high altar to await the preparation of special tombs in the new chapel. The seven martyrs were moved with great ceremony to their new resting place in 1712, and on 13 December 1713, Diemut followed. The abbot commissioned a stone portrait of a nun holding a stylus in her right hand to mark the tomb.[2] Diemut, the recluse-scribe of Wessobrunn, had become a local saint.

[1] "III Cal. April. Obiit pie memorie Diemut inclusa, que suis manibus Bibliothecam S. Petro hec fecit." This inscription is cited in Cölestin Leuttner, *Historia monasterii Wessofontani*, 4 vols. (Augsburg and Freiburg, 1753), vol. I, p. 174, and in Joseph von Hefner, "Ueber die Nonne Diemud von Wessobrunn und ihr literarisches Wirken mit einem Facsimile ihrer Handschrift," *Oberbayerische Archiv* 1 (1839): 359–360. There is no contemporary record of the placement of these tablets in the grave, and they are no longer extant.

[2] Wolfgang Winhard, *Die Benediktinerabtei Wessobrunn im 18. Jahrhundert* (Munich, 1988), p. 33. Abbot Boelzl was a major promoter of the cult of the saints in Bavaria, and also the head of the Confraternity of the Mother of Beautiful Love, a group dedicated to encouraging devotion to Mary and the celebration of the Immaculate Conception. See Winhard, *Die Benediktinerabtei Wessobrunn*, pp. 31–45.

## WESSOBRUNN'S EARLY HISTORY

Wessobrunn – Diemut's home during the first half of the twelfth century – was a thriving Benedictine community situated between the Amer and Lech rivers in the diocese of Augsburg.[3] The early history of the monastery is obscure, as few documents survive to tell the story of its first three centuries. We hear no more than the names of some eighth- and ninth-century abbots,[4] and that the community, a Carolingian imperial monastery since the late eighth century, was made the *Eigenkloster* of the bishop of Augsburg in the early tenth century. Already weakened by a secularization ordered by Duke Arnulf of Bavaria (d. 937), the community collapsed in 955 in the wake of the Hungarian raid that had led to the martyrdom of the seven monks. For the next hundred years, Wessobrunn operated as a house of secular canons directed by a series of priors. The last of these was Adalbero (1065–1110), who repopulated the monastery with a group of monks from Saint Emmeram in Regensburg, restored Benedictine observance, and stayed on himself as abbot.

Through its connection with Saint Emmeram, Wessobrunn came into contact with the reform ideas associated with the monastery of Gorze.[5] During the twelfth century, and possibly during Diemut's time there, the monastery joined the Hirsau reform. While the establishment of an adjoining cenobitic community for women in *c.* 1138 may signal the beginning of this conversion,[6] the process was certainly complete by 1161, when Liutold of Hirsau, who would serve as abbot from 1161 to 1165, arrived with six of his monks.[7]

We can imagine, in the absence of any contemporary customary or narrative source from Wessobrunn itself, that like most Benedictines, the community's monks and nuns divided their day among liturgical celebration, manual labor, reading, and prayer. As a monastery within the Regensburg filiation of the Gorze reform, the community likely embraced some version of Saint Emmeram's customs. Saint Emmeram's tenth-century customary, which like all Benedictine customaries was intended to be followed in conjunction with the Rule, set forth an elaborate

3 The monastery was founded in *c.* 753 by the Bavarian duke Tassilo III, or perhaps by a member of the Huosi family, who founded nearby Benediktbeuren. For a history of Wessobrunn, see Leuttner, *Historia monasterii Wessofontani*; Pirmin Lindner, *Monasticon Episcopatus Augustani antiqui. Verzeichnisse der Aebte, Pröpste und Aebtissinnen der Klöster der alten Diözese Augsburg*, vol. I (Bregenz, 1913), pp. 96–100; *Germania Benedictina* (Augsburg, 1970– ), vol. II, pp. 336–342.

4 Ilsung (*c.* 753), Snello (806–810), Benedict (933–944), Thiento (to 955).

5 On the monastery of Gorze and Lotharingian monastic reform, see John Nightingale, *Monasteries and Patrons in the Gorze Reform: Lotharingia c. 850–1000* (Oxford, 2001). See also the classic work of Kassius Hallinger, *Gorze-Kluny. Studien zu den monastischen Lebensformen und Gegensätzen im Hochmittelalter*, Studia Anselmiana 22–25 (Rome, 1950), pp. 158–159.

6 On the connection between Hirsau and the founding of double monasteries, see pp. 26–28 above.

7 Romuald Bauerreiss, *Kirchengeschichte Bayerns*, 7 vols. (Munich, 1949–1970), vol. III, p. 13.

liturgical schedule for the entire year. The text specified the time that the religious were to read and pray, with variations reflecting the liturgical obligations of the changing seasons.[8]

Documentary sources have more to say, especially about the economic status and social range of the monastery: twelfth-century Wessobrunn was an expanding community, enjoying the patronage of many local nobles and *ministeriales*,[9] as well as individuals of lower social status. The monastery's medieval charters, however, are preserved only in a sixteenth-century *liber traditionum* compiled from scattered archival documents by the monk Stephen Leopold.[10] By the time Stephen began his work, some of the medieval charters may already have been lost, especially since two major fires destroyed parts of the monastery during the twelfth century. Stephen may also have been selective in his compilation, including only the documents that he thought were relevant to the monastery's history.[11] He transcribed only three diplomata dating from the abbacy of Adalbero, Sighard (1110–1128), and Adalbero II (1128–1129), although we cannot know whether others existed that did not pass through Stephen's filter. But the substantial number dating from 1130 to 1200 reflect a house that was thriving financially. Stephen's *liber traditionum* includes thirty-four donations from the twenty-six year period (approximately 1.3 per year) of Waltho's abbacy (1130–1156). Sixteen of these were gifts of landed estates made by noble men and women. Under Waltho's successor, Norbert (1156–1161), the house was equally successful at bringing in donations; during his abbacy, patrons made at least eight gifts to the monastery (approximately 1.3 per year). Donations appear to have decreased to approximately one every two years under Abbots Liutold (1161–1165), Conrad I (1165–1166), and Sigibald (1172–1200), although this could signal nothing more than a gap in the documentation. Another indicator of economic health is the remains of an extensive program of carefully executed Romanesque sculpture, which many art historians consider to be among the finest examples from Germany – a luxury that only a well-endowed community could afford.[12]

8 See Kassius Hallinger, ed., *Corpus Consuetudinum Monasticarum* 7/3 (Siegburg, 1984), pp. 187–256. On the other hand, this text survives in only one manuscript, a tenth-century copy from Einsiedeln (Einsiedeln, Stiftsbibliothek 235), and it is unclear how widespread its use was in the tenth and later centuries.

9 On the nature of these *ministeriales*, see John B. Freed, *Noble Bondsmen: Ministerial Marriages in the Archdiocese of Salzburg, 1100–1343* (Ithaca, NY, 1995); see also Timothy Reuter, *Germany in the Early Middle Ages, 800–1056* (New York, 1991), pp. 231–232.

10 For a discussion of this genre, see above Chapter 3, p. 75 and following.

11 On the problems associated with omissions, intentional and unintentional, from *libri traditionum* compiled from earlier, now lost charters, see Patrick Geary, *Phantoms of Remembrance: Memory and Oblivion at the End of the First Millennium* (Princeton, 1994), pp. 81–114, esp. at p. 82.

12 G. Hager, "Die Bautätigkeit und Kunst im Kloster Wessobrunn," *Oberbayerisches Archiv* 48 (1892): 195–521.

## THE EXPANSION OF THE FEMALE COMMUNITY

Although an anonymous sixteenth-century historian claimed that there were women at the monastery already during its first Benedictine period (753–*c.* 955),[13] there is no surviving documented female presence at Wessobrunn until Diemut.[14] She may have been the only woman during her first years there, or perhaps other female recluses escaped the notice of, or failed to interest, the medieval and early modern record-keepers. Around 1138, however, we can see the women's community begin to grow. Some women may have been attracted to Wessobrunn by Diemut herself, for it was common for a single recluse to provide the nucleus around which a larger community of women might develop, or perhaps they arrived in response to the growing influence of the Hirsau reform.[15] The first surviving record of a female profession can be dated to 1138/1139, when a nobleman donated a piece of land to the community on the occasion of the entrance of his sister, Richinsa.[16] It is unclear what type of community Richinsa joined – the charter indicates only that she was admitted to the spiritual life at Wessobrunn. She may have lived as a professed nun within a newly established cenobitic community for women, or like Diemut, she may have lived as a recluse. It is also possible that she joined as a lay sister, or *conversa*, a type of convert whose presence at Wessobrunn is reflected in the necrology.[17] The next wave of professions began in 1147 when a daughter of Adalbert of Mammendorf, and the noblewoman Adelheid and her daughter, joined the community.[18] A charter from 1156/1157 states that Mechtild, a noble woman from Weilheim, joined a group of virgins already in residence.[19] These were local women, as both Mammendorf and Weilheim are towns near the monastery. By 1163, the female community had grown large enough to support a satellite house, which was colonized with twelve nuns and two priests.[20] This period of flowering, however, appears to have been short-lived: no charter documenting the admission of a woman after the middle of the thirteenth century has survived. It is unclear why the monastery discontinued its support of women's religious life, but possibly,

[13] The chronicler speaks of a cloister for women (*clausura sanctimonialium feminarum*) at the monastery under Abbot Ilsung. Cölestin Leuttner, the eighteenth-century historian of Wessobrunn, claimed that the anonymous author was Stephen Leopold, the compiler of the 1502 tradition book. For a brief history of the female community at Wessobrunn, see Irma Bühler, "Forschungen über Benediktiner-Doppelklöster im heutigen Bayern," *Zeitschrift für bayerische Kirchengeschichte* 5 (1930): 243–248.

[14] *Necrologium Wessobrunnense*, ed. Franciscus Ludovicus Baumann. MGH, Necrologiae Germaniae 1, p. 45.

[15] Giles Constable, *The Reformation of the Twelfth Century* (Cambridge, 1996), pp. 69–70.

[16] Reinhard Höppl, ed., *Die Traditionen des Klosters Wessobrunn*. Quellen und Erörterungen zur bayerischen Geschichte. NS 32/1 (Munich, 1982), Tr. 17.

[17] These women were of a status similar to that of *conversae* at Premonstratensian communities such as Schäftlarn. See the related discussion in Chapter 4, p. 111 and following.

[18] Höppl, *Traditionen*, Tr. 27. [19] Höppl, *Traditionen*, Tr. 41a.

[20] Höppl, *Traditionen*, Tr. 49.

like so many other female communities at that time, it fell victim to the sentiment against double monasteries that characterized the major religious orders of the time.[21]

## DIEMUT AS *INCLUSA*

In supporting Diemut as an *inclusa*, Wessobrunn stood in a long tradition of facilitating religious seclusion within a Benedictine context.[22] Benedict's Rule makes room for individuals who, after a period of spiritual preparation in a cenobitic community, are called to a life of greater solitude and rigor.[23] We know that there were Benedictine recluses, male and female, throughout Europe between 700 and 1000,[24] and while the extent of their involvement in the activities of the wider community varied from place to place, many of the Rule's precepts influenced their way of life.[25] The Benedictine Rule exerted its influence primarily through the inclusion of many of its major precepts in later rules written specifically for solitaries. The earliest of these was the work of a ninth- or tenth-century monk named Grimlaic, whose *Regula solitariorum* stipulated that a hermit divide the day among prayer, devotional reading, and manual labor. Education was essential; a recluse was expected to be learned in both the Old and the New Testament.[26] Grimlaic devoted two chapters of his rule to manual labor, which was intended to combat the perils of idleness.[27] For a female recluse, this labor could include weaving, basket-making, spinning, embroidery, and book copying. The community could then use the items produced, or sell them and apply the profit toward her upkeep.[28] The placement of a cell with a window into the monastery church could provide a view of the altar for mass, facilitate participation in the sacrament of communion, and enable the solitary to take part in the Divine Office. One Bavarian anchorhold had three windows: one opening into the choir, one for passing food and other materials in and out, and a third for light.[29]

21 See related discussion in Chapter 3, pp. 68–69.

22 Both eremitical and cenobitical forms of religious life flourished in the West beginning in late antiquity. In the eleventh and twelfth centuries, the eremitical impulse gave rise to new orders of hermits. These eremitical orders were especially successful in Italy, England, and France. See Peter F. Anson, *The Call of the Desert: the Solitary Life in the Christian Church* (London, 1964) and Henrietta Leyser, *Hermits and the New Monasticism: A Study of Religious Communities in Western Europe, 1000–1150* (London, 1984). For a discussion of hermits and other solitaries in the context of the twelfth-century monastic reforms, see Constable, *Reformation*, pp. 60–65.

23 RB 1980 1: 2–5. 24 Anson, *Call of the Desert*, p. 63.

25 Ann K. Warren, *Anchorites and their Patrons in Medieval England* (Berkeley, 1985), p. 23.

26 PL 103, col. 599. 27 PL 103, col. 629.

28 Ottmar Doerr, *Das Institüt der Inklusen in Suddeutschland* (Münster, 1934), p. 55, although Doerr did not list book-copying as a type of manual labor undertaken by women.

29 Anson, *Call of the Desert*, pp. 62 and 169.

German religious clearly shared an interest in the solitary life with other Western Europeans during the eleventh and twelfth centuries, but organized orders of hermits never took hold in German lands.[30] In Bavaria, solitaries of both sexes tended to remain independent or to seek refuge in single cells attached to monasteries.[31] Contemporary and near-contemporary sources name as *inclusae* women who lived in a variety of settings, with and without overseeing institutions. The recluse Herluca (d. 1127), for example, was permitted to leave her cell at the Benedictine monastery of Bernried, and she traveled extensively, involving herself with contemporary church politics through a series of visions. Herluca was a vocal supporter of the Hirsau reform and a well-known spiritual figure in the region.[32] The late-eleventh-century widows Judith (or Jutta) and Salome of Niederaltaich, a Benedictine community with connections to the reform ideas associated with Gorze and Saint Emmeram, on the other hand, were said to be permanently enclosed in separate cells in which they worked in the service of the monastery.[33] And the recluse Edigna of Puch (d. 1109) lived alone in the woods, enclosed in a hollow linden tree, independent of any organized religious community.[34] The names of many other eleventh- and twelfth-century female recluses appear in the

[30] The congregations of Camaldoli (the first eremitical order founded in the West) and Vallombrosa were founded and gained popularity during the eleventh century, especially in Italy, but communities of both types of congregation were also founded in France and Spain. C. H. Lawrence, *Medieval Monasticism: Forms of Religious Life in Western Europe in the Middle Ages*, second edition (London and New York, 1989), pp. 152–156.

[31] Bauerreiss, *Kirchengeschichte*, vol. III, p. 47; Armin Basedow, *Die Inclusen in Deutschland vornehmlich in der Gegend des Niederrheins um die Wende des 12. und 13. Jahrhunderts* (Heidelberg, 1896); the annals of the Premonstratensian abbey of Windberg report that, by the middle of the eleventh century, an Armenian archbishop had founded a colony of hermits near Passau. This same document goes on to mention a hermit called William who took up residence in Bogen and enjoyed the financial support of Liutkart, the local countess. A chapel Luitkart's son built over William's grave was incorporated into Windberg at its founding in 1140: *Historiae et Annales Windbergenses*, ed. Philipp Jaffé. MGH, Scriptores 17, pp. 560–561; Bauerreiss, *Kirchengeschichte*, vol. III, p. 43. Two hermits, both named Henry, lived near Starnbergersee and Beuerberg during the twelfth century, but nothing is known of their history. A necrology from Baumburg, a house of regular canons, identifies a third Henry as an *inclusus* at that community. A rule associated with Baumburg survives in one twelfth-century copy, and this may provide some clues as to the daily life of these men: Doerr, "Inklusen in Suddeutschland," p. 108; Bauerreiss, *Kirchengeschichte*, vol. III, p. 44.

[32] Paul of Bernried, the biographer of Pope Gregory VII, wrote a Life of Herluca just after her death, and he tells us of her visions, which included warnings about the morals of local parish priests. Herluca had become involved in the reform through her acquaintance with William of Hirsau and with Dietger, a reforming abbot of St. George in the Black Forest. See *Vita Beatae Herlucae*, AASS, 2 April, pp. 549–554; see also *LThK* 5, p. 249.

[33] Both women were enclosed at Niederaltaich in adulthood after undertaking a pilgrimage to Jerusalem. Neither appears to have been a professed nun prior to enclosure: AASS, 5 June, pp. 492–498.

[34] Edigna was allegedly the daughter of a French king, Henry I or Philip I, and fled an unwanted marriage as a young adult. When her ox cart stopped beside the hollow linden tree, Edigna interpreted it as a divinely inspired sign and settled there. A brief biography can be found in AASS, 3 February, p. 668.

necrologies of Nonnberg, St. Peter, and St. Rupert and St. Florian (in Salzburg), and Schäftlarn (near Munich), but we know little about their lives.[35]

Because there is no contemporary biography, Diemut's way of life at Wessobrunn is almost as obscure.[36] Wessobrunn was associated at the time of her arrival, like Judith and Salome's Niederaltaich, with the Gorze reform, whose advocates asserted that strict enclosure provided needed insulation from corrupting worldly pursuits. Removed from the world in the extreme, the recluse represented for the reformers the highest level of spiritual praxis, and many reformed houses supported one or more of these isolated individuals.[37]

It is impossible to say with certainty when or why Diemut came to Wessobrunn. Her sixteenth-century biographer claimed that she had joined the community as a young child, but it is difficult to imagine that the monks would have undertaken the care and education of just one young girl. Perhaps as a young woman, Diemut, like Edigna, fled an unwanted marriage or other difficult family situation and found the monks of Wessobrunn willing to shelter her as a recluse and to provide her with food and spiritual guidance. But another, less dramatic, scenario seems more plausible: Diemut was a proficient scribe when she copied the first of her manuscripts for the monastery, and was thus able to offer the monks a valuable commodity – books – in exchange for her spiritual and physical upkeep. Examples of her work from this period display a skilled, consistent hand, and the parchment that she was given to use was of good quality.[38] This was not the work of a student, or even a merely competent scribe, but of an experienced copyist. This level of skill may indicate that Diemut had reached adulthood by the early twelfth century. It is possible that Diemut was trained as a copyist at Wessobrunn, but no examples of her work from her early, less experienced phase have survived. It seems more likely that she had received a monastic education, possibly at a women's or double monastery in the area before her arrival at Wessobrunn.[39] Having received her initial spiritual and intellectual training at another community, she may have

35 On Willa, see Nora Watteck, *Einsiedler. Inklusen, Eremiten, Klausner und Waldbrüder im Salzburgischen* (Salzburg, 1972), pp. 15–21.

36 Because a *Regula solitariorum*, probably that of Grimlaic, is first documented at Wessobrunn in a list of books drawn up in 1180 (i.e. after Diemut's death), it is questionable whether she followed that specific Rule. The 1180 list is found in MBKr, p. 184.

37 On the Gorze reform's interest in and support of eremitism, see Bauerreiss, *Kirchengeschichte*, vol. II, pp. 24–25.

38 For a full description of Diemut's hand, see below, pp. 47–48; see Appendix A, Table A1 for statistics reflecting the quality of the parchment used for these volumes.

39 On the educational background of English recluses during this period, see Bella Millett, "Women in No Man's Land: English Recluses and the Development of Vernacular Literature in the Twelfth and Thirteenth Centuries," in *Women and Literature in Britain, c.1150–1500*, ed. Carol M. Meale (Cambridge, 1993), pp. 86–103. Millett demonstrates that while some recluses, like Eve of Wilton, appear to have had some degree of monastic education before becoming anchoresses, others entered without education directly from lay life (pp. 88–90).

sought a higher degree of spiritual rigor as a recluse. She died on 30 March, but the year of her death is unknown. Scholars have suggested dates ranging from 1130 to 1150.[40]

While the details of Diemut's daily life are elusive, we can imagine that she, like other female Benedictines, devoted considerable energy to prayer and reading. But manual labor – and especially scribal work – must have consumed a large portion of her time. The sheer number of manuscripts she produced (see Table 2.1) indicates that book copying was a primary focus of her life. For spiritual companionship and guidance, Diemut may have exchanged letters with fellow recluse Herluca of Bernried.[41] Their correspondence, for which the earliest evidence is from the sixteenth-century biographer, was said to be preserved at Bernried, but it had disappeared by the early eighteenth century.[42] Perhaps lacking a suitable spiritual companion at Wessobrunn, Diemut may have used a letter exchange with Herluca to fill this void.[43] This connection between Diemut and Herluca may have provided one point of contact between Wessobrunn and the Hirsau reform circle.[44]

## BUILDING A LIBRARY AT WESSOBRUNN

As an affiliate of two successive monastic reforms, Wessobrunn was certainly influenced by the interest in literary pursuits that tended to accompany those movements. Wessobrunn is not known to have produced any original literary work during the Middle Ages.[45] The rapid growth of its library, both in the size and scope of its holdings, however, suggests Wessobrunn experienced its own intellectual flowering in the twelfth century. One focus of this revival was devotional reading, an activity that held an important place in the ideals of both the Gorze and Hirsau reforms. The biography of John of Gorze describes a course of devotional

[40] For a discussion of the possible dates of her death, see Elisabeth Klemm, *Die romanischen Handschriften der Bayerischen Staatsbibliothek*, 3 vols. (Wiesbaden, 1980–), vol. II/1, p. 163.
[41] Leuttner, *Historia monasterii Wessofontani*, p. 173; von Hefner, "Diemud," p. 367. On Herluca, see p. 37 above.
[42] Bernard Pez investigated the report of letters exchanged by the two *inclusae*, but all evidence was lost. See p. 62 below.
[43] As Grimlaic shared the conviction that complete seclusion was not spiritually beneficial, he suggested in his Rule that a monastery ought to accommodate at least two or three hermits in individual cells close enough to one another to permit communication through the small window or windows. See Grimlaic, *Regula solitariorum*, PL 103, col. 595.
[44] On Herluca as a supporter of Hirsau monasticism, see n. 32 above.
[45] It is possible that the author of the ninth-century *Wessobrunner Gebiet*, one of the oldest prayers written in Old High German, was a monk of Wessobrunn. The monastery preserved for almost one thousand years a copy of the prayer made by scribes associated with the scriptorium of the archdiocese of Augsburg.

Table 2.1 *Books copied by Diemut*

| | Booklist A<br>"Isti sunt libri, quos scripsit et sancto Petro tradidit Diemot, ancilla Dei" | Booklist B<br>"Hi sunt libri, quos scripsit Diemoth, ancilla Dei" | Notes |
|---|---|---|---|
| 1 | Liber missalis cum graduali et sequentiis. | Quinque libros missales. Tres ex his cum gradualibus et sequentiis, cum epistolis et evangeliis, II sine epistolis et evangeliis. | 1221 booklist includes seven missals, which may include the four copied by Diemut that remained at Wessobrunn |
| 2 | Alius liber cum graduali et sequentiis, qui datus est episcopo Treverensi. | — | |
| 3 | Item missalis liber cum epistolis et evangeliis et graduali et sequentiis. | — | |
| 4 | Item alius liber missalis cum epistolis et evangeliis per totum annum et graduali et sequentiis et baptisterio integro. | — | |
| 5 | Item missalis liber cum epistolis et evangeliis. | — | |
| 6 | Officialis liber. | Duos libros officiales | 1221 booklist includes 3 libri officiales, which may include the one copied by Diemut that remained at Wessobrunn |
| 7 | Alius liber officialis cum baptisterio, qui datus est episcopo Augustensi. | — | |
| 8 | Liber cum evangeliis et lectionibus. | Lectionarium, I volumen | |
| 9 | Liber cum evangeliis. | | **Clm 22044**<br>Diemut only (except illuminated first page of each Gospel), *c.* 1120.<br>1221 booklist includes a Gospel, which might be the one copied by Diemut |
| 10 | Liber cum epistolis. | Epistolarium et evvangelia, II volumina | 1221 booklist includes an epistolarium, which might be the one copied by Diemut |
| 11–12 | Bibliotheca in duobus voluminibus, que data est in pretio predii ad Bisinberc. | | |
| 13–15 | Bibliotheca in tribus voluminibus. | Testamentum <in> III voluminibus | **Clm 22005**<br>**Clm 22006**<br>Collaborative, *c.* 1126–1150<br>In 1240 inventory |

Table 2.1 (*cont.*)

| | Booklist A<br>"Isti sunt libri, quos scripsit et sancto Petro tradidit Diemot, ancilla Dei" | Booklist B<br>"Hi sunt libri, quos scripsit Diemoth, ancilla Dei" | Notes |
|---|---|---|---|
| 16–21 | Moralis in sex partibus. | Moralia in VI voluminibus | **Clm 22009**, 17th c. ex-libris<br>**Clm 22010**, 17th c. ex-libris<br>**Clm 22011**, 17th c. ex-libris<br>**Clm 22012**<br>Diemut only, *c.* 1100<br>In 1221 inventory (lists vols. II–VI = vol. I missing by 1221)<br>In 1240 (lists five volumes)<br>In 1513 booklist (vols. II and IV–VI = vol. I and III missing by 1513) |
| 22<br>23 | Gregorius ad Regaredum.<br>Gregorius super Ezechielem. | Gregorium super Hezechielem, I volumen | **Clm 22008**, 17th c. ex-libris<br>Diemut only, *c.* 1100<br>In 1221 inventory<br>In 1240 inventory |
| 24–26 | Omeliae in tribus voluminibus. | Omelias sanctorum patrum in tribus voluminibus | **Clm 22002**<br>**Clm 22003**<br>Collaborative, 1126–1150<br>In 1221 inventory (?)<br>In 1240 inventory (?) |
| 27 | Originem super vetus testamentum. | Origenem super vetus testamentum, I volumen | In 1221 inventory<br>In 1240 inventory |
| 28 | Origenes super cantica canticorum. | Origenem super cantica canticorum, I volumen | In 1221 inventory<br>In 1240 inventory |
| 29–31 | Augustinus super psalterium in tribus voluminibus. | Augustinum super psalterium, III volumina | **Clm 22007**, 17th c. ex-libris<br>Diemut only, 1100–1125<br>In 1240 inventory |
| 32–33 | Augustinus super evangelium et super epistolam Johannis in duobus voluminibus. | Augustinum super evvangelium et epistolam Johannis, I volumen | In 1221 inventory<br>In 1240 inventory |
| 34 | Epistolae Augustini numero LXXV | Epistolas Augustini in uno volumine | Stams Fragments (?)*<br>In 1221 inventory (?)<br>In 1240 inventory (?) |
| 35 | Augustinus de verbis Domini, in quo etiam continetur liber de sermone Domini in monte, etc. | Augustinum de verbis domini. De sermone Domini in monte habito. De opere monachorum. De agone Christiano. De adorando Deo ad Probam. | In 1240 inventory |
| 36 | Epistolae Jeronimi numero CLXIIII. | | Stams Fragments (?)<br>In 1240 inventory (?) |

(*cont.*)

Table 2.1 (*cont.*)

| | Booklist A "Isti sunt libri, quos scripsit et sancto Petro tradidit Diemot, ancilla Dei" | Booklist B "Hi sunt libri, quos scripsit Diemoth, ancilla Dei" | Notes |
|---|---|---|---|
| 37–38 | Tripartita historia. (Cassiodorus) | Tripartitam hystoriam, II volumina | **Clm 22015**<br>Diemut only, 1126–1150<br>In 1221 inventory |
| 39 | Ecclesiastica hystoria. (Eusebius) | Ecclesiasticam <histo>riam | **Clm 22014**<br>Collaborative, 1126–1150<br>In 1221 inventory |
| 40 | Quinquaginta sermones Augustini, in quo continetur vita sancti Silvestri. In eodem Jeronimus contra Vigilantium. In eodem Jeronimus de consolatione mortuorum. In eodem vita S. Basilii et vita Johannis Elemosinarii. | L sermones Augustini. Hieronimum de laude virginum. Vitam Basilii. Vitam Johannis Eleymonis [sic]. Hieronimum contra Vigilantium. Augustinum contra diffinitiones, I volumen. | |
| 41 | Paschasius de corpore et sanguine Domini. In eodem conflictus Lanfranci contra Beringerum. In eodem passiones martyrum Dionisii et sociorum eius et Adriani et Stephani paparum. | [Two Separate Volumes:] Pascasium, I volumen. Passiones martirum Dionisii, Mauritii, Alexandri, Adriani, I volumen. | Probably divided into two parts between the compilation of List A and List B.<br>In 1221 inventory (Pascasius and Passionarium)<br>In 1240 inventory (Pascasius and Passionarium) |
| 42 | Johannes Chrisostimus. | Johannem Crisostomum de lapso et cetera, I volumen | In 1221 inventory<br>In 1240 inventory |
| 43 | Jeronimus de hebraicis questionibus. | Librum hebraicarum questionum Jeronimi | **Clm 22016?**<br>Collaborative, 1126–1160<br>In 1221 inventory<br>In 1240 inventory |
| 44 | Confessionum liber Augustini. | Augustinum de confessionibus, I volumen | In 1221 inventory<br>In 1240 inventory |
| 45 | Canones. | Canones | In 1221 inventory? (Corpus canonum)<br>In 1240 inventory (Corpus canonum) |
| 46 | Glossa per a b c composita. | Glossam cum alfabeto de ignotis <nom>inibus | |
| 47 | Plenarium in uno volumine. | Plenarium I | |

Spellings as in the original lists have been retained.

* See the discussion of the origin of manuscript fragments preserved at Stams on p. 46 below.

reading that focused heavily on certain patristic texts – particularly Gregory, Ambrose, Jerome, and the less complex texts of Augustine.[46] Twelfth-century readers at Wessobrunn would have had access to some of these texts, but only after a dramatic expansion of the library. At the end of the eleventh century, more than three-quarters of the books at the monastery seem to have been liturgical or biblical texts, with a smaller number of volumes containing patristic and hagiographical texts and biblical commentaries.[47] As the library grew, its focus shifted from liturgical texts to texts used for the devotional reading of the Bible.

The most striking evidence of the expansion of Wessobrunn's library is found in two lists of the works that Diemut copied. The earlier of the two lists (Booklist A, Clm 22001[d]) was copied by a fellow nun-scribe, who must have had firsthand knowledge of Diemut and her work. The second list (Booklist B) was copied in the first years of the thirteenth century by a third scribe on a free page in a manuscript of Sulpicius Severus' *Life of Saint Martin* (Clm 22059, f. 72v). Both list over forty books, giving credence to the claim voiced on the plaques that marked her grave that Diemut built an entire library for the monastery with her own hands. This collection, most of which evidently remained in the monastery library in the twelfth and early thirteenth centuries, reflects the changing needs and interests of her community.

Table 2.1 lists each of the texts named in the two inventories (columns 1 and 2),[48] and notes any appearance in later booklists or seventeenth-century ex-libris entries (column 3).[49]

The range of texts represented – whether those texts were chosen by Diemut or by someone else at Wessobrunn – is interesting. Roughly half were biblical and liturgical books. Diemut copied twelve service books, enough to allow for the gift of a surplus missal with graduals and sequences to the bishop of Trier (number 2)

[46] John's *Vita* provides a high level of detail regarding the ideal daily practices within Gorze-affiliated communities. The Life is an important source of this information, since we lack a customary from Gorze at this period. See Lin Donat, "Vie et coutume monastique dans la Vita de Jean de Gorze," in *L'Abbaye de Gorze au Xe siècle*, ed. Michel Parisse and Otto Gerhard Oexle (Nancy, 1993), pp. 159–182.

[47] This observation is based on a single list, which might not reflect all of the monastery's books. The list might, for example, represent the contents of a single armarium among two or more. For an edition of the list, see MBKr, pp. 177–178: "Liber genesis, actus apostolorum / epistolae canonicae, apocalysis in uno volumine, Libri regum, expositio ecclesiastes, Job, Tobias, Judith in uno volumine, Libri Machabeorum, Libri Prophetarum, Collectarium, Epistolae Pauli, Psalterium, Omeliae II, De quadraginta XXI, Liber sancti Martini, Canones apostolorum, Expositio psalterii, Liber Smaragdus, Passionarium apostolorum, Prognosticum futuri saeculi, Isidorus, Dialogus, Missalia III, Missale, graduale, lectionarium in uno volumine, Lectionaria cum evangeliis II, Plenaria II, Gradualia IIII, Matutinales libri II, Offitiale, Sequentionarius, Libri baptismales cum commendatione animarum II."

[48] MBKr, pp. 181–182 (Booklist A, Clm 22001[d]) and p. 183 (Booklist B, Clm 22059, f. 72v).

[49] For the production of these later lists, see p. 60.

and a *liber officialis* with the baptismal rite to the bishop of Augsburg (number 7). In *c.* 1130 the monastery exchanged a two-volume copy of the Bible (numbers 11–12) for an entire estate in Peissenberg owned by the widow Hademut.[50] It seems that, beyond meeting the needs of the monastery's own literate monks, nuns, and priests, Diemut's books also provided a means of fostering good relations with ecclesiastical authorities and a tangible source of wealth for the community.

Patristic works comprised over half of Diemut's total output and reflect a clear interest at Wessobrunn in biblical study – specifically the meditative, devotional monastic *lectio* to which, in the tenth century, John of Gorze's (d. 977) abbot insisted John limit himself. When John ventured too deeply into Augustine's *De trinitate* – even going so far as to undertake a study of Porphyry's *Isagoge* to help him to grasp Augustine's logic – his abbot sharply warned him back into a more restricted realm of monastic devotional reading.[51] So strikingly conservative and reflective of Gorze's ideals was Diemut's choice of books (if, in fact, it was her choice, and not the choice of the *armaria* or *armarius*) that continued ties between Wessobrunn and Gorze reform circles during Diemut's time appear highly probable.

The hypothesis of continued Gorze influence is supported by the order in which the compiler of Booklist A listed Diemut's codices: the first non-liturgical book on Booklist A is a six-volume copy of Gregory's *Moralia in Job* (Booklist A, numbers 16–21), a text that John of Gorze's biographer claimed John had memorized. Others of Gregory's works follow immediately on the list, notably his commentary on Ezekiel (number 23) to which John had returned – and memorized – after his reproof by the abbot.[52] The works of Gregory appear, in fact, to have been given a particular prominence, at least by the scribe who wrote the booklist. Only after the works of Gregory (numbers 16–23) and a mixed compilation of patristic homilies (numbers 24–26) do the individual works of other church fathers appear. First listed are Origen's commentaries on the Old Testament (number 27) and on the Song of Songs (number 28), followed by Augustine's commentaries on the Psalms

[50] The following entry appears in the list of Diemut's books, identified here as Booklist A: *Bibliotheca in duobus voluminibus, que est in pretio predii ad Bisinberc* (a Bible in two volumes, which was given in payment for an estate in Peissenberg); the donation of the land is recorded in the tradition book, although no reference is made in the charter to the books: "Notum sit omnibus Christi fidelibus, quod quedam vidua nomine Hademot tradidit sancto Petro tale predium, quod in Bisenberch habuit, cum omnibus redditibus suis in proprietatem fratrum pro remedio anime sue et parentum suorum." (May it be known to all the faithful of Christ, that a certain widow named Hademut gave a certain estate that she had in Peissenberg, with all its revenues to Saint Peter for the salvation of her soul and the souls of her relatives.) There is no notice of this set of books in Booklist B, which was probably copied several decades later.

[51] Teresa Webber, "The Patristic Content of English Book Collections in the Eleventh Century: Towards a Continental Perspective," in *Of the Making of Books: Medieval Manuscripts, their Scribes and Readers. Essays Presented to M. B. Parkes*, ed. P. R. Robinson and Rivkah Zim (Aldershot, 1997), pp. 196–197.

[52] Webber, "Patristic Content of English Book Collections," p. 196.

(numbers 29–31) and the Gospel of John, and others of his sermons (number 32–33). Significantly, Diemut copied none of Augustine's more theological works, such as his treatise on the Trinity, and his *Confessions* appears close to the end of the list (number 44). Diemut also copied the letters of Jerome (possibly interesting, in part, to Diemut or her community because of their instructions and advice regarding female education) (number 36), and his *Hebraicae quaestiones in Genesim* (number 43) which appears near the end of the list, but just before Augustine's *Confessions*. Diemut also copied more recent theological works by Paschasius Radbertus and Lanfranc of Bec (number 41), reflecting a concern within the community for orthodox teaching on the nature of the transformation of the bread and wine in the mass. The *Historia ecclesiastica tripartita* of Cassiodorus (number 37–38) and Eusebius' *Historia ecclesiastica* (number 39), and the alphabetical glossary, which provided explanations of unfamiliar names from sacred writings, may have served as aids to deeper meditation on the Bible, further supporting the image of this collection as one geared toward the meditative reading of the monastic *lectio*. This is a collection of books of which even John of Gorze's abbot would have approved, which gives it a distinctly conservative character in the context of its twelfth-century production. It may be that, even after the advent of the Hirsau reform at Wessobrunn, the spiritual and intellectual ideals of a previous generation of nuns and monks prevailed.

## IDENTIFYING DIEMUT'S MANUSCRIPTS

In 1220, soon after the compilation of Booklist B, a fire destroyed much of the monastery's library – a disaster to which the charred edges and burned pages of many of Diemut's surviving books bear witness. In the year following the fire, the monk Conrad Pozzo began the work of assessing the damage and compiling a list of salvaged books. The four missals copied by Diemut for use at the monastery may have been among the seven that survived the fire. The *evangeliarium*, *liber officialis*, and *epistolarium* that were saved may also have been hers, although it is not possible to determine this from the information provided in Conrad's list. Four of her manuscripts were destroyed in the fire, including the first volume of her six-volume *Moralia in Job* (number 16), fifty sermons by Augustine (number 40), the alphabetical glossary (number 46), and the one-volume *plenarium* (number 47). Her three-volume Bible (numbers 13–15), which was not included in the post-fire inventory, does appear in Conrad's second booklist, which he compiled in 1240. This suggests either that he initially overlooked it, or that it was on loan outside the community at the time of the fire and subsequently returned.

The 75 Letters of Augustine (number 34) and 164 Letters of Jerome (number 36) may have been combined to form a single volume by 1221, as Conrad listed a one-volume collection of letters of Jerome and Augustine, but no independent collection of letters by either author. While this volume was not listed in the inventory of 1240, fragments of a similar collection were discovered at the Cistercian monastery of Stams. Stams had acquired a number of books from Wessobrunn during a period of financial difficulty during the fourteenth century,[53] and conservators in the early nineteenth century discovered two double leaves, the remnants of a manuscript containing the letters of Jerome and Augustine, when they replaced the binding of a seventeenth-century book preserved in Stams' archives.[54] Bruno Griesser identified Diemut as the scribe of these fragments based on paleographical similarity to her work preserved in Munich, and suggested that they originated in the single codex created by the combination of two initially independent books of letters (number 34 and 36) described above.[55] Two other surviving manuscripts, Cassiodorus' *Historia ecclesiastica tripartita* and Eusebius' *Historia ecclesiastica*, do not appear in Conrad's 1240 inventory, but are still extant, suggesting that they were perhaps off-site at the time, and subsequently returned to the monastery.[56] Between 1240, when Conrad conducted his second inventory, and 1803, when the collection was transferred to the Bayerische Staatsbibliothek in Munich, Diemut's books continued to disappear from Wessobrunn's library. Today only fourteen of Diemut's manuscripts – a fraction of her original corpus – are known to survive.

### *Isolating Diemut's hand*

Diemut did not sign any of her books, a fact that her sixteenth-century biographer attributed to her great humility. How, then, can we identify her work among the remnants of Wessobrunn's library? A comparison of the contents of the two twelfth-century lists with extant twelfth-century books from the library yields fourteen volumes that correspond to entries in the lists, five of which contain a seventeenth-century ex-libris identifying them as the work of Diemut.[57] The one scribe common to all fourteen was Diemut. Bernhard Bischoff, who conducted a spot-check of these books, was right to note, however, that not all of these were the

[53] On Wessobrunn's financial difficulties and its time under the direction of Stamms, see p. 61 below.

[54] On the contents and origin of these fragments, see Bruno Griesser, "Fragmente einer Diemuthandschrift aus dem Kloster Stams mit Hieronymus- und Augustinusbriefen," *StM* 53 (1935): 241–256.

[55] Abbot John of Stams wrote a letter in 1325 promising to return three books – a copy of the Letters of Jerome, Isidore's *Etymologiae*, and excerpts from an unnamed text of Ivo of Chartres – to the abbot of Wessobrunn, but this was evidently not done. MBKr, p. 190; Griesser, "Fragmente," pp. 252–253.

[56] MBKr, p. 188.

[57] The shelfmarks of the fourteen extant manuscripts that contain texts from the medieval lists are identified in boldface type in Table 2.1 beginning on p. 40. The five volumes containing ex-libris entries are Clm 22007, 22008, 22009, 22010, and 22011 and are also noted in Table 2.1.

work of a lone scribe.[58] She worked closely with other scribes in four manuscripts (Clm 22002, 22003, 22005, and 22006), showing that, although she was a recluse, Diemut did not always work alone.[59]

Examples of Diemut's hand can be divided into two categories. Manuscript Group 1 contains her earlier books, copied between 1100 and 1130, although they cannot be dated precisely. Group 2 contains her later books, copied perhaps between the 1130s and her death around the middle of the century. The quality of her script in the Group 2 volumes is not as high as that found in the Group 1 codices. Diemut's advancing age provides the most likely explanation for this difference. Because she was an active scribe over the course of as many as five decades, we witness in her manuscripts the decline in her physical abilities – from the peak of her skill to those copied when advanced age and perhaps illness had robbed her work of its earlier precision and clarity. In her later work, the duct more often slants to the right and appears to have been written by an unsteady hand.

Her consistency in the formation of specific letters and abbreviations, however, links the two groups as the work of a single scribe. Particularly distinctive is Diemut's abbreviation for *-orum*, which consists of an L-shaped stroke extending from the bottom of the **o** down to the right crossed with a second straight diagonal stroke to form an x. A short hook extends from the top of the **o** [Figure 1, lines 5 and 6; Figure 2, line 15]. The tail of the **y** curves up at its terminus, which frequently extends underneath the letter to the left [Figure 1, line 2; Figure 3, line 4]. Her ampersand resembles a lower case **a** with a short foot that does not extend below the text line. One very short arm extends up and to the right out of the top of the **a** and a second, longer arm, extends up to the right from the center of the right side of the **a** and terminates with a small ball. Diemut's abbreviation for the *-us* ending of the dative and ablative plurals is generally a semicolon following the **b**. The comma stroke of the semicolon is shaped like the number 7 tipped to the right [Figure 1, line 4; Figure 3, line 9]. An alternate form, a curved stroke, almost like a number 9, attached to the lobe of the **b** also appears in Group 2 manuscripts, alternating with the form found in Group 1 [Clm 22014, f. 6r, col. 1, line 8 and 12]. The descending stroke of her **g** bends to the right. The lower lobe of the **g** is generally ovoid and, in places, is not closed. The long **s** and the **t** are joined [Figure 1, lines 2, 4, 6–8, 10–12; Figure 2, line 7; Figure 3, lines 4, 8, 11]. The limb of Diemut's minuscule **h** curves around toward the bottom of the ascender with a slight hook, but remains near the text line, sometimes terminating slightly above or below [Figure 1, lines 4 and 7; Figure 2, lines 7 and 9; Figure 3, lines 4 and 10]. In the abbreviation for *pro-*, an arm crosses the descender (following the formation

58 Raymund Kottje, "Klosterbibliotheken und monastische Kultur in der zweiten Hälfte des 11. Jahrhunderts," *Zeitschrift für Kirchengeschichte* 80 (1969): 151, n. 29.

59 See related discussion on pp. 50–56 below.

of the lobe) and curves down at its terminus [Figure 1, line 12; Figure 2, lines 1 and 8]. The crossbar of the minuscule **e** frequently extends into the next letter to the right. When **e** is not immediately followed by another letter (i.e. at the end of a word) the crossbar is likewise elongated, but in this case, extends out into the blank space to the right of the letter. Most of Diemut's books contain simple pen-and-ink intitials, many of which were probably the work of the scribe herself.

### *Group 1 manuscripts: codicology and patterns of collaboration*

Diemut alone copied each of the Group 1 manuscripts. As a recluse, Diemut would probably not have had ready access to collaborators, female or male, or use of the resources of the monks' scriptorium. The monks, rather, may have provided her with the necessary facilities for copying – a desk, seat, tools, and ink – within her cell. Her life of seclusion was ideally suited to scribal work, as her high level of productivity suggests.

#### Clm 22007

Clm 22007 was originally the second of a three-volume set of Augustine's *Enarrationes* on the Psalms, divided into units of fifty psalms each. This is probably identical with the three-volume commentary on the Psalms by Augustine listed both in Booklists A and B (numbers 29–31). This identification is supported by the presence of a seventeenth-century annotation on folio 1r identifying the book as her work.

This volume contains 341 folios measuring 385 by 255 mm, with the text block measuring 280 by 170 mm and arranged according to pattern A (p. 145). The quires are uniform quaternions (except the final gathering) with no visible quire marks remaining. The manuscript was modestly decorated with a few, simple red initials, some with curvilinear floral or leaf motifs. The parchment is of high quality; the surface is smooth and white, making it difficult to differentiate between the hair and flesh sides, and 43 percent of the folios contain no significant flaws or repairs. Noteworthy is the uniformity of her hand, the high quality of the material entrusted to her, and the fact that she worked alone – characteristics shared by all of the Group 1 manuscripts – and evidence that Diemut was already a mature and highly skilled copyist at the time of their production.

#### Clm 22008

Clm 22008 is a single-volume copy of Gregory's Homilies on *Ezekiel* that appears in both contemporary booklists (number 23). The volume contains 178 folios, each measuring 340 by 245 mm with a text block of 255 by 150 mm, arranged in gatherings of four bifolia. Each folio contains twenty-eight long lines ruled, like Clm 22007, according to pattern A (see p. 145). The parchment is of very good quality, with 54 percent of the folios free of significant imperfections. The same seventeenth-century hand seen in Clm 22007 identified the manuscript as the work of Diemut of folio 1r.

### Clm 22009, 22010, 22011, 22012

Diemut copied a six-volume set of Gregory the Great's *Moralia in Job* of which four volumes have survived: volume two (books 6–9), volume four (books 17–22), volume five (books 23–27), and volume six (books 28–35). Booklists A and B describe an identical set (numbers 16–21), and Conrad Pozzo also lists a six-volume group, noting that volume one was no longer extant. By 1513 volume three was also missing.[60] A seventeenth-century ex-libris identifies Clm 22009 (f. 2r), 22010 (f. 1r), and 22011 (f. 1v) as Diemut's, although Clm 22012, the final volume in the series and clearly copied by the same scribe, was not similarly marked. The ruling and parchment size are not entirely consistent; the parchment varies between 335 and 350 mm by 220 and 245 mm, and is ruled according to pattern A, $A_1$, or $A_2$ (see p. 145).[61] The gatherings are mainly uniform quaternions, but the quality of the parchment is inconsistent, with between 39 and 49 percent of the folios free from visible flaws. These variations probably resulted from changes in parchment supply or techniques of manufacture during the extended period over which the six volumes were executed. Perhaps Diemut took several years to complete the entire set, and conditions in the monastery (i.e. finances, staffing, and quality of available animal skins) may have changed over time.

### Clm 22044

Clm 22044 is a richly illuminated copy of the Gospels made during the first quarter of the twelfth century. The volume measures 250 by 175 mm, with each of its 270 leaves ruled for twenty-three long lines of text. The text area is 195 by 100 to 110 mm, arranged in a variation of ruling pattern A (see p. 145). The quire structure is somewhat irregular with six of its gatherings differing from the standard quaternion. E. F. Bange claimed that this volume was incorrectly attributed to Diemut, but his judgment seems to have been based on an examination of only the illuminated initial pages with lettering done by a second scribe.[62]

The evangelist portraits, and the initial pages that follow them, raise interesting questions about illumination at Wessobrunn, and the relationship between Diemut and the painters. Each of the four portraits was painted on an independent folio, and

60 When the anonymous author of the *Collectanea de viris illustribus* listed Diemut's books, he noted that volumes one and three of her six-volume *Moralia* were missing. For a transcription of this list (from Clm 22103, f. 164r), see von Hefner, "Diemud," p. 364.

61 For data listed by individual manuscript, see Appendix A, Table A1.

62 E. F. Bange, *Eine bayerische Malerschule des XI. und XII. Jahrhunderts* (Munich, 1923), p. 128. Bange's full analysis of the manuscript is found on pp. 128–133.

these single leaves were added to the quires containing the text. These leaves may have been painted at Wessobrunn or commissioned from, and executed, elsewhere. More complicated is the connection between Diemut and the scribe who copied, on a purple field in gold lettering, the initial pages for each of the Gospels. This is very likely the hand of a female scribe who collaborated elsewhere with Diemut and who wrote the earliest list of Diemut's books.[63] The appearance of this hand writing gold letters – and her thus seemingly integral connection to the bordering decoration on these folios – raises the possibility that she was both a scribe and an illuminator.

### *Group 2 manuscripts: codicology and patterns of collaboration*

It is clear from following Diemut's hand through one of her later (Group 2) manuscripts that she experienced good days and bad days. In places she writes with the precision and clarity seen in the Group 1 books, but then the characters begin to slant and grow irregular, sometimes returning a few lines or folios later to her normal quality. It is easy to imagine her as an older scribe beginning a work session with a strength that would wane as copying progressed. This pattern, together with the likelihood that Diemut was a solitary recluse during her early years at the monastery, strongly suggests that the Group 2 manuscripts were produced later in her life when she had passed the peak of her skill. Later in her career, when a community of women had formed, she had female collaborators, either to teach or to share the work. This general dating is compatible with that suggested by Elisabeth Klemm, who based her judgment on the style of the initials in each volume.

Two scribes appear to have worked closely alongside Diemut to produce these books, and these were probably fellow recluses or nuns of Wessobrunn. The copyist who did the gold lettering in Clm 22044, anonymous Nun-Scribe 2, was a close and frequent collaborator who appeared with Diemut in four manuscripts. Nun-Scribe 2 wrote Booklist A, which further reflects the close connection between the two women.

### Clm 22002 and 22003

Clm 22002 and 22003, which contain a collection of patristic homilies, are probably the surviving two volumes of the three-volume homiliary (numbers 24–26) listed in Booklists A and B. Both are laid out in two columns of forty-one lines of text, with the parchment measuring 345–355 by 215 mm. The folios are generally arranged

[63] For the identification of Nun-Scribe 2 and her close collaborative relationship with Diemut, see pp. 57–68 below. Thanks are due to Adam Cohen for his insights regarding text and illumination in this manuscript.

Table 2.2 *Bayerische Staatsbibliothek Clm 22002*

| Location in manuscript | Scribe | Comments |
|---|---|---|
| 1v–106r, col. 1<br>Quires 1–15 | Diemut | |
| 106r, cols. 2–110r, col. 2, line 41<br>Quires 15–16 | Anonymous Nun-Scribe 1 | |
| 110r, col. 2, lines 42–110v, col. 1<br>Quire 16 | Anonymous Nun-Scribe 2 | |
| 110v, cols. 2–112v<br>Quire 16 | Anonymous Nun-Scribe 1 | |
| 113r–214v<br>Quires 16–29 | Diemut | |

in gatherings of four bifolia, although several quires are irregular. Clm 22002 was ruled according to pattern B, and Clm 22003 according to pattern $C_1$.

A total of five hands are in evidence in these two volumes, with Diemut as the principal scribe of both. In Clm 22002, a second scribe (identified in Table 2.2 as anonymous Nun-Scribe 1) copied a short section of the text, working alongside Diemut in quires 15 and 16. Four scribes appear in Clm 22003, with scribe 2 collaborating very closely with Diemut within quires 7, 8, 11, and 29 (see Table 2.3), again suggesting that the two worked together in a single scriptorium and that scribe 2 was also a nun.

## Clm 22005 and 22006

Clm 22005 and 22006 are two volumes of what was once a three-volume Bible, listed both in Booklist A and B (*Bibliotheca in tribus voluminibus* in Booklist A and *Testamentum in III voluminibus* in Booklist B, numbers 13–15). Clm 22005 contains 155 leaves, each measuring 335–345 by 210–220 mm and ruled according to pattern B. Clm 22006, also ruled according to pattern B, contains 271 345–350 by 215 mm parchment leaves. The quire structure of both volumes is based on quaternions, although a significant number (five of twenty-two quires in 22005 and seven of thirty-six quires in 22006) are irregular.[64] The quality of Diemut's hand in these manuscripts is more uneven and inconsistent than that found in any other of her surviving manuscripts. Although this makes paleographical attribution to Diemut less certain, some letters (especially **g** and **y**) and other abbreviation and

[64] One of the several fires at Wessobrunn damaged Clm 22006, making an assessment of the quality of the parchment impossible.

Table 2.3 *Bayerische Staatsbibliothek Clm 22003*

| Location in manuscript | Scribe | Comments |
|---|---|---|
| 1r–53v, col. 1, line 12<br>Quires 1–7 | Diemut | |
| 53v, col. 1, lines 12–54v<br>Quire 7 | Anonymous Nun-Scribe 2 | |
| 55r–64r<br>Quires 7–8 | Diemut | |
| 64v<br>Quire 8 | Anonymous Nun-Scribe 2 | |
| 65r–84v, col. 2, line 8<br>Quires 8–11 | Diemut | |
| 84v, col. 2, lines 11–93v<br>Quires 11–12 | Anonymous Nun-Scribe 2 | |
| 94r–125v<br>Quires 13–16 | Scribe 3 | Titles by scribe 2 |
| 126r–227v, col. 2, line 8<br>Quires 16–29 | Diemut | |
| 227v, col. 2, lines 8–229v<br>Quire 29 | Anonymous Nun-Scribe 2 | |
| 230r–238r, col. 1, line 12<br>Quires 29–30 | Diemut | |
| 238r, col. 1, lines 16–243r, col. 1, line 6<br>Quire 30 | Anonymous Nun-Scribe 2 | |
| 243r, col. 1, lines 8–243v<br>Quire 30 | Scribe 4 | |

ligature forms (*-orum* and ampersand) remain sufficiently consistent to identify these volumes as her work.

Collaboration within quires in both manuscripts was limited, and generally in evidence only at the end of a quire where blank spaces were left for excerpts from various texts, most frequently from Jerome's commentary on the preceding or following book, as well as material from the breviary. Diemut seems to have left these spaces blank at the beginning and end of books in anticipation of the addition of commentary by another scribe. The possibility that scribe 5's contributions to the two volumes were made after the completion of the main text makes it impossible to determine his or her sex. Scribe 5 appears in Clm 20005 at the end of quires 5 and 22 and in Clm 20006 on a stub following folio 133, in chapter titles, and in additions to the text (see Table 2.6). Diemut used quire 5, a binio, to begin a new chapter on folio 30; but to keep this text together with the following chapter, she began to write on the verso of the folio, leaving the recto blank. This left blank parchment after the last line of the previous text, which provided scribe 5

Table 2.4 *Bayerische Staatsbibliothek Clm 22005*

| Location in manuscript | Scribe | Comments |
|---|---|---|
| 1r–30v, col. 2, line 29<br>Quires 1–4 | Diemut | |
| 30v, col. 2, lines 30–31r<br>Quires 4–5 | — | Later addition (Gothic) |
| 31v<br>Quire 5 (binio) | Diemut | |
| 32r–32v<br>Quire 5 (binio) | Scribe 5 | Wrote marginal glosses elsewhere in text |
| 32v<br>Quire 5 (binio) | — | Later additions (Gothic) |
| 33r–91r, col. 1, line 6<br>Quires 6–14 | Diemut | |
| 91r, col. 1, line 7–end<br>Quire 14 | Scribe 5 | |
| 91r, col. 2, lines 7–91v<br>Quire 14 | Anonymous Nun-Scribe 2 | |
| 92r–120r, col. 2, line 10<br>Quires 14–17 | Diemut | |
| 120r, col. 2, line 11–end of col.<br>Quire 17 | Anonymous Nun-Scribe 2 | |
| 121v–155r, col. 1, line 12<br>Quires 17–22 | Diemut | |
| 155r, col. 1, lines 16–155v<br>Quire 22 | Scribe 5 (?) | |

with space to make later additions. Scribe 5 is very likely Lodevicus, the main scribe of Clm 22004, a copy of Flavius Josephus' *De bello iudaico*. Lodevicus was still active at Wessobrunn's scriptorium during the last quarter of the twelfth century, after Diemut's death.[65] This allows for the possibility that Lodevicus' contributions to Clm 20005 and 20006 were made after the completion of the main text. If this was the case, he and Diemut did not work side by side. A later hand, scribe 6, added a section of text in a later cursive hand in a small blank space before Diemut's text on folio 32v.[66]

Anonymous Nun-Scribe 2 also appears in both Clm 20005 and 20006, although the extent of her work in these two volumes was limited to lists of chapter titles and sporadic short sections of the text (see Tables 2.4 and 2.5).

65 For a discussion of Lodevicus' career, see pp. 59–60 below.
66 This same scribe also wrote numerous marginal glosses in both volumes.

Table 2.5 *Bayerische Staatsbibliothek Clm 22006*

| Location in manuscript | Scribe | Comments |
|---|---|---|
| 1r–20r, col. 2., line 22<br>Quires 1–3 | Diemut | |
| 20r, col. 2, line 23–end of col.<br>Quire 3 | Anonymous Nun-Scribe 1 | List of chapter titles only |
| 21r–29r, col. 1<br>Quires 3–4 | Diemut | |
| 29r, col. 2<br>Quire 4 | Anonymous Nun-Scribe 1 | List of chapter titles only |
| 30r–103v, col. 1, lines 9<br>Quires 4–13 | Diemut | |
| 103v, col. 1, lines 9–36<br>Quire 13 | Anonymous Nun-Scribe 1 | Brief section of text |
| 103v, col. 1, lines 37–104r, col. 1<br>Quire 13 | Diemut | |
| 104r, col. 2, lines 1–13<br>Quire 14 | Anonymous Nun-Scribe 1 (?) | Brief section of text |
| 104r, col. 2, lines 14–189v, col. 2, line 10<br>Quires 14–25 | Diemut | |
| Stub following f. 133 | Scribe 5 | Corrects omission |
| 189v, col. 2, lines 15–195v<br>Quires 25–26 | Scribe 5 | Adds to text on 189v and then copies next quire |
| 196r–254, col. 2, line 19<br>Quires 27–34 | Diemut | |
| 254, col. 2, line 20–end of col.<br>Quire 34 | Scribe 5 | List of chapter titles only |
| 254v–270v<br>Quires 34–36 | Diemut | |

## Clm 22014

Clm 22014 is a copy of Eusebius' *Historia ecclesiastica,* which corresponds with a volume listed in Booklists A and B (number 39). The manuscript is composed of 133 leaves each measuring 350 by 235 mm and organized, with the exception of the first quire, in quaternions. Each leaf was ruled according to pattern D, with the text area of the two columns measuring 165 by 75 mm. 48 percent of the leaves are without significant imperfections. Diemut was the sole scribe of the text, but a later copyist (scribe 6 in Table 2.6) made additions to the text, possibly during the thirteenth or fourteenth century, on folios 7 and 8v. Diemut's hand is particularly erratic in this manuscript, as is also the case with

Table 2.6 *Bayerische Staatsbibliothek Clm 22014*

| Location in manuscript | Scribe | Comments |
|---|---|---|
| 1r–6v<br>Quire 1 | Diemut | |
| 7r–7v<br>Quire 1 | Scribe 6<br>(later addition) | 13th or 14th c. hand |
| 8r<br>Quire 2 | Diemut | |
| 8v<br>Quire 2 | Scribe 6<br>(later addition) | |
| 9r–133v<br>Quires 2–17 | Diemut | |

her work in Clm 22015 and 22016, but less so than in Clm 22005 and 22006 (see Table 2.6).

## Clm 22015

According to Booklists A and B, Diemut made a copy of Cassiodorus, *Historia ecclesiastica tripartita* (numbers 37–38). This manuscript remained in the library following the 1221 fire. Produced between 1125 and 1150, it contains 167 folios (the foliation, however, ends erroneously with 170) measuring 345 by 230 mm with a text area measuring 265–270 by 165 mm. The quire structure is not consistent; while most of the gatherings are quaternions, quire 1 consists of a single bifolium, quires 22 and 23 are binios (two bifolia), and quire 21 is a ternio (three bifolia). The text is arranged in two columns of forty lines following ruling pattern $D_1$. The quality of the parchment is also inferior to that used in Diemut's Group 1 manuscripts, with only 32 percent of the folios unflawed. Changing conditions in the scriptorium, or in the monastery itself, may account for this difference in materials. Folios 1v–2v and 169v–180v contain entries made later in the twelfth century.[67]

## Clm 22016

Diemut copied this collection of short theological treatises before the middle of the twelfth century (Elisabeth Klemm dates the manuscript to between *c.* 1130 and 1150).[68] The manuscript contains 159 leaves measuring 345 by 230 mm, organized, with the exception of four gatherings, in quaternions. The text area, which measures 260–270 by 165–175 mm, is ruled according to pattern C.

67 Klemm, *Die romanischen Handschriften* II/1, p. 169 suggests this dating for the two sections not copied by Diemut.

68 Stegmüller 11638, 11639, 11015, 9333, 11773, 11636, and 11637.

Table 2.7 *Bayerische Staatsbibliothek 22015*

| Location in manuscript | Scribe | Comments |
|---|---|---|
| 1v–2v<br>Quire 1 | (later addition) | Later 12th c. hand |
| 3r–169r<br>Quires 2–23 | Diemut | |
| 169v–170r<br>Quire 23 | (later addition) | Later 12th c. hand |

Table 2.8 *Bayerische Staatsbibliothek Clm 22016*

| Location in manuscript | Scribe | Comments |
|---|---|---|
| 1v–2r<br>Quire 1 | Scribe 7<br>(later addition) | Inexperienced hand from later 12th c. |
| 2v<br>Quire 1 | Scribe 8<br>(later addition) | Inexperienced hand from later 12th c. |
| 3r–156r<br>Quire 2–21 | Diemut | |
| 157r–v<br>Quire 21 | Scribe 7<br>(later addition) | |
| 158r–159r<br>Quire 21 | Various<br>(later addition) | Inexperienced hands from later 12th c. |

The texts included in the volume are as follows: Jerome's *Hebraicae questiones in Genesim* (3r–22v), *De decem tentationibus Israel* (22v–24r), *De canticum Debborae* (24r–26r); Pseudo-Jerome's *Hebraicae questiones in libros regum et paralipomenon* (26r–54r), commentary on Habakkuk (54v–55v), *De ieiuniis disputatio* (55v–56r), *Chronica succinta de regno hebraeorum* (56r–v), Isidore of Seville's *In libros veteris ac novi testamenti prooemia* (57v–63r), and *De litteris hebraicis* (63r), Jerome's *Interpretatio hebraicorum nominum* (63v–85r), and *De situ et nominibus locorum hebraicorum* (85r–107r), Bede's *Nomina regionum atque locorum de actibus apostolorum* (107r–110r), *De decem nominibus dei* (110r), and *Interpretationes hebraeorum nominum secundum Esdram* (110r), Eucherius of Lyons' *Formulae spiritualis intelligentiae* (110r–139v), Isidore's *De ortu et obitu sanctorum patrum* (139v–148r), *Allegoriae sacrae scripturae* (148r–155v), and the anonymous *De quattuor temporibus* (155v–156r). A later hand added Hildebert of Lavardin's *Conversio sanctae Mariae Ægyptiacae* in space left blank by Diemut on folios 1v–2v and 156v–159r.

## *Other female scribes at Wessobrunn*

### Anonymous Nun-Scribe 1

Anonymous Nun-Scribe 1 worked alongside Diemut in Clm 22002. She and anonymous Nun-Scribe 2 collaborated within several quires. Her abbreviation for *-orum* consists of a small, generally closed loop extending from the side of the **o** and an unserifed stroke that extends from the attachment point of this loop down to the right. This stroke extends below the text line and is crossed by a short stroke to form an **x** [Figure 4, col. 1, line 17]. The tail of Scribe 1's **y** is unserifed and curves to the left. Serifs on the **y**'s two arms extend to the left. She does not usually dot her **y**, as Diemut did in both Group 1 and Group 2 [Figure 4, col. 2, lines 2, 11, 15]. The ampersand resembles a lower case **a** with a short foot that does not extend below the text line. A short line or tiny loop (almost a tick mark) extends from the top of the **a**, and a second, longer arm extends up to the right from the center of the right side of the **a** and terminates with a short movement of the pen to the left. Nun-Scribe 1's abbreviation for the *-us* ending of the dative and ablative plurals generally resembles a semi-colon tight against the lobe of the **b** [Figure 4, col. 1, lines 6, 12, 14]. The descending stroke of the **g** curves to the right. The lower lobe of the **g** is closed and varies between round and oval. The tall **s** and **t** are joined, but the cross bar of the **t** does not penetrate across the shaft as it does in Diemut's hand [Figure 4, col. 1, line 3 and col. 2, lines 11, 15]. The limb of the **h** curves around toward the bottom of the ascender with a slight hook, generally terminating slightly above the text line [Figure 4, col. 1, lines 6, 8 and col. 2, lines 1, 2, 4, 7, 12, 13, etc.]. In her abbreviation for *pro-*, an arm crosses the descender (following the formation of the lobe) and terminates with a short stroke to the left [Figure 4, col. 1, line 15]. The crossbar of the minuscule **e** frequently extends into the next letter to the right to form a slight ligature. When the minuscule **e** stands alone (i.e. at the end of a word) the crossbar is likewise elongated, but in this case, extends out into the blank space to the right of the letter. The minuscule **c** and **t** are joined by a hairstroke from the top of the **c** and the left side of the headstroke of the **t**. She occasionally uses a more dramatic stroke to join **c** and **t** [Figure 4, col. 2, line 11].

### Anonymous Nun-Scribe 2

Nun-Scribe 2 collaborated with Diemut in Clm 22002 and 22003, and wrote Booklist A, the closest contemporary witness we have to the extent of Diemut's work. Her abbreviation for *-orum* is similar to Diemut's. It consists of a curved (in places L-shaped) stroke extending from the bottom of the **o** down to the right crossed with a second stroke that terminates with a ball at the right. A short hook (a loop in places) extends from the top of the **o** [Figure 6, line 16]. The unserifed tail of the **y** curves up to the left at its terminus, and frequently extends underneath the letter to the left. The arms of the **y** both splay out and down [Figure 5, line 15].

The ampersand resembles a lower case **a** with a short foot that extends slightly below the text line. One short arm (almost a tick mark) extends up and to the right out of the top of the **a** and a second, longer arm, extends up to the right from the center of the right side of the **a** and terminates in a small ball. Nun-Scribe 2's abbreviation for the *-us* ending of the dative and ablative plurals generally resembles a semi-colon following the **b** [Figure 7, line 9]. The descending stroke of the **g** bends sharply to the right as it leaves the upper lobe. The lower lobe of the **g** is generally round and closed, and in some cases, is attached directly to the upper lobe with little or no descending stroke. Tall **s** and **t**, and **c** and **t** are joined [Figure 5, lines 6, 7, 13; Figure 6, line 14; Figure 7, lines 2, 6, 7; Figure 5, lines 3, 7]. The limb of her **h** curves around toward the bottom of the ascender with a slight hook, but remains near the text line, sometimes terminating slightly above or below [Figure 5, lines 7, 8, 15; Figure 6, line 6; Figure 7, line 6]. In Scribe 2's abbreviation for *pro-*, an arm crosses the descender (following the formation of the lobe) and curves down at its terminus, and touches (or comes close to) the descender to form a small loop [Figure 6, line 10; Figure 7, line 6]. The crossbar of the minuscule **e** frequently extends into the next letter to the right. When an **e** is not immediately followed by another letter (i.e. at the end of a word) the crossbar is likewise elongated, but in this case, extends out into the blank space to the right of the letter.

In addition to collaborating with Diemut in Clm 22002, 22003, 22005, 22006, and 22044, and writing Booklist A, this scribe also copied Clm 22040 and portions of Clm 23411. She was the sole scribe of Clm 22040, a ritual book that contains 133 folios measuring 245 by 160 mm ruled for seventeen long lines according to pattern A and $A_2$. The text area, which measures 160 by 100 mm, contains seventeen long lines. The manuscript is mainly made up of unmarked quaternions. The quality of the parchment this scribe used is very high, with 65 percent of the folios without serious imperfections. Elisabeth Klemm has dated this manuscript to *c.* 1120, which, if correct, suggests that this scribe was a fellow recluse of Diemut's prior to the formation of a cenobitic women's community in the 1130s.

Nun-Scribe 2's hand also appears in Clm 23411, a collection of saints' lives produced around the middle of the century by at least three scribes. This book, measuring 230 by 165 mm and ruled according to pattern A, contains eighty-three folios normally organized in gatherings of four bifolia. The text area, which measures 165–175 by 110 mm, is set out for twenty-four or twenty-three long lines. With 71 percent of its folios free from serious flaws, Clm 23411 was produced with excellent quality parchment. Nun-Scribe 2 copied all of quires one through six, but was replaced by a second scribe on folio 53v. Because her hand does not reappear in the manuscript after this point, it is not possible to determine whether women or men completed it.

## Lodevicus

The only other named scribe from Wessobrunn was the monk Lodevicus, active during the last quarter of the twelfth century. In the fifteenth century, when Stephen Leopold transcribed an unidentified list of books from 1180, he gave it the title, *Index bibliothece Ludovici monachi* in his transcription, suggesting that this was a reckoning of books brought to the monastery by Lodevicus, but there is no evidence to suggest that this scribe copied all of the books named.[69] In fact, several of the books on the list (the Missal of Snello, for example) were clearly the work of a scribe other than Lodevicus.[70] Paul Ruf, in his introduction to the collection, went so far as to suggest that Leopold assigned the collection to Lodevicus in the unfounded hope that he had found evidence that there had been a male scribe at Wessobrunn on a par with Diemut.[71]

Whoever copied this collection of books, it was clearly geared toward the study of the liberal arts, and entirely different in character from the collection of books that Diemut copied earlier in the century. Included in Lodevicus' collection were numerous non-Christian classical texts, including works by Aristotle, Terence, Juvenal, Homer, Vergil, Sallust, and Cato. Even more significantly in this context, the collection included the works of both Priscian and Donatus, and Boethius' commentary on the *Isagoge* of Porphyry. That many of these works were inventoried after the fire of 1221 indicates that the books had been integrated into Wessobrunn's library by that date.

At Wessobrunn, Lodevicus did in fact copy a number of texts, including Clm 22004, Flavius Josephus' *De bello iudaico* and Clm 22034, Jerome's *De viris illustribus*. Clm 22004, measuring 475 by 320 mm, contains 174 leaves ruled in two columns (text area 320–345 by 205–215 mm) according to pattern D. The manuscript is composed mostly of quaternions, marked at the bottom center of the first and last folio of each gathering. Although Lodevicus was a skilled scribe who worked alone, the parchment he used for this volume was not of high quality, with only 26 percent of the folios free from significant imperfections. Clm 22034 is a small volume containing only sixty-one leaves and measuring 235 by 160 mm. The folios, organized into quaternions marked on the bottom center of the first and last folio of each gathering, are ruled according to pattern A. The text area, measuring 150–155 by 90–95 mm, contains twenty long lines. Although 54 percent of the folios are without serious flaws, the parchment is thick and yellow and

69 MBKr, pp. 184–185.

70 The transfer of a personal library with its owner to a new monastery was not uncommon. For example, the monk Otloh brought to St. Emmeram in the eleventh century a large book collection, which also included a large number of classical non-Christian writings. Like Lodevicus, Otloh proceeded to work as a scribe in the service of his new community. See Kottje, "Klosterbibliotheken," pp. 152–153.

71 MBKr, p. 184.

not of high quality. While Diemut's parchment was, in general, of higher quality than Lodevicus', this may simply reflect changes in the availability of materials at Wessobrunn from the early to the late twelfth century.[72]

## REMEMBERING DIEMUT

Even with her outstanding scribal productivity, it would have been easy for Wessobrunn to forget Diemut. She never recorded her name in any of her books, and the only truly contemporary witness to her life and accomplishments – beyond a corpus of unsigned manuscripts – is a booklist that survives on a mere fragment of parchment. This modest memorial could easily have been destroyed, discarded, or used in binding by someone who was unaware of, disinterested in, or even hostile to, its contents.[73] But the story of her remembrance is as much about the institutional needs of her monastery during her lifetime and in the centuries following her death as it is about the accomplishments of the nun-scribe herself.

The story begins either just before, or just after Diemut's death, when her sometime collaborator Nun-Scribe 2 detailed her accomplishments by compiling a list of her books. The wider community mirrored Nun-Scribe 2's esteem for Diemut. Indeed, in the years surrounding her death she seems to have been a person of great importance to the community, as witnessed by the honor of the burial she is said to have received in the abbey's oldest chapel. This esteem is readily understandable when we place her achievements in the intellectual context of twelfth-century Wessobrunn. Her books made possible the biblical study and devotional reading so central to the intellectual and spiritual life prescribed by monastic reformers in the eleventh and twelfth centuries.

During the thirteenth century, librarian Conrad Pozzo and the monastery's literate monks, who in 1221 established and endowed a yearly commemoration, noted the magnitude of her contribution to the intellectual life of the monastery.[74] Perhaps it was as he sifted through and cataloged the books that had been salvaged from the fire of 1220 that the scope of Diemut's contribution came to Conrad Pozzo's attention. Perhaps Conrad knew her as the major contributor to the monastery's library from oral tradition, passed down during the intervening sixty years. Whether through continuing oral tradition among the monastery's scribes and readers, new discovery of the extent of her work following the fire, or a combination of these, the

72 A statistical examination of the parchment quality used in manuscripts from Wessobrunn's scriptorium across the twelfth century suggests that the monastery may have had access to parchment of slightly declining quality. Manuscripts from the first quarter of the century contain an average of 48.5 percent unflawed folios. This average dropped to 43.6 percent during the second quarter, and to 39.8 percent during the last two quarters of the century.

73 Clm 22001[d]. 74 Höppl, *Traditionen*, Tr. 75.

memory of Diemut was strong at Wessobrunn in the early decades of the thirteenth century.

Diemut then disappears from Wessobrunn's surviving written records for nearly three hundred years. During this period, the monastery experienced a cycle of severe financial difficulty and recovery. The trouble started in the early fourteenth century, when the monks were forced to sell or mortgage much of their property, including many manuscripts, to the Cistercian monastery of Stams in order to generate income. In 1313, when the community was unable to meet its financial obligations, Stams took over its operation and attempted unsuccessfully to convert Wessobrunn into a Cistercian house. By the end of century the monastery had reestablished its independence. With its identity as a community badly shaken, the monastery entered the fifteenth century under the leadership of Abbot Ulrich V (1384–1414). The financial situation improved significantly during Ulrich's abbacy, and the fifteenth century, generally, was a time of recovery and rebuilding.

By the first decade of the sixteenth century, Wessobrunn had regained its former economic strength and status as an important intellectual and spiritual center. But with many of its written records and manuscripts lost or scattered, the monastery had, in a sense, lost its history. In the spirit of recovering that lost past, Stephen Leopold, one of the community's monks, turned to what remained of the archives to construct one. There he came upon Conrad's charter for Diemut's anniversary. He copied this document, along with many others from the central Middle Ages, into the *liber traditionum* that he was compiling. The motive was probably similar a decade later when an anonymous monk began work on a compendium of the biographies of Wessobrunn's most important men (*Collectanea de viris illustribus*). The monk-historian evidently noticed Conrad Pozzo's commemorative charter in the *liber traditionum*, and was interested enough in the nun-scribe to include an imaginative version of her life story – the only one for a woman – in his work. In it, he transformed a mere name and list of books into a fully formed holy woman in a biography that reads like a saint's life. He presents Diemut as a pious recluse, totally devoted to a life of work and prayer. Three days a week, he tells us, she fasted, consuming nothing but bread and water, and never taking meat or wine. She was permitted to speak only from None until Vespers, a time that she used to discuss doctrine with the abbot, to give counsel to the community's monks and nuns, or for other pious conversation.[75] During the harsh winter she wore a simple tunic of fur, and her only source of heat and light was a candle – a detail that seems highly implausible for such a prolific scribe. This strict regimen fatigued her body, which was already taxed by her ceaseless scribal work. Whatever the underlying reality of the story, the author's purpose seems clear: to construct a history to rival those of the great religious houses of his day. Other monasteries in the

[75] Leuttner, *Historia monasterii Wessofontani*, pp. 172–173.

region could claim their own holy women: St. Emmeram had St. Aurelia, Bernried had Herluca, and Niederaltaich had Judith and Salome. At Hohenwart it was Richild, and at Admont, Agnes of Wolfratshausen.[76] Wessobrunn would now have Diemut.

There are several interesting parallels between the pattern of recognition of Diemut and of Herluca of Bernried. Paul of Bernried wrote Herluca's Life, it seems at least in part, for its reflection of a pro-Gregorian stance. Paul also wrote the Life of Gregory VII, so it seems likely that Herluca's story suited his ecclesiastical–political agenda. Following a long hiatus, Herluca's Life evidently returned to light through its "rediscovery" in the early seventeenth century by Jesuit scholar Jacob Gretser. The Life appeared in the *Acta Sanctorum* in 1675.[77] Jean Mabillon encountered the text on his journey through Augsburg in August of 1683, and wrote about it in his *Iter germanicum.*[78]

Once Abbot Boelzl and the monks moved Diemut to her resting place in a newly built chapel in the early years of the eighteenth century, her future visibility was assured, for just four years after the translation of her relics, Bernard Pez, the famous monk-historian from Melk, visited Wessobrunn and saw her newly prepared tomb. Intrigued by the story of the prolific nun-scribe, he attempted to find the books Diemut copied among the volumes in the library, an effort that may be related to a series of early modern notes in some of her books identifying her as scribe.[79] Pez wrote of Diemut in the account of his visit to the monastery in his *Thesaurus anecdotorum novissimus*, in which he quoted extensively from the sixteenth-century *De viris illustribus.*[80] Pez thus provided what became a readily available source of information about Diemut for subsequent historians,[81] especially after his work was incorporated into the history of Wessobrunn written by the monk Cölestin Leuttner, which was published in 1753.[82] Together, the published work of Leuttner

[76] Ibid., pp. 171–172. [77] AASS Apr. II (1675): 552–557.

[78] Jean Mabillon, *Iter Germanicum* (Hamburg, 1717), pp. 49–52 (not seen). See Horst Fuhrmann, "Zur handschriftlichen Verbreitung der Vita B. Herlucae des Paul von Bernried," *Analecta Bollandiana* 73 (1956): 362–369.

[79] For a description of these annotations see von Hefner, "Diemud," p. 372. While Elisabeth Klemm dates the annotations to the seventeenth century (see, for example, Klemm, *Die romanischen Handschriften*, p. 163), it is entirely possible that they were written – even by Pez himself – in the early eighteenth century. It is unclear how the annotater arrived at this determination, but it seems likely that he was relying on tradition, which would be consistent with an attribution to Pez.

[80] Bernard Pez, *Thesaurus anecdotorum novissimus: seu Veterum monumentorum, praecipue ecclesiasticorum, ex germanicis potissimum bibliothecis adornata collectio recentissima*, 6 vols. (Regensburg, 1721–1729), vol. I, pp. XVII and XX–XXII.

[81] See, for example, the account of Magnoald Ziegelbauer, in *Historia rei literariae ordinis S. Benedicti*, 4 vols. (Augsburg, 1754), vol. I, p. 549, which is entirely derived from Pez. See also Samuel R. Maitland, *The Dark Ages: A Series of Essays Intended to Illustrate the State of Religion and Literature in the Ninth, Tenth, Eleventh, and Twelfth Centuries* (London, 1853), pp. 419–422, which is simply an English translation of Pez.

[82] Leuttner, *Historia monasterii Wessofontani.*

and Pez brought Diemut to the attention of late-nineteenth-century historians, including Joseph von Hefner (1839), Wilhelm Wattenbach (1875),[83] John Bradley (1887),[84] and Lina Eckenstein (1896).[85] Diemut is now the best-known female scribe of the Middle Ages, despite the fact that she never recorded her own name.[86]

It may have been the strength of the oral tradition surrounding Diemut that kept her memory alive – this in itself may have been enough to ensure the preservation of the few early documents that name her and identify her work. I think it more likely that she was remembered because the monks of Wessobrunn found in her a source of pride for their community. Remembering Diemut suited Wessobrunn's need to re-create its history centuries after her death. For Conrad and monks of the early sixteenth century, Diemut provided evidence of the monastery's great past, and a useful tool for rebuilding the house's history in the wake of difficult times. For Abbot Boelzl and the eighteenth-century monks who paid her so much attention, her importance was as a pious producer of books – an ideal "saint" for the learned monks of the Enlightenment.

* * *

Diemut and the books she copied offer a fascinating look into the intellectual and spiritual world of twelfth-century Wessobrunn. The conservative character of the scope of her life's work may point either to a continued connection between her community and Gorze reform ideas, or to the ongoing influence of those ideas among at least some members of the community despite an official shift to connection with the Hirsau reform. In either case, Diemut played an essential role, providing as she did the basic raw material for intellectual and spiritual practice at Wessobrunn: a library.

It may be that Diemut's skill as a copyist – whether she attained it before taking up her monastic vocation or during her time as a recluse at Wessobrunn during the early twelfth century – enabled her to give the monastery's spiritual life some of its shape and direction. Did Diemut select the books she copied herself, or did she merely take orders from a librarian, school director, or abbot? Neither the lists nor the books themselves tell us. What is clear is that Diemut's books reflect the

83 Wilhelm Wattenbach, *Das Schriftwesen im Mittelalter*, third edition (Leipzig, 1896), p. 445. Wattenbach published the first edition of this work in 1875.

84 John W. Bradley, *A Dictionary of Miniaturists, Illuminators, Calligraphers, and Copyists, with References to their Works, and Notices of their Patrons, from the Establishment of Christianity to the Eighteenth Century*, 3 vols. (London, 1887), vol. I, p. 283.

85 Lina Eckenstein, *Woman under Monasticism: Chapters on Saint-Lore and Convent Life between A.D. 500 and A.D. 1500* (Cambridge, 1896), pp. 236–237.

86 Griesser, "Fragmente," pp. 243–256, an analysis of several fragments found at Stams thought to have originated in Diemut's corpus of manuscripts, is the only detailed study from the twentieth century. She is nevertheless now frequently cited in passing as an example of a medieval female scribe. See, for example, Joan M. Ferrante "The Education of Women in the Middle Ages in Theory, Fact, and Fantasy," in *Beyond their Sex: Learned Women of the European Past*, ed. Patricia H. Labalme (New York and London, 1980), p. 16.

intellectual and spiritual interests of at least some members of the community, and her ability to create an entire library with her own hands won her their esteem. We glimpse her only partially through the words she copied and through the lens of the community that remembered her. But Diemut the individual – the woman who lived as a recluse and nun – remains a shadow, a fact that would, perhaps, have pleased her.

# 3

## *Claustration and collaboration: the nun-scribes of Admont*

On a forgotten day around 1570, or perhaps somewhat earlier in the sixteenth century, Admont's last nun lay dying. Her death, whenever it occurred, would mark the end of approximately four hundred and fifty years of women's religious life at this Benedictine monastery on the Enns River in the medieval archdiocese of Salzburg. As Admont's modern librarians have told the story, a group of monks gathered outside the women's enclosure awaiting this nun's passing. As soon as they received word that she was dead, they went in, loaded all of the books onto a cart, and wheeled them off to add to their own collection. The evident enthusiasm of the waiting monks reflects the richness of the library that they were about to inherit – Admont's nuns had amassed an enviable library during their centuries of participation in the community's vigorous intellectual life.

The collection of books that the monks were so eager to appropriate is one of several witnesses to the presence at Admont of literate women. I use the term "literate" here to cover a range of overlapping levels of training and ability in manipulating written words, beginning with the ability to form letters following a model without comprehension of their meaning and culminating with the ability both to read and understand a variety of texts written by others, and to compose original ones.[1] Both narrative sources and manuscript evidence suggest that many

[1] On the difficulties of defining literacy, see Walter Ong, "Orality, Literacy, and Medieval Textualization," *New Literary History* 16 (1984): 5. On the terminology of literacy and illiteracy in the Middle Ages, see Herbert Grundmann, "Litteratus-illitteratus. Der Wandel einer Bildungsnorm vom Altertum zum Mittelalter," *Archiv für Kulturgeschichte* 40 (1958): 1–65. Franz H. Bäuml, "Varieties and Consequences of Medieval Literacy and Illiteracy," *Speculum* 55 (1980): 237–265 both draws on and modifies Grundmann's analysis. Rosamond McKitterick's introduction to *The Uses of Literacy in Early Mediaeval Europe* provides a useful summary of recent scholarly efforts to define literacy in medieval contexts. See Rosamond McKitterick, ed., *The Uses of Literacy in Early Mediaeval Europe* (Cambridge, 1990), pp. 2–5. On the literacy of medieval women in particular, see Bella Millett, "Women in No Man's Land: English Recluses and the Development of Vernacular Literature in the Twelfth and Thirteenth Centuries," in *Women and Literature in Britain, c. 1150–1500*, ed. Carol M. Meale (Cambridge, 1993), pp. 86–103, and Grundmann's earlier work, "Die Frauen

of Admont's twelfth-century nuns participated in – and helped to shape – their local religious and intellectual environment by copying texts, studying the Bible, helping to give written form to the exegetical sermons of some of the community's monks, and composing and delivering their own sermons.

## ADMONT'S EARLY HISTORY

As active as they were in the lively intellectual life of the monastery during the twelfth century, women were not included in the original plan for the community, which was founded in 1074 by Archbishop Gebhard of Salzburg (1060–1088) as a male monastery with an endowment made earlier in the century by a local patron, Emma of Gurk (d. 1045). Emma had specified that a monastery should be built on her land in the "Admonter-Tal," but her request was not carried out until twenty-five years after her death, when the first buildings went up and twelve monks from the monastery of Saint Peter in Salzburg arrived to colonize the new community.[2] Gebhard, who was a partisan of the papal party in the contemporary struggle for church reform and thus an opponent of the German emperor Henry IV, ensured that the monks would remain independent of all secular power by establishing Admont as an episcopal *Eigenkloster*, or proprietary monastery, over which he and his successors maintained authority, ordaining and investing its first five abbots (1075–1115).[3] The last of the proprietary abbots was Wolfhold (d. 1137), whom Archbishop Conrad I (d. 1147) selected and installed in 1115. Wolfhold was

und die Literatur im Mittelalter. Ein Beitrag zur Frage nach der Entstehung des Schrifttums in der Volkssprache," *Archiv für Kulturgeschichte* 26 (1936): 129–161. For broader studies of the history and functions of literacy in the Middle Ages, see the now classic studies by M. T. Clanchy, *From Memory to Written Record: England 1066–1307*, second edition (Oxford, 1993), and Brian Stock, *The Implications of Literacy: Written Language and Models of Interpretation in the Eleventh and Twelfth Centuries* (Princeton, 1983). See also Rosamond McKitterick, *The Carolingians and the Written Word* (Cambridge, 1989), and Patrick J. Geary, *Phantoms of Remembrance: Memory and Oblivion at the End of the First Millennium* (Princeton, 1994).

2 For a history of St. Peter in Salzburg, see Reinhard Rinnerthaler, ed., *St. Peter in Salzburg: das älteste Kloster im deutschen Sprachraum* (Salzburg, 1986).

3 Godfrey (1138–1165) was the first to be elected by the monks themselves. See *Vita Gebehardi, Thiemonis, Chunradi, Eberhardi, Chunradi II Archiepiscoporum cum chronico Admuntensi*, ed. Philipp Jaffé. MGH, Scriptores 9, pp. 34–51. On Admont as a center of twelfth-century church reform, see Klaus Arnold, "Admont und die monastische Reform des 12. Jahrhunderts," *Zeitschrift der Savigny-Stiftung für Rechtsgeschichte* 89. Kanonistische Abteilung 58 (1972): 350–369; Walter Steinböck, *Erzbischof Gebhard von Salzburg (1060–1088). Ein Beitrag zur Geschichte Salzburgs im Investiturstreit*, Veröffentlichungen des Historischen Instituts der Universität Salzburg 4 (Vienna and Salzburg, 1975); and Stephan Weinfurter, *Salzburger Bistumsreform und Bischofspolitik im 12. Jahrhundert*, Kölner historische Abhandlungen 24 (Cologne, 1975). For orientation in the enormous literature on the history of Salzburg, see Heinz Dopsch, ed., *Geschichte Salzburgs: Stadt und Land*, 7 vols. (Salzburg, 1981), vol. I. Admont is in the modern diocese of Graz-Seckau.

called to Admont from St. George in the Black Forest, an important center of the monastic reform emanating from the nearby Benedictine monastery of Hirsau. His successor Godfrey (1138–1165) would be elected by the monks, not appointed by the archbishop, as a direct result of the community's new affiliation with the Hirsau reform.[4]

Abbot Wolfhold's decision to add a cenobitic women's community to the men's house between 1116 and 1120 seems also to have coincided with the advent of the reform. The first nuns may have come either from the region of Swabia or from the monastery of Nonnberg in Salzburg,[5] or possibly from the cells of scattered recluses who had been living near the men's monastery.[6] Whatever the source of these first arrivals, the daughters and widows of local noble families began to join, and the population of the community began to rise in the 1130s and 1140s. The highest-born nun admitted during this period was Sophia, the daughter of King Bela II of Hungary, who arrived between 1137 and 1147 in the wake of a failed plan for her to marry Henry, the son of the German emperor Conrad II.[7] During the decades that followed, the expanding community remained primarily, though not exclusively, noble.[8] The years between 1155 and 1165 saw renewed expansion, with ten new professions in *c.* 1155–1156 alone, and twenty-six during the entire ten-year period.[9] To meet the needs of the growing female population, Abbots Godfrey, Liutold (1165–1171), and Irimbert (1172–1176) each increased the nuns' endowment, which had been set originally by Wolfhold.[10]

4 For the most complete discussion of Admont's role in twelfth-century monastic reform, see Arnold, "Admont und die monastische Reform," 350–369; between *c.* 1074 and 1115 the house may have been influenced by the reform ideas associated with the Lotharingian monastery of Gorze. Some scholars have argued that the connection between Admont and Hirsau predated the arrival of Wolfhold. It is possible that founder Gebhart's choice of Saint Blaisius as one of the new community's patrons reflects ties with Saint Blasien in the archbishop's Swabian homeland. On the possible influence of Hirsau on Admont prior to 1115, see Helmut J. Mezler-Andelberg, "Admont und die Klosterreform zu Beginn des 12. Jahrhunderts," *Zeitschrift des historischen Vereines für Steiermark* 47 (1956): 28–42.

5 Jakob Wichner, "Das ehemalige Nonnenkloster O.S.B. zu Admont," *StM* 2 (1881): 76.

6 Giles Constable, *The Reformation of the Twelfth Century* (Cambridge, 1996), p. 69.

7 Jakob Wichner, *Geschichte des Benediktiner-Stiftes Admont*, 4 vols. (Graz, 1874–1880), vol. I, pp. 95–96.

8 Between 1150 and 1160, a bondsman dedicated his sister to the monastery, and during this same decade three servants dedicated theirs. See Wichner, "Das ehemalige Nonnenkloster," p. 289.

9 Wichner, "Das ehemalige Nonnenkloster," pp. 86 and 289. To put these recruitment figures into perspective, see Constable, *Reformation*, p. 91, where Constable states that "a hundred monks constituted a very large community, and fifty was still a good size. Most houses probably had between ten and twenty-five members . . ." He also cites the examples of St. Martin at Tournai, which averaged five new male recruits per year between 1092 and 1105, and Zwiefalten, which averaged two new female recruits during the mid-twelfth century (pp. 90–91).

10 Under Irimbert, the nuns received annually one half of the sheep's wool and all of the lamb's wool from two estates, nine marten skins and the wool of eighty sheep from the men's flocks, all for making clothes for the monks and for themselves. The monks also provided them with a peck of salt for preserving fur, 10 pecks of bran, 200 cheeses, and 4 pecks of rye flour, and for their lay

Throughout the twelfth century the community as a whole enjoyed enthusiastic and ready patronage. After a catastrophic fire swept through and destroyed many of the monastery's buildings during matins on 11 March 1152, a local nobleman named Gregory of Wetterfeld stepped in at the urging of both Abbot Godfrey and Archbishop Eberhard (d. 1164) to fund the rebuilding. Gregory's resolute patronage ensured that the disruption to the community was brief, and the first mass was celebrated in the new church by the end of the same year.[11] Prosperity and patronage afforded Admont's monks and nuns the leisure (*otium*) to pursue intellectual and artistic activities, and following Hirsau's lead, the monastery became one of the most important spiritual and intellectual centers in Bavaria.[12]

## ADMONT'S LEARNED NUNS

Contemporary sources claim that Admont's women were strictly cloistered – locked in an enclosure with a single three-lock door. The *magistra*, the head of the women's community, had one key, and two senior monks were entrusted with the others. According to Irimbert's account of the fire of 1152, this arrangement necessitated the dramatic last-minute rescue of the nuns when the disoriented and frightened monks were unable to find the keys. As the flames threatened to engulf the enclosure, Abbot Godfrey ordered the door broken down and the women freed. Once outside the familiar confines of their cloister, the nuns did not know where to go – their sudden freedom seems to have been as upsetting and disorienting as the fire itself.[13]

Irimbert went on to explain that this door was normally opened only for a woman to enter to make her profession, for a priest to enter to administer last rites, or to remove a nun's body for burial.[14] All communication with the outside world, he alleged, took place through a single small window in the enclosure. This opening, and the bolted door, provided the only physical link to the world beyond the cloister. Irimbert's account is particularly interesting for its reflection of contemporary

workers 2 pecks of rye flour, 15 cheeses, 5 measures of millet and legumes, 13 pecks of oats, as well as 7 loaves of bread every Saturday. They also received rents totaling forty-four marks from estates owned by the monastery. See Wichner, "Das ehemalige Nonnenkloster," p. 86.

11 Wichner, "Das ehemalige Nonnenkloster," pp. 84–86.

12 For a discussion of the connection between monastic leisure (*otium monasticum*) and literary activity, see Jean Leclercq, "*Otium Monasticum* as a Context for Artistic Creativity," in *Monasticism and the Arts*, ed. Timothy Gregory Verdon (Syracuse, NY, 1984), pp. 63–80.

13 See Bernard Pez, ed., *Bibliotheca ascetica antiquo-nova*. 12 vols. (Regensburg, 1723–1725), vol. VIII, pp. 454–464. Fire that threatens nuns locked in their enclosure is a literary *topos* in medieval writing about holy women. See Penelope D. Johnson, *Equal in Monastic Profession: Religious Women in Medieval France* (Chicago, 1991), pp. 154–155. We know from monastery records, including the report of the consecration of the rebuilt abbey church, that a fire did, in fact, destroy a number of buildings at Admont in 1152.

14 Pez, *Bibliotheca*, vol. VIII, p. 454.

anxiety about the proximity of men and women in double monasteries. He made it clear that there was no direct interaction between men and women at Admont, not mentioning, for example, the arrangements for necessities such as food, materials for making clothes, and other essential supplies passing into the women's enclosure. Refuse, clothing made by the nuns for the monks, and other materials must likewise have found their way out by some other means. Clearly, these entered and exited through something other than the small window in the chapter house. While Irimbert may well have exaggerated the drama of the rescue or the confusion of the released nuns in the interest of emphasizing the separateness of the sexes, it does appear that the monastery's nuns and monks did not interact freely. The issue in this context is not active enclosure, that is whether nuns occasionally left the cloister to defend their interests, visit ailing family members, or tend to other pressing business, but that when they were in residence, a separation between men and women was maintained.[15]

Given this emphasis on keeping the nuns physically isolated from the larger community, it is surprising to learn that they were active players in the spiritual and intellectual life of the monastery during the twelfth century. Some degree of literacy was required by the Rule of Saint Benedict. At a minimum, a woman who was to participate in the liturgy would have needed to know enough Latin to sing the Psalms. The Rule further prescribed daily periods of private devotional and mealtime reading, and as interpreted from the Carolingian period onward, the distribution of a book to each monk (or nun) during Lent.[16] But some of the nuns moved well beyond this required monastic *lectio*. From the nun Gertrude we have evidence of both strong interest and pride in female intellectual ability at Admont, as well as some of the particulars of the shape and scope of education there. Gertrude wrote a biography of an unnamed *magistra* who, she tells us, was so well trained in the study of sacred Scripture that she was sought after as a model for nuns of other communities. She praises both the *magistra*'s devotion to serving God and her extensive training in liberal studies.[17] It was in this capacity that she

[15] On the types of enclosure, see Johnson, *Equal in Monastic Profession*, p. 151, and Jane Schulenburg, "Strict Active Enclosure and its Effects on the Female Monastic Experience (ca. 500–1100)," in *Distant Echoes*, Medieval Religious Women 1, ed. John A. Nichols and Lillian Thomas Shank (Kalamazoo, 1984), pp. 51–52.

[16] RB 1980 38: 1–12 (mealtime reading) and 48: 4 and 10–23 (private daily and lenten reading). It has been argued that Benedict's requirements for Lenten reading comprised a program of reading from the books of the Bible: see A. Mundo, "'Bibliotheca'. Bible et lecture du carême d'après saint Benoît," *Revue Bénédictine* 60 (1950): 65–92; Benjamin Victor, "Aux origines de la bibliothèque monastique: la distribution du carême," *Scriptorium* 50 (1996): 247–253.

[17] "Et quia in divinis cultibus, studiis quoque liberalibus nulli secunda habebatur, aliquotiens ad alia loca aedificationis exemplo transmittebatur." (And because she was regarded as second to none in the service of God and in liberal studies, she was sent on several occasions to other places to serve as an edifying example.) *Vita, ut videtur, cuisdam Magistrae Monialium Admuntensium in Styria saeculo, XII.* Analecta Bollandiana 12 (1893), 361.

was first called to Admont, where she would serve as a model of piety and a teacher of the novices.[18]

While Gertrude makes frequent reference to the *magistra*'s intellectual abilities in very positive terms, she was careful to stress that piety always took precedence over literary activities.[19] She tells us that the *magistra* wrote verse and prose in both Latin and German, composing texts late at night and dictating them to a scribe. Gertrude is careful to point out that she always dictated in Latin during periods of silence, suggesting that speaking Latin was acceptable when speaking German was not.[20] The *magistra* complied more fully with the letter of the rule of silence on other occasions, responding to her students' requests and inquiries by writing on tablets rather than dictating. Gertrude's association of learning with piety reflects her own ideas about how a pious, praiseworthy *magistra* should behave – a positive evaluation of intellectual activity that was shared by others, both female and male, within her community. Abbot Irimbert, for example, tells us that the nuns held their own daily chapter, a gathering that in Benedictine circles normally entailed reading aloud both a lesson from Scripture and a chapter of the Rule before the delivery of a sermon.[21] On feast days, when a monk could not do the job, one of the nuns preached. "They are exceedingly lettered," Irimbert states, "and wonderfully trained in the knowledge of sacred Scripture."[22]

From the beginning the nuns operated their own school in which students were taught skills ranging from basic reading and writing to biblical

[18] "transmittebatur in coenobium quarundam noviciarum in commune viventium; quas scholaribus disciplinibus instruxit et omnium bonorum augmentis promovit." (she was sent into a monastery of novices living the communal life. She instructed them in the scholarly disciplines and encouraged them in the increase of all good things.) *Vita Magistrae*, p. 363.

[19] See p. 75 below for the *Vita Magistrae* in the contex of Admont's community of authors.

[20] "Aliquando enim intempesta nocte litteras composuit et scribenti praedixit, silentii tamen observantiam retinens numquam aliqua theutonica verba protulit. Praeterea licet post completorium secundum regulam perpetuum haberet silentium, tamen cum rogaretur a parvulis, ut versus et prosas praediceret illis, sicut erat plena caritate et dilectione, accepit tabulas et scripsit eis reddendos in crastino versus et prosas." (Sometimes in the dead of night she composed a letter and dictated to a scribe. In spite of this she maintained the observation of silence since she never uttered German words. In addition, although after compline she kept perpetual silence according to the rule, when, nevertheless, she was asked by the girls to dictate verse and prose for them, since she was full of love and concern, she took up tablets and wrote verse and prose to be handed over to them the next day.) *Vita Magistrae*, pp. 363–364.

[21] C. H. Lawrence, *Medieval Monasticism: Forms of Religious Life in Western Europe in the Middle Ages*, second edition (London and New York, 1989), pp. 114–115.

[22] "Capitulum suum inter se quotidie habent, Magistra vel ejus Vicaria praesidente. Et in festis diebus, cum Abbas ad eas non poterit venire, sunt inter eas personae ad verbum exhortationis faciendum dispositae. Valde quippe sunt litteratae, and in scientia sacrae scripturae mirabiliter exercitatae." (They hold chapter themselves each day, with the magistra or her representative presiding. On feast days, when the abbot is not able to come to them, there are persons among them able to give the sermon. Indeed, they are exceedingly literate and wonderfully trained in the knowledge of sacred Scripture.) Pez, *Bibliotheca*, vol. VIII, p. 460.

interpretation.[23] Like the monks, Admont's nuns were probably schooled in grammar and rhetoric – for, as Gertrude and Irimbert both tell us, they demonstrated many skills compatible with these arts: the ability to write formal letters, to deliver sermons based on their own study of Scripture, and to assist with the composing of exegetical works.[24] But the details of the operation of the nuns' school are less clear than the fact of their education. For this we must turn to the *Constitutions* of Hirsau, a set of rules intended to amplify the Rule of Saint Benedict, to which the community had adhered since Wolfhold's arrival in 1115.[25] Although both Benedict's Rule and the *Constitutions* were addressed to monks, they also regulated life in the nuns' community, and the women themselves probably owned a copy of both.[26] The *Constitutions* set forth general guidelines for operating a school both for novices and for externs. The monk (or nun) charged with overseeing the training of the novices was the *magister*, and a schoolroom was required, regardless of the number of students.[27] The *magister* was permitted to give literate novices manuscripts to read a few days after their arrival,[28] and the librarian could call upon those who could copy or bind books to put these skills to use.[29] The singling out of some entrants as literate suggests that not all were. Some non-literate newcomers were trained in the

[23] The training of German nuns in the liberal arts was not without precedent. For example, the tenth-century canoness Hrotsvit of Gandersheim was trained in both grammar and rhetoric. Pierre Riché, *Les écoles et l'enseignement dans l'Occident chrétien de la fin du Ve siècle au milieu du XIe siècle* (Paris, 1979), p. 151. See also p. 19 and p. 21 above.

[24] Many current and deceased abbots from twelfth-century monastic reform circles were praised for their erudition and their training in the liberal arts. See Peter Johanek, "Klosterstudien im 12. Jahrhundert," in *Schulen und Studium in sozialen Wandel des hohen und späten Mittelalters*, ed. Johannes Fried (Sigmaringen, 1986), pp. 35–68. Several of the abbots of Admont, whose administrations were summarized by the author of the *Vita Gebehardi*, were so distinguished. See p. 75 below. For a useful (though somewhat out of date) summary in English of medieval education under the Rule of Saint Benedict, see Frank Pierrepont Graves, *History of Education during the Middle Ages and the Transition to Modern Times* (New York, 1919), pp. 14–21.

[25] *Constitutiones Hirsaugienses*. PL 150, cols. 923–1146; Abbot Wolfhold probably introduced this text and its customs to Admont upon his arrival in 1115.

[26] There are two twelfth-century copies of the Rule of Saint Benedict (Admont MS 184 and MS 567) and the *Constitutiones Hirsaugienses* (Admont MS 497 and MS 518) in Admont's present collection. In two fourteenth-century lists of books in the monks' library, the list's compiler, Peter von Arbon, noted only one copy of both texts. It is possible that the second copy belonged to the nuns. See the edition in ÖMBK, pp. 15–65.

[27] "Novitii, sive sint pauci, sive multi, in praedicta cella instruuntur. Quotidie namque docendi omnes ibi conveniunt" (Novices, whether there be few or many, are to be instructed in the cell mentioned above. All gather there daily to be taught) *Constitutiones Hirsaugienses*, col. 935.

[28] "Post tres autem quatuor dies adventus eorum, his qui litterati inter eos sunt, magistro admonente, codices ad lectionem ab armario dantur . . ." (Three or four days after their arrival, those among them who are literate, at the discretion of the *magister*, are given codices by the librarian for reading.) *Constitutiones Hirsaugienses*, col. 935.

[29] "Si quis eorum scribendi vel libros ligandi est sciolus, in cella novitiorum potest a magistro illis injungi hoc opus: si tamen rogaverit eum armarius." (If any of them is skilled in writing or binding books, this work may be assigned to them by the *magister* in the novices' cell, if indeed the librarian asks him.) *Constitutiones Hirsaugienses*, col. 938.

monastery's school, while others probably received no education at all: the *Constitutions* refer to unlettered lay brothers (*conversi litteras nescientes*) whose role within the community centered around manual tasks for which reading was not required.[30]

## ADMONT AS A COMMUNITY OF AUTHORS

From among these educated nuns and monks emerged a number of prolific biblical exegetes. Of the fifty-two volumes of medieval commentary that survive in the monastery library, thirteen contain the work of in-house biblical scholars. Abbot Irimbert was Admont's best-known twelfth-century author, and he focused his efforts on the canonical books of the Old Testament. Irimbert's major works, which come down to us in six Admont manuscripts, include commentaries on the books of Kings, Joshua, Judges, Ruth, and the Song of Songs. Nuns, who took dictation and made copies, assisted him in composing much of this work. Irimbert was a beginner in biblical exegesis when he undertook his collaboration with the women, whom he himself described as skilled in scriptural study. This and the short time in which he produced his commentaries suggest that he could have received extensive editorial help from the nuns.[31] Considering the important role that the women seem to have played as the work was written down, we may consider them, to some degree, as co-authors,[32] and it may be that, along with Irimbert's own words, we hear echoes of the exegetical voices of the nuns.

Others wrote anonymously. Preserved in eleven of Admont's twelfth-century manuscripts are nearly 260 unattributed biblical commentaries and sermons written by one or more Admont authors.[33] Bernard Pez, who printed the majority

[30] *Constitutiones Hirsaugienses*, col. 988. Lay brothers generally entered the religious life in adulthood, as opposed to child-oblates who entered early in life and were reared in a monastery. The *conversi* took monastic vows and wore the habit, although they did not participate in the singing of the liturgy, and unlike the choir-monks, they were usually illiterate. See Lawrence, *Medieval Monasticism*, pp. 178–181; on the use of *conversi* within the Hirsau movement, see Stephanus Hilpisch, *Benedictinism through Changing Centuries*, trans. Leonard J. Doyle (Collegeville, MN, 1958), pp. 62–63.

[31] Johann Wilhelm Braun, "Die Überlieferung der Schriften Gottfrieds und Irimberts von Admont mit einem Lebesabriß Irimberts," Ph.D. diss. (University of Giessen, 1967), p. 149. On the role of the scribe in the process of recording sermons, see Nicole Bériou, *La prédication de Ranulphe de la Houblonnière: sermons aux clercs et aux simples gens à Paris au XIIIe siècle*, 2 vols. (Paris, 1987), vol. I, pp. 59–64.

[32] Stephan Borgehammar, "Who Wrote the Admont Sermon Corpus – Gottfried the Abbot, his Brother Irimbert, or the Nuns?" in *De l'homélie au sermon: Histoire de la prédication médiévale*, ed. Jacqueline Hamesse and Xavier Hermand (Louvain, 1993), pp. 47–51, and "The Admont Sermon Corpus." Paper presented at the International Congress on Medieval Studies. Kalamazoo, MI, 8 May 1993.

[33] On the Admont sermon corpus, see Ulrich Faust, "Gottfried von Admont: ein monastischer Autor des 12. Jahrhunderts," *StM* 75 (1964): 273–359, and Alf Härdelin, "God's Visiting. A Basic Theme in the Homilies Ascribed to Godfrey of Admont," in his *Munkarnas och mystikernas medeltid. Tjugofyra kapitel om teologi, spiritualitet och kultur*. Opuscula Selecta 1 (Skellefteå, 1996), pp. 201–218.

of these texts in 1725, attributed them to Abbot Godfrey, apparently selecting, in the absence of any contemporary attribution, the community's best-known man as the most likely author. When Jacques-Paul Migne reprinted Pez's edition in the *Patrologia Latina* (volume 174), Godfrey's name remained attached to the anonymous texts. As recent scholars have noted, however, there is no contemporary evidence to link them to Godfrey, or even to suggest that the abbot ever wrote anything.[34] The commentaries must now be considered to be the work of an anonymous author or authors at Admont, who may have been either male or female.

A strong argument can be made for female authorship of at least some of these anonymous works.[35] Admont MS 58 and MS 62 contain images of nuns – one holding a book (Admont MS 62) and one preaching (Admont MS 58) – which might suggest that the texts contained in them, and possibly the illustrations themselves, were the work of Admont's women (see Figure B). We know from Irimbert that the women were skilled biblical exegetes, and that a nun could deliver the homily when a male preacher could not be present on feast days – the very days for which the sermons in Admont MS 58 and MS 62 were written.[36] Several scholars have also suggested that the *St. Trudperter Hohelied*, a vernacular commentary on the Song of Songs may be localized to the women's community.[37]

Like Irimbert, Admont's anonymous biblical commentators showed particular interest in explicating the books of the Old Testament. Their careful training and intellectual sophistication is reflected in the elegant, rhetorically complex Latin and a highly developed exegetical style, which closely followed patristic models, particularly the allegorical homilies of Gregory the Great.[38] Following a brief introduction, the sermons focus on a short passage of biblical text in which the author provides a close, and sometimes word by word allegorical, and in places mystical, explication. But to say that Admont's exegetes were intellectually conservative

[34] Bernard Pez's edition was reprinted in PL 174, cols. 21–1210 under the name of Godfrey. On the question of attribution, see Alf Härdelin, "God's Visiting," pp. 201–202, Borgehammar, "Admont Sermon Corpus," pp. 8–9, and Fritz Peter Knapp, *Die Literatur des Früh- und Hochmittelalters in dem Bistümern Passau, Salzburg, Brixen, und Trient von den Anfängen bis zum Jahre 1273*, Geschichte der Literatur in Österreich 1 (Graz, 1994), pp. 75–77.

[35] See Alison I. Beach, "Listening for the Voices of Admont's Twelfth-Century Women," and John Van Engen, "The Voices of Women in Twelfth-Century Europe," in *Voices in Dialogue: New Approaches to Women's Cultural History*, ed. Linda Olsen and Kathryn Kerby-Fulton (Notre Dame, IN, forthcoming).

[36] See the related discussion on p. 70 above.

[37] On the possible connections between Admont and the *St. Trudperter Hohelied*, see Friedrich Ohly, *Hohelied-Studien. Grundzüge einer Geschichte der Hohelied-Auslegung des Abendlandes bis um 1200* (Wiesbaden, 1958), 269–271; see also Urban Küsters, *Der verschlossene Garten: volkssprachliche Hohelied-Auslegung und monastiche Lebensform im 12. Jahrhundert.* Studia Humaniora 2 (Düsseldorf, 1985), p. 69 and pp. 88–99; Hans-Jörg Spitz, "Zur Lokalisierung des St. Trudperter Hohenliedes im Frauenkloster Admont," *Zeitschrift für deutsches Altertum und deutsches Literatur* 121 (1992): 174–177.

[38] Faust, "Gottfried von Admont," pp. 294–297.

Figure B Image of a nun preaching from a twelfth-century manuscript produced at Admont, possibly by the community's nuns and preserved in their library. The volume contains anonymous homilies written at Admont for feast days.

would miss the breadth of their learning – reading not only the Church Fathers, but also many contemporary theologians as well. While the methods of gloss and *quaestio* were taking on greater importance at Bec, Chartres, Paris, and other more progressive monasteries and cathedral schools, Admont looked both to these centers and to models from the patristic era for inspiration. Biblical exegetes here and at other Hirsau monasteries, while turning to old methods of critique, nevertheless built from them a practice of commentary and homiletic that reflected their new reformed context.[39]

[39] On developments in interpretation in the eleventh and twelfth centuries, see Smalley, *The Study of the Bible in the Middle Ages* (Notre Dame, IN, 1964), pp. 46–82. I am grateful to Rachel Fulton of the University of Chicago for her helpful insights on this issue.

But Admont's nuns and monks did not restrict their writing to the genre of biblical exegesis. From the nuns' enclosure we have Gertrude's Life of the anonymous *magistra*, and later in the century, one of the monks wrote the Life of the monastery's founder Gebhard, his successors, and a number of Admont's abbots.[40] From the middle of the twelfth century to the beginning of the thirteenth century, scribes maintained a Chronicle, a running record of events of contemporary importance placed within the context of world history.[41] And at the end of the century, the monastery began to maintain a necrology, a record of the death of monks, nuns, patrons, and other individuals connected with the house.[42] A religious community could use a necrology to remember liturgically the names of departed monks, nuns, and benefactors for whose souls the community was to pray, an activity central to the monastery's intercessory function.[43] Through these writings, the monks and nuns of Admont recorded and imagined their collective history.

Writing also served the community's economic and legal needs. Scribes maintained written records of transactions involving the donation of land, money, and revenue from estates, the settlement of border disputes, and the entry of new members.[44] The resulting charters, and later, the *libri traditionum* in which they were recorded, provided written documentation of matters of vital importance to Admont's material well-being.[45] Such charters generally included a brief description of the transaction and a list of witnesses, which could serve to prevent property disputes and to provide witnessed documentation of their rights when problems did, inevitably, arise.

Material welfare was also a primary purpose of writing and preserving letters. Surviving in the monastery's archives are four leaves of a nuns' twelfth-century letter copybook, which contain copies of nineteen complete and fragmentary letters.[46]

40 *Vita Gebehardi*, pp. 34–51.

41 For an edition of this text, which is found in Admont MS 501, see MGH, Scriptores 9, pp. 569–579 and 580–593. These annals were part of a long tradition of chronicle writing, strongly, though not exclusively, associated with the learned world of Benedictine monasticism. The majority of surviving examples of this genre from the mid-ninth through the mid-twelfth century were the work of the Benedictines. Geary, *Phantoms of Remembrance*, pp. 81–84, provides a discussion of the development of this genre and its place in Benedictine intellectual life.

42 *Necrologium Admuntense*, ed. Sigismund Herzberg-Fränkel, MGH, Necrologiae Germaniae 2, pp. 287–309: the practice of commemorating the deceased in a written calendar had evolved by the late eighth century. See N. Huyghebaert, *Les documents nécrologiques*, ed. L. Genicot, Typologie des sources du moyen âge occidental 4 (Turnhout, 1972), esp. pp. 46–47, for the use of necrologies as a source of social history.

43 John Van Engen, "The 'Crisis of Cenobitism' Reconsidered: Benedictine Monasticism in the Years 1050–1150," *Speculum* 61 (1986): 296–297.

44 Number I *Liber traditionum* (16th-c.) was also lost in the fire. Number III (date uncertain) had already been lost before the fire of 1865. Wichner, "Das ehemalige Nonnenkloster," p. 77, n. 1.

45 See pp. 67–68 and following for a discussion of the *libri traditionum* as a source for the monastery's economic history.

46 Admont, Stiftsarchiv Ii/1. Wichner transcribed two letters from the fragments and published them in the appendix to his article, "Das ehemalige Nonnenkloster," pp. 318–319.

One focus of this correspondence was patronage – ensuring that old patrons continued their support and seeking new sources of assistance. But the nuns also wrote to a variety of individuals, both secular and religious, on a range of topics unrelated to economics: they admonished a bishop to remember his religious duties, exhorted a kinsman to consider the spiritual consequences of renouncing his monastic vows, and pleaded with the archbishop of Salzburg for the return of a child left behind in the care of strangers when her mother joined the community.[47] Admont's women used their training in writing letters – a branch of rhetoric known as the *ars dictaminis* – to reach beyond their enclosure, making their voices heard in the management of their affairs, both personal and communal.

A number of letters *to* the nuns have also survived. Between 1139 and 1144, the theologian Gerhoch of Reichersberg (1093–1169) wrote to the nuns in response to a question that they had posed regarding the interpretation of Psalm 50.[48] His reply is preserved in two twelfth-century Admont manuscripts.[49] In a letter written between 1145 and 1169 and addressed to his "beloved sisters in Christ," Gerhoch explained the image of the centurion in Matthew 8: 5–13. This may also have been directed to Admont's women.[50] He wrote to a group of nuns from another community in or around 1160. In this third letter, Gerhoch responded to an inquiry made by his "beloved sisters" about the meaning of the readings for the liturgy for the feast of the Assumption. The survival at Admont of two copies of this letter suggests that, although it was not addressed to the community's nuns, it was sent both to them and to the original inquirers in the tradition of the open letter of the Middle Ages, or shared by the nuns to whom it was addressed.[51] Admont's nuns may also have corresponded with a lesser-known theologian, Liutold, the prior of the Benedictine abbey at Mondsee.[52]

47 For a study of these letters and a consideration of their social, intellectual, and religious context, see Alison I. Beach, "Voices from a Distant Land: Fragments of a Twelfth-Century Nuns' Letter Collection," *Speculum* 77 (2002): 34–54.

48 Gerhoch was prior of Reichersberg, a house of Augustinian canons in upper Austria, and a friend of Abbot Godfrey. See Peter Classen, *Gerhoch von Reichersberg. Eine Biographie* (Wiesbaden, 1960).

49 Admont, Stiftsbibliothek MS 579 and MS 602.

50 Classen, *Gerhoch*, pp. 404–405 and Damien Van den Eynde, *L'œuvre littéraire de Géroch de Reichersberg*, Spicilegium Pontificii Athenaei Antoniani 11 (Rome, 1957), p. 288. Van den Eynde suggests Reichersberg while Bernard Pez suggests Admont. The matter has not been resolved. See Classen, *Gerhoch*, p. 405.

51 Classen, *Gerhoch*, pp. 403–404, see also Van den Eynde, *L'oeuvre*, pp. 245–246, who argues that the letter and accompanying sermon were addressed to nuns at Reichersberg. The survival of two copies of this letter at Admont (MS 602, ff. 15r–21r and MS 579, ff. 3r–38r), together with the known relationship between Gerhoch and the nuns of Admont, suggest that the letter could have been addressed originally to them. Van den Eynde's assertion that Gerhoch's protestation that he had no jurisdiction over what they read at the Feast of the Assumption was a mere posture of humility (p. 245, n. 3) is not convincing.

52 See Hans Radspieler, "Regilind aus Admont, Äbtissin von Bergen und Hohenburg. Reformerin – Lehrerin – Dichterin," *Neuburger Kollektaneenblatt* 115 (1962): 35.

Admont's monks also wrote and preserved letters. In 1162, Archbishop Eberhard presented Godfrey with copies of correspondence sent or received by the archdiocese between 1119 and 1162.[53] It is hard to imagine that Eberhard's motive for the transfer of this letter collection was other than to ensure its preservation, and where better to deposit these texts than in the hands of a group of literate, diligent record-keepers? If preservation was what the archbishop had in mind, his plan succeeded; under the direction of Godfrey, Admont's scribes made a copy of the letters, adding numerous letters of their own.[54] Formal letters were seen as a literary genre, and like other such genres, they were considered worth keeping as models for further correspondence, or simply for the enjoyment of reading them.

## ADMONT'S TWELFTH-CENTURY LIBRARIES

The monks' letter collection is still preserved among the approximately two hundred twelfth-century books that survive from the monastery – a number far larger than for any other contemporary Bavarian library (see Table 3.1),[55] including St. Emmeram and Tegernsee, both known for their scribal productivity. When we compare the sizes of these surviving collections, we must consider that Admont's twelfth-century books (aside from ten sold during a period of financial difficulty in the 1930s) have been preserved on site at a monastery that has remained in continuous operation since the eleventh century. Unlike the monasteries of modern Bavaria, Admont was not secularized under Napoleon, although the monastery's property, including all of the manuscripts and early printed books, was appropriated during World War II, moved to Graz, and returned to the monastery in 1947.[56] Even the two fires – one medieval and one modern – that destroyed many of the buildings spared the books. The fire of 1865 left nothing of town or monastery standing except the beautiful baroque library, which had been completed in 1776. Just as the flames began to threaten the building's main frescoed dome, the wind shifted, and the library was saved.

We thus have at Admont the opportunity to study, essentially intact, the books that comprised this twelfth-century library. What was available for the monks and

53 *Die Admonter Briefsammlung*, ed. Günther Hödl and Peter Classen, MGH, Die Briefe der deutschen Kaiserzeit 6 (Munich, 1983). On the wider context of the making and dissemination of letter collections in the twelfth century, see Giles Constable, *Letters and Letter-Collections*, Typologie des sources du moyen âge occidental 17 (Turnhout, 1976).

54 Vienna, Österreichische Nationalbibliothek, MS 629.

55 Although Wichner was not a paleographer and his dating is often questionable, his catalog still provides an indispensable starting point for research. The Admont manuscripts in other libraries have not been systematically charted.

56 ÖMBK, p. 11.

Table 3.1 *Surviving twelfth-century manuscripts from Bavarian monasteries*

| Monastery (provenance) | # Surviving twelfth-century mss. |
|---|---|
| Admont | 203 |
| Schäftlarn | 66 |
| St. Emmeram | 64 |
| Windberg | 53 |
| Prüfening | 47 |
| Benediktbeuern | 44 |
| Tegernsee | 37 |
| Aldersbach | 36 |
| Wessobrunn | 32 |
| Oberaltaich | 29 |
| Weihenstephan | 27 |
| Ranshofen | 23 |
| Kaisheim | 19 |
| Beuersberg | 12 |
| Indersdorf | 12 |
| Dießen | 7 |
| Polling | 7 |
| St. Nikola, Passau | 6 |
| Herrenchiemsee | 6 |
| St. Ulrich and St. Afra | 6 |
| Ottobeuern | 6 |
| Ebersberg | 5 |
| St. Peter, Salzburg | 4 |
| Nonnberg, Salzburg | 4 |
| Scheyern | 4 |
| Stadtamhof, Regensburg | 3 |
| Asbach | 2 |
| Altomünster | 2 |
| Rottenbuch | 2 |
| Michaelbeuern | 1 |
| Seeon | 1 |
| Hohenwart | 1 |
| Holy Cross, Augsburg | 1 |
| St. George, Augsburg | 1 |

nuns to read?[57] First, there are the standard authors that we expect to see in a well-stocked monastic library of this date: there were the old standards such as

[57] Jakob Wichner, *Catalogus codicum manu scriptorum Admontensis* (Admont, 1888). Wichner's hand-written catalog has been microfilmed and printed under the title *Catalog of Manuscripts in Stift Admont, Austria* (Ann Arbor, 1982).

Ambrose, Jerome, Augustine, Eusebius, Gregory the Great, Isidore of Seville, and Bede.[58] More surprising is the extent of the library's collection of more contemporary authors: Anselm, Bernard of Clairvaux, Rupert of Deutz, Hugh of St. Victor, Honorius *Augustodunensis*, Peter Lombard, and even Peter Abelard.[59] Admont's readers – to judge by their libraries – were willing to take in a wide range of theological opinion and method in the interest of enhancing their *lectio*, a willingness that is evident, if not in the form of their written exegesis, then in its spirit.

Notably only two volumes containing the work of non-Christian authors survive, but this is consistent with the general lack of interest in classical Latin pagan texts reflected in other surviving evidence for book collections assembled at monasteries associated with the Hirsau reform.[60] Without the standard classical works used for teaching grammar and rhetoric, the schools in these reformed communities seem to have taken an approach to teaching Bible study that veered significantly away from the traditional framework of the liberal arts curriculum.

### *Reconstructing the nuns' library*

Returning briefly to the image of the impatient sixteenth-century monks and their book cart, we recall that Admont's libraries were combined after the closing of the nuns' community. The books that the monastery now preserves as a unified collection were once divided between the men and the women. Which of these surviving books belonged to Admont's women? There is no straightforward answer to this question, as no inventory of the nuns' library has survived. This is not at all surprising: reconstructing medieval libraries, especially those in women's religious houses, is rarely, if ever, so tidy – a fact well illustrated in David Bell's, *What Nuns Read: Books and Libraries in Medieval English Nunneries*.[61] The nuns' library was, at least by the end of the twelfth century, large enough to necessitate designating one of the nuns as "armaria." Her office was considered of great enough importance to warrant mention in the monastery's necrology for 22 May: "Adlheit, a nun of our community, an *armaria*."[62] If the passage on the *armarius* in Hirsau's *Constitutions* accurately describes Adlheit's duties, she oversaw the library,[63]

58 Teresa Webber, *Scribes and Scholars at Salisbury Cathedral, c. 1075–1125* (Oxford, 1992), pp. 31–32, provides a useful discussion of the texts that were considered (according to the guidelines set forth by Cassiodorus) essential for biblical exegetes. Although Webber's study focuses on Salisbury Cathedral's twelfth-century library, the discussion provides insight into the choice of texts copied at Admont.

59 Faust, "Gottfried von Admont," p. 282. Faust based his list of authors on Wichner's reconstruction.

60 Kottje, "Klosterbibliotheken und monastische Kultur in der zweiten Hälfte des 11. Jahrhunderts," *Zeitschrift für Kirchengeschichte* 80 (1969): 150–151.

61 David N. Bell, *What Nuns Read: Books and Libraries in Medieval English Nunneries*, Cistercian Studies Series 158 (Kalamazoo, MI, 1995).

62 "Adlheit m.n.c. armaria," *Necrologium Admuntense*, p. 297.

63 "Praecentor, qui et armarius, armarii nomen obtinuit, eo quod in ejus manu solet esse bibliotheca, quae et alio nomine armarium appellatur," *Constitutiones Hirsaugienses*, PL 150, col. 1072A.

Table 3.2 *Reconstructed nuns' library*

| Shelfmark | Author | Text | Comment |
|---|---|---|---|
| 16 | Irimbert of Admont | Commentaries on 1–4 Kings | Ex-libris |
| 18 | — | *liber matutinalis* | Colophon |
| 58 | Anonymous Admont school | Homilies for feast days | Image of preaching nun |
| 62 | Anonymous Admont school | Homilies for feast days | Image of nun holding book |
| 63 | Anonymous Admont school | Homilies for Sundays | |
| 232 | Ambrose, Augustine, Bede, Bernard of Clairvaux, Gregory the Great, Haimo of Auxerre, Jerome, John Chrysostom, Leo, Maximus Confessor | Homilies | Notice of monks borrowing book from nuns |
| 243 | | Partial Hebrew Bible | Ex-libris |
| 274 | Gregory the Great | *Dialogues* | Ex-libris |
| 376 | | Passional | Ex-libris |
| 579 | Gerhoch of Reichersberg | *Letter to the Admont Nuns* | Inclusion of letter to the nuns together with absence from monks' library |
| | Honorius *Augustodunensis* | *Hexameron, Sign of St. Mary* | |
| 602 | | Passional | Inclusion of letter to the nuns together with absence from monks' library |
| | Gerhoch of Reichersberg | *Letter to the Admont Nuns* | |
| 638 | | *Miracles of the Blessed Virgin* | Image of nuns praying at the feet of the virgin |

directed the scriptorium,[64] and took charge of liturgical music.[65] But neither Adlheit nor any other librarian left an inventory of the books in her charge.

[64] "Si quis eorum scribendi vel ligandi est sciolus, in cella novitiorum potest a magistro illis injungi hoc opus: si tamen rogaverit eum armarius." *Constitutiones Hirsaugienses*, PL 150, col. 938.

[65] The Constitutions of Hirsau list a single hand signal for the cantor and *armarius* together: to the basic sign for a monk should be added the signs for singing and keeping the beat – both gestures clearly emphasizing the cantor's, rather than the librarian's duties. *Constitutiones Hirsaugienses*, col. 953B. On the changing duties associated with the office of the *armarius* and its growing association with the office of cantor, see Margot E. Fassler, "The Office of the Cantor in Early Western Monastic Rules and Customaries: A Preliminary Investigation," *Early Medieval Music* 5 (1985): 29–51.

Only a single book, a beautiful *liber matutinalis* (Admont, MS 18) contains a contemporary annotation naming Admont's women as owners.[66] Placing other books in the nuns' library requires the creative use of the less direct evidence that is available. The process of reconstructing the nuns' library is best begun by an examination of the evidence for the monks' library. In the late Middle Ages, librarian Peter of Arbon compiled two systematic lists of the men's books: the first in 1376, and the second and more comprehensive in 1380.[67] These lists begin with copies of the Old Testament, followed by Gospel books and epistolaries. After the biblical texts come patristic authors, beginning with Gregory, and followed by Augustine, Jerome, and Ambrose. Next are listed volumes containing the work of primarily medieval biblical commentators and theologians: Origen, Bede, Isidore of Seville, Bernard of Clairvaux, Hugh of St. Victor, and Rupert of Deutz. Following these entries are the books of sentence collections, sermons (a particularly large category), saints' lives, histories, decretal collections, and a final miscellaneous group of authors only represented in a few volumes (Honorius *Augustodunensis*, John Cassian, Rhabanus Maurus, Anselm of Canterbury, among others). This is not a librarian's optimistic "wish list" but a catalog of the monks' library, including manuscript *incipits* for nearly all of the volumes.

Admont's nineteenth-century librarian Jakob Wichner attempted to derive a list of the monks' twelfth-century book collections by matching surviving volumes with those listed on Peter's booklists. His reconstruction would include those books listed in the late medieval booklists that matched surviving volumes in the library. There are limits to Wichner's approach. First, Peter's catalog may not have included within its scope all of the various book collections within the community.[68] Second, not all of the books that the monks owned were on the premises at all times. Some may have been on loan to other communities for use as exemplars, and others may have been in the nuns' enclosure to be read or copied. Any book that was out on loan and returned after 1380 would have escaped Peter's notice. Further, by 1376, some of the books that had been in the library in the twelfth century may have been destroyed or given away, and conversely, others may have been purchased by or given to the monastery after the twelfth century. Even with these uncertainties, the reconstructed list provides a good, if not exact, idea of the nature of the monks' library and reflects the main contours and boundaries of their religious and intellectual world.

66 Two scribes – Johannes and Udalricus – recorded their names and stated that they had made the book expressly for the women. See note 69 below.

67 For a critical edition of Peter of Arbon's catalogs, see ÖMBK, pp. 15–34.

68 On the existence of multiple book collections within a single community and their implications for reading and interpreting medieval library inventories, see A. J. Piper, "The Libraries of the Monks of Durham," in *Medieval Scribes, Manuscripts and Libraries: Essays Presented to N.R. Ker*, ed. M. B. Parkes and Andrew Watson (London, 1978), pp. 213–249.

As Wichner attempted his reconstruction, he noted that there were a significant number of twelfth-century books – many of which had been copied at Admont itself – that were not listed in either of Peter's inventories. He hypothesized that these "missing" twelfth-century books were owned, not by the monks, but by the nuns. To test Wichner's hypothesis, I repeated his matching process using his catalog and the fourteenth-century booklists. The inclusion of manuscript *incipits* in all three sources made this job easier and allowed for a high degree of precision in matching. My attempt yielded forty-seven twelfth-century books that may not have been part of the monks' book collections. I compared my list with a second list of surviving books with ex-libris annotations or other indications of connection to the nuns' library. MS 18, for example, which contains two scribal subscriptions that identify the scribes as Johannes, who copied the first section, and Udalricus, who completed the work in 1180, was not inventoried by Peter.[69] Likewise, several volumes that contain visual hints of female ownership – images of nuns holding books, preaching, and praying – do not appear in the monks' lists. In fact, none of the books with demonstrable links to the women appear in either of the fourteenth-century inventories. The books on both the list of volumes "missing" from the monks' lists, and the list of volumes with possible links to the women may well be the remnants of the nuns' twelfth-century library.

What, then, might the nuns' book collections have contained? The reconstructed list includes liturgical books such as the nuns' *Liber matutinalis*. This volume is actually an antiphoner and lectionary that contains both chants and readings, which the women would have used in the daily celebration of the Divine Office. It is clear from the wear at the corners of each folio that the manuscript was used frequently, although it is unclear exactly where the volume would have been placed during the nuns' liturgy. One can imagine the women clustered around the book as they chanted, but the reader would also have needed to see the lessons.[70]

Another of their liturgical books is a passional (Admont, Stiftsbibliothek MS 376) with the lives of both early Christian martyrs and medieval saints organized by date, which contains a fourteenth-century ex-libris annotation placing it in their collection. The nuns would have used this book either in chapter or during the celebration of the Divine Office, reading aloud the life on the appropriate day for each saint. They may also have read aloud from MS 243, which, as suggested by an

[69] "Notum sit omnibus tam futuris quam presentibus, qualiter ego frater Johannes prior Admuntensis hunc matutinalem librum sumptu et labore meo perfecti et carissimis sororibus nostris hic deo militantibus contradidi quatinus orationibus earum adiutus cum ipsis in libro vitae merear conscribi et eterne beatitudinis premia adipisci. Amen." f. 1r; "Rogo vos dilectissime sorores ut memores sitis Uldarici peccatoris in orationibus vestris, qui vobis presentem librum cunctis in eo Christo servientibus cum magno labore conscripsit. Librum hunc descripsimus anno ab incarnatione domini Millesimo Centesimo Octogesimo. Scriptoris memores Udalrici queso sorores, Hoc optate sibi nomen super ethere scribi." f. 295r.

[70] Thanks are due to Rachel Fulton for her suggestions on the liturgical use of this manuscript.

ex-libris, was their copy of Proverbs, Ecclesiastes, Song of Songs, Sirach, Wisdom, Job, Tobit, Judith, Esther, and Ezra. They also seem to have owned a compendium of patristic and medieval sermons and homilies (Admont, Stiftsbibliothek MS 232). This book may have served multiple purposes; the nuns may have read from it at chapter, during the office, or in private devotion, or they may have used it for their scriptural studies. A fifteenth-century annotation in the volume indicates that the monks had borrowed it from the nuns.

The nuns probably also held Admont MS 579 in their library. This volume contains Honorius *Augustodunensis' Hexameron* and *Sigillum Beatae Mariae* and a letter of Gerhoch of Reichersberg explaining the liturgical readings for the feast of the Assumption, addressed to a group of nuns. This and several others point both to their interest in biblical exegesis and to their assistance with Irimbert's exegetical work. A sixteenth-century ex-libris in the final recension of Abbot Irimbert's commentaries on Kings 1–4 (Admont, Stiftsbibliothek MS 16) indicates that it was kept in the women's library.[71] In Admont MS 58, one of the manuscripts of anonymous sermon-commentaries not listed in the fourteenth-century monks' inventories, a nun holding a book in her left hand and extending her right in a gesture of speaking or preaching stands above the center of the arch that frames the book's table of contents (see Figure B). Could this image suggest that the book had been made for, and possibly belonged to, the nuns? The image could even point to connections between the women and the writing of the book's anonymous texts. Admont MS 62 contains a similar image, this time of a nun holding a book, in what seems to be a visual statement of the nuns' intended ownership.

Images of women also appear in two additional volumes missing from the monks' lists. Both of these books provided material primarily for personal devotional reading. The neumes in what may have been the nuns' collection of Anselm of Canterbury's *Meditationes et Orationes* (MS 289), a book *not* copied at Admont, suggest that a reader might sing part of the text as a part of private devotion. The clothing worn by the women in this volume, however, suggests that these were not nuns, but canonesses, and this weakens the hypothesis of a connection with Admont's women. This book may have arrived at Admont after the twelfth century, accounting for its absence from the lists. The *Miracles of the Blessed Virgin* (MS 638), which shows nuns, these shown in garb compatible with that of Admont, at the feet of the teaching Virgin Mary, may have served a similar devotional purpose.[72]

Some of the nuns' books drifted from the monastery, either on loan or as gifts between the twelfth and sixteenth centuries, or after the closure of the women's community. Among these may have been the so-called Millstätter Psalter

[71] On Irimbert as biblical exegete and author, see pp. 72–74 above.

[72] I am grateful to Prof. Dr. Ursula Nilgen for her observations on this manuscript during a study session at the conference, Manuscripts and Monastic Culture: Admont and the Twelfth-Century Renaissance in Germanic Lands, held at Admont on 7–10 August 2002.

(Österreichische Nationalbibliothek, MS 2682), which was probably copied at Admont between 1173 and 1200.[73] A calendar within the manuscript lists prominently several feast days of importance to Admont's nuns – those of St. Martin, St. Rupert, and Saint Erintrude.[74] Another clue is an entry in the calendar for 24 February noting the death of a nun, Bertha of Leoben, which helps to localize the manuscript both to the region of Steiermark (in which both Leoben and Admont are located), and to Admont's women's community (since the *libri traditionum* record the profession of several women from Leoben).[75]

The breadth of the reconstructed library reflects the active liturgical, spiritual, and intellectual life within the nuns' enclosure. But these surviving books can only suggest the range of their needs and interests, as the women were probably not limited to the books held in their own library. Given the climate of support and exchange at Admont, it seems likely that the women could borrow books from the men. We know from the note in Admont MS 232 stating that the volume had been borrowed from the women's cloister that, at least in the fifteenth century, the exchange could also go the other way.

## ADMONT AS A COMMUNITY OF SCRIBES

Admont's men and women used written forms of expression to control and make sense of their world, and to seek greater wisdom and knowledge of God – a primary function of the monastic *lectio*. We can see this clearly in the range and number of books in their libraries, in the impressive corpus of sermon-commentaries they wrote, in the way they used biographies, necrologies, and charters both to remember and imagine a collective past, and to control and shape a present and future. This was a community that was bounded and defined, shaped and informed by the written word in its various forms. We can imagine, then, the importance to the monastery of its scribes.

During Godfrey and Irimbert's time at Admont, the community's copyists were trained to write a highly uniform book hand in the calligraphic tradition of the monastic schools of south Germany and Austria from the tenth through the twelfth

[73] Österreichische Nationalbibliothek Cod. Pal. Vind. 2682. See Peter Wind, "Zur Lokalisierung und Datierung des Millstätter Psalters," *Codices manuscripti: Zeitschrift für Handschriftenkunde* 8 (1982): 115–134.

[74] St. Erintrude was patron of the monastery from which the anonymous *magistra* came to Admont. *Vita Magistrae*, p. 363.

[75] *Libri traditionum* are books that record copies or summaries of original documents. For a discussion of the nature and impact of this kind of archival memory, see Geary, *Phantoms of Remembrance*, pp. 81–84.

century.[76] Paleographers refer to this regional form of Caroline minuscule as the *Schrägoval*, or Tilting Oval style, in reference to the frequent appearance of a distinctive flat-topped, slanted **o**. The conservative character of this regional form of Caroline minuscule, as it was written at Admont during the last three-quarters of the twelfth century, is best illustrated through contrast with contemporary examples from France and England, where at the beginning of the century the transition from Caroline minuscule to Textura had already begun.[77]

Admont's late-twelfth-century necrology names two nun-scribes – Diemut and Mathilt – entries that reflect both the esteem in which Admont's scribes were held and the fact of female participation in this highly valued activity. We also hear about female scribes from Irimbert, who acknowledged their support in the prologue to several of his sermons and commentaries. "Several years ago," he wrote, "the Admont sisters heard certain of my expositions from the same book of Kings, which they committed to parchment without my knowledge."[78] To understand how Irimbert could possibly have been unaware of the nuns' plans to record his sermons, we must imagine the setting: he probably preached to the women through a small window in their chapter house. One or two scribes, writing quickly to keep pace with the exposition, could have placed themselves outside his line of vision.[79] And it would certainly have been possible to transfer their notes, presumably taken down on wax tablets, onto parchment without Irimbert's knowledge. It is also possible that his claim of ignorance was no more than a formulaic expression of modesty. Or perhaps he was trying to shift the responsibility for what must have been a rather unconventional collaborative effort onto the women. Whatever his degree of awareness of the nuns' intentions, Irimbert here alerts us to the presence at Admont of nun-scribes.

In the prologue to his commentary on 4 Kings, Irimbert again acknowledged the help he had received from the women's community:

[76] For comparison, see the example from the middle of the eleventh century at Tegernsee (Clm 18005) and the third or fourth quarter of the eleventh century at St. Emmeram (Clm 14399), in Bernhard Bischoff, *Kalligraphie in Bayern: achtes bis zwölftes Jahrhundert* (Wiesbaden, 1981), p. 36 (#26) and p. 37 (#27). On the development of the south German "monastic school" of calligraphy, see Christine Eder, *Die Schule des Klosters Tegernsee in frühen Mittelalter im Spiegel der Tegernseer Handschriften*, Münchener Beiträge zur Mediävistik und Renaissance-Forschung (Munich, 1972); Bischoff, *Kalligraphie in Bayern*; Hartmut Hoffmann, *Buchkunst und Königtum im ottonischen und frühsalischen Reich*, 2 vols., MGH, Schriften 30–31 (Stuffgart, 1986).

[77] Michelle Brown, *A Guide to Western Historical Scripts: From Antiquity to 1600* (London, 1993), pp. 73–78.

[78] ". . . sorores Admuntenses capitula quedam ex eodem libro Regum ante annos aliquot a me audierant, que me nesciente ipse in membranis exceperant . . ." Johann Wilhelm Braun, "Irimbert von Admont," *Frümittelalterliche Studien* 7 (1973): 319.

[79] Braun, "Irimbert von Admont," p. 288.

In the very great difficulty of this work, I was refreshed thoroughly by the liberality of the aforementioned sisters, since they appointed to me two sisters free from every occupation, who continually and diligently transcribed on tablets what was spoken by me.[80]

These two women must have been skilled writers, for taking dictation is a complex task requiring simultaneously careful listening, interpretation, and fast writing.[81] Their task was further complicated by the use of a stylus on wax tablets.[82] We know that monks, too, assisted Irimbert with this work, as it was a male secretary who was with him when the fire that delayed the completion of the project broke out in the night in 1152. To judge by the particular mention Irimbert made of them in his prologues, however, it was two of the nuns who did much of the initial *reportatio*, and at least some of the manuscript work – if the production of a manuscript copy was indeed what Irimbert meant by the expression *in membranis exceperant*. The argument that Admont's nuns participated in the actual production of books is supported by Stefanie Seeberg's recent study of the illuminations in the nuns' breviary (Admont, MS 18). Seeberg argues, based on an analysis of the unusual themes depicted in the volume's many initials, that they were painted by the nuns.[83]

We may also see nun-scribes at work in manuscripts of other of Irimbert's exegetical writings, as two nuns also helped him to record his commentaries on Ruth and on Judges 19–21. It is not from Irimbert, however, that we learn the names of these women. The rubricator of the manuscript containing the final version of these two texts, Admont MS 17, identified them in large red letters as sister Irmingart and sister Regilind.[84] The wording chosen by the rubricator – *Explanatio*

[80] "In difficultate earundem sororum utrimque recreatus sum liberalitate, ut duas michi sorores ab omni occupatione liberas deputarent, que continue ac diligenter transscriberent, que a me dicta in tabulis excipi potuissent." Braun, "Irimbert von Admont," p. 320.

[81] Malcolm Parkes describes the process of converting spoken words to written ones as a form of translation. See, "Tachygraphy in the Middle Ages: Writing Techniques Employed for *Reportationes* of lectures and Sermons" in *Scribes, Scripts and Readers. Studies in the Communication, Presentation and Dissemination of Medieval Texts* (London, 1991), p. 25.

[82] The sisters recorded the commentary on 2 Kings on parchment (see n. 78 above) and 4 Kings on tablets (see n. 80 above); wax tablets, constructed of a wooden frame with a wax-filled recess, were frequently used for schoolroom exercises. The writer used a special stylus to scratch letters into the wax. Authors and scribes commonly used wax tablets for composition and first drafts, reserving costly parchment for a more polished version. When the contents of the wax tablet were no longer needed or had been transferred to a more permanent support such as parchment, the wax was smoothed and reused. For a detailed description of wax tablets and their various uses, see Richard A. Rouse and Mary A. Rouse, "Wax Tablets," *Language and Communication* 9 (1989): 175–191. For a history of the use of wax tablets, see David Diringer, *The Book Before Printing: Ancient, Medieval and Oriental* (New York, 1982), pp. 26, 29, 192, 217, 258, 544, and 553.

[83] Stephanie Seeberg, *Die Illustrationen im Admonter Nonnenbrevier von 1180. Marienkrönung und Nonnenfrömmigkeit – Die Rolle der Brevierillustration in der Entwicklung von Bildthemen im 12. Jahrhundert*, Imagines Medii Aevi. Interdisziplinäre Beiträge zur Mittelalterforschung 8 (Wiesbaden, 2002), pp. 3–4, 18–19, and 161–162.

[84] "Explanatio huius hystorie descripta a sorore Irmingarte." (The interpretation of this *historia* was copied by sister Irmingart.) Admont MS 17, p. 420; Braun, "Irimbert von Admont," p. 288;

*huius hystorie descripta a sorore Irmingarte* and *Explanatio huius hystorie descripta a sorore Regilinde* – is ambiguous. *Descripta* can be taken to mean either copied (in the sense of copying a manuscript) or took down (in the sense of *reportatio*, taking dictation), or possibly a combination of both. Was the rubricator telling us that Irmingart and Regilind took dictation, copied manuscript drafts, or both? An initial in MS 17, which depicts Irimbert dictating to a monk in the initial F in Judges 19–21 (p. 389), suggests that it was not only the nuns who took the dictation.[85] It seems unlikely that the rubricator of the last version, writing years after the first version was taken down, would find these two women worthy of such prominent mention if their role had been limited to the initial *reportatio*.

Even in the face of an absence of colophons, we can rely on a combination of textual and paleographical evidence to identify the hands of Irimbert's assistants Regilind and Irmingart, whose work we would expect to find in the earliest copies of the earliest version of his commentaries on Ruth and Judges 19–21.[86] It is then possible to identify sections of other manuscripts within this textual tradition as the work of these two women. Copyists who worked closely with Regilind and Irmingart (i.e. whose hands alternated with that of either Regilind or Irmingart within a quire) can also be identified, though less securely, as female scribes.[87]

Vorau MS 193 contains the earliest extant version of Irimbert's Ruth and Judges commentaries, and Admont MS 650 and MS 682 contain slightly different later versions. Vorau 193, which was probably made from the notes dictated by Irimbert to the nuns, reveals two principal hands.[88] The first scribe (to whom I shall refer temporarily as Scribe 1) copied the bulk of the Judges commentary, and the second (Scribe 2) copied the bulk of the Ruth commentary (see Table 3.3). Both

"Explanatio huius hystorie descripta a sorore Regilinde." (The interpretation of this *historia* was copied by sister Regilind.) Admont MS 17, p. 393; Braun, "Irimbert von Admont," p. 288.

85 For an alternative analysis of the placement of this image of a monk-secretary, see Jeffrey F. Hamburger, "Art, Enclosure and the Cura Monialium: Prolegomena in the Guise of a Postscript," *Gesta* 31 (1992): 108–109.

86 Writing colophons seems not to have been common practice at Admont, or, indeed at most twelfth-century centers of manuscript production, for copyists of either sex. Only a small fraction of Admont's many monk-scribes signed their work, and only seven of the manuscripts copied in the monastery's prolific twelfth-century scriptorium bear a name. No female scribes are listed by Maria Mairold, *Die datierten Handschriften in der Steiermark ausserhalb der Universitätsbibliothek Graz bis zum Jahre 1600*, 2 vols., Katalog der datierten Handschriften in Lateinscher Schrift in Österreich 7 (Vienna, 1988), vol. I, pp. 9–13. Two recent master's theses have helped to identify scribal hands within this large corpus of manuscripts: Gerhard Gonsa, "Einige paläographische Beiträge zur Erforschung der Admonter Schreibschule des 12. Jahrhunderts," MA thesis (University of Vienna, 1989). Gonsa's work treats Admont MS 15, MS 164, MS 380, MS 497, and MS 786; Andrea Scheichl, "Studien zu Handschriften des 12. Jahrhunderts aus der Stiftsbibliothek Admont," MA thesis (University of Vienna, 1989), discusses Admont MS 18, MS 23, MS 33, MS 40, MS 43, MS 271, MS 281, MS 292, and MS 786.

87 For a description of the primary hands identified, see pp. 87–91.

88 Braun, "Irimbert von Admont," p. 271.

Scribe 1 and Scribe 2 worked alongside two other scribes (Scribes A and B), whose hands appear sporadically. Similarly, in Admont MS 650, Scribe 1 copied most of the Judges commentary and Scribe 2 copied most of the Ruth commentary (see Table 3.4). The pattern in Admont 682 is slightly different (See Table 3.5). Here it is Scribe B who is the main hand, and Scribe 2 appears only briefly. Scribe A again copied the Judges commentary in its entirety. Finally, in MS 17 (see Table 3.6) a hand very highly similar to that of Scribe 2 (though writing slightly later and with more attention to calligraphic style and neatness) copied the entire Ruth commentary. Based on the association of Scribe 2 with the earliest versions of the Ruth text, I have identified her as Irmingart.

Irmingart's hand appears in Vorau MS 193,[89] Admont MS 650,[90] Admont MS 651,[91] Admont MS 682,[92] and possibly Admont MS 16 and MS 17.[93] Several features distinguish her hand, which is a typical south German monastic Tilting Oval script representing a stage in the development from Caroline minuscule to Gothic Textura.[94] Her abbreviation for *-orum* consists of the letter **o**, a small oblong loop extending up to the right, and two straight and unembellished lower oblique strokes. The two straight lower stokes extend below the text line [Figure 8, line 15; Figure 10, lines 2, 7, 13; Figure 11, line 9; Figure 12, lines 4, 9, 13]. The ampersand is tipped to the right and the foot extends below the text line. A small closed loop, a wedge-shaped arm, and a slightly upturned foot are attached to the main lobe. The arm of the ampersand is slightly different in Admont MS 17 where it curves up at the end rather than terminating with a wedge [Figure 11, lines 9, 11, 12]. In Irmingart's abbreviation for the *-us* ending of the dative and ablative plurals, the attachment point for the curved stroke is the lobe of the **b** [Figure 8, line 9; Figure 9, lines 11, 17, 23; Figure 11, lines 3, 4, 5, 8, 13]. The descending stroke of the **g** bends to the right, and though usually quite rectangular, the shape of the **g**'s lower lobe is not consistent. In Admont MS 17, the descender is shorter, and the upper and lower lobes almost touch. In her abbreviation for *per*, the horizontal stroke is made at the very end of an unserifed descender of the **p** [Figure 8, line 5; Figure 9, lines 5, 7, 19, 23; Figure 10, lines 25, 26; Figure 11, lines 11, 13; Figure 12, lines 1, 2, 9, 12], but the horizontal stroke is made closer to the middle of the descender in Admont MS 682. The limb of the **h** curves around toward the bottom of the ascender like a hook, but does not drop below the text line [Figure 8, lines 1, 4, 5, 11, 12, 14;

[89] ff. 170v–174v, 186r–196r, and 211r–214v.

[90] ff. 1v–25r, 48r–49v, and 56r–64r.

[91] ff. 117r–124r and 129r–143r.

[92] ff. 18r–25v and 91r.

[93] MS 17, pp. 36–71 (?), p. 149–215, and 224–386.

[94] The scriptoria of Bavaria were slow to be influenced by the new Gothic bookhand that was rapidly gaining popularity elsewhere (Bischoff, *Latin Palaeography: Antiquity and the Middle Ages*, trans. Dáibhí Ó Cróinín and David Ganz (Cambridge, 1990), pp. 120–121). Still, some Gothic elements (e.g. more elongated and compressed letters) did begin to appear before the end of the twelfth century. See Karin Schneider, *Gotische Schriften in deutscher Sprache*, 2 vols. (Wiesbaden, 1987), vol. I, pp. 24–53, for a discussion of Bavarian book hands in the last quarter of the twelfth century.

Figure 9 lines 1, 8, 15, 18, 19, 25; Figure 10, lines 1, 4, 6, 8, 10, etc.; Figure 11, lines 3, 12; Figure 12, lines 1, 8]. Her **s** and **t** are barely joined by a light hairstroke [Figure 8, line 7; Figure 9, lines 9, 17, 21; Figure 10, line 22; Figure 11, lines 5, 6; Figure 12, lines 1, 8]. The **y** is unserifed and curves to the left at both top and bottom [Figure 8, line 5; Figure 9, lines 6, 19; Figure 10, line 10], though in Admont MS 16 and Admont MS 17 it moves slightly to the right at its termination [Figure 11, line 4; Figure 12, lines 7, 9]. The lobe of the **b** is slightly wider at the top than at the bottom, making it appear wedge-shaped.

Irmingart attained a high degree of consistency in her writing. The variations that are present, as they are in the hand of all scribes, can be explained by differences in writing speed and other environmental factors. The case of both Admont MS 16 and Admont MS 17 is difficult because these manuscripts were more carefully produced than the other four discussed here. They were also copied up to a decade later, during which time Irmingart's writing could easily have changed, especially in view of the growing influence of Gothic Textura in the region.

Regilind is more difficult to identify – Scribe 1 was clearly the main scribe of the earliest version (Vorau 193) and one of the intermediate versions (Admont 650), but not of the second intermediate version (Admont 682) or the final recension (Admont 17). On the strength of the appearance of Scribe 1 in the earliest version, as well as on the continuing association of her hand with the Judges text, I have identified her as Regilind.

Regilind's work is somewhat inconsistent. The slight differences in appearance among the folios provided as examples probably result from the relative speed of their execution. However, the common formation of the letters and abbreviations outlined above suggest that each was the work of a single scribe. Her hand is found in five manuscripts: Vorau MS 193,[95] Admont MS 650,[96] Admont MS 651,[97] Admont MS 682,[98] and possibly Admont MS 16 and MS 17.[99]

Regilind was, in general, not as neat a copyist as Irmingart. Her transitional script often appears to have been written quickly, with an absence of penlifts from one letter to the next. The letters **u** and **s** are occasionally joined at the end of a word. This ligature resembles a **v** with its right side curved in the shape of an **s** [Figure 13, line 19; Figure 14, line 3]. She also linked the letters **c** and **t** with a hairstroke extending from the top of the **c** to the top of the shaft of the **t** [Figure 13, lines 1, 11; Figure 14, lines 5, 12, 23, 24]. The **c** and **t** are not consistently connected in this way, particularly in Admont MS 16 and Admont MS 17. In most places the shaft of the **t** terminates with a small movement of the pen to the left [Figure 15, lines 2, 6, 11, 17]. Both forms are sometimes present on a single page [Example: Admont MS 17, p. 2, col. 1, line 2 (no hairstroke) and

[95] ff. 157r–167r and 175r–182v. [96] ff. 26r–47v and 50r–55r.
[97] ff. 87r–116r and 144r–154r. [98] ff. 69r–82v and 122r–137v. [99] MS 17, pp. 1–35 and 72–149.

col. 1, lines 3 and 27 (hairstroke)]. Both forms are also present in Admont MS 682 [Example: Admont MS 682, f. 82r, lines 4 and 6 (no hairstroke) and line 16 and 17 (hairstroke)]. The absence of the hairstroke joining **c** and **t** may have resulted from the lengthening of the shaft of the **t**, again, perhaps reflecting the influence of Gothic Textura, and may thus reflect a later stage in the scribe's development. In Regilind's abbreviation for *-orum*, the final two strokes extend below the line and these strokes are attached to the **o** below a closed loop. The stroke that extends from the **o** down to the right curves up towards the text line at its termination point [Figure 14, lines 18, 19, 23; Figure 16, lines 11, 18]. The attachment point for the curved stroke in the abbreviation for the *-us* ending of the dative and ablative plurals is the stem of the **b** [Figure 13, lines 2, 3, 15, 18; Figure 14, line 5; Figure 15, line 7]. The foot of her ampersand extends slightly below the text line, and a long arm curves upward with either a round or forked terminal. The lower lobe of the **g** is a slightly flattened oval or wedge that slants sharply down to the left. In Admont MS 16 and Admont MS 17 the lower lobe of the **g** is proportionally larger and slightly rounder. The strokes that form the top of the **y** are slightly serifed, and an unserifed descender makes a wide sweep from right to left [Figure 13, lines 5, 6; Figure 14, lines 2, 9, 10; Figure 15, lines 1, 13; Figure 16, lines 4, 6, 8, 11, 13, etc.]. Regilind occasionally used an uncial-type **d** (with a curved ascender brought back over the lobe of the letter) [Figure 13, lines 4, 9]. The lobe of the **b** is wider at the top than at the bottom, giving it a wedge shape.

The hand of two additional scribes, identified above as anonymous Nun-Scribes A and B appear in more than one of the manuscripts linked to the Admont nuns' scriptorium. The repeated juxtaposition of their work with Irmingart and Regilind's work strongly suggests that they were co-workers in the nuns' scriptorium.

The work of the anonymous Nun-Scribe A is found in both Vorau MS 193 (ff. 167v–170v, 183r–185r, and 197r–206v) and Admont MS 682 (ff. 30r–68v and f. 139r). Her *-orum* abbreviation consists of an **o** with a small closed loop above two hairstrokes. The first hairstroke extends from the bottom of the **o**, drops below the text line, and turns up at an angle towards the text line before its termination [Figure 17, line 19; Figure 18, lines 3, 15, 18]. The point of attachment for the curved stroke in the abbreviation for the *-us* ending of the dative and ablative plurals is the stem of the **b** [Figure 17, line 2; Figure 18, line 14]. Scribe A frequently (but not always) used the tironian notes for *et* (resembling a 7) [Figure 17, lines 14, 16] and *con* (resembling a backwards **c**) [Figure 17, line 14; Figure 18, line 1]. The foot of her ampersand touches but does not drop below the text line and its top stroke is a hook rather than a loop. Her **c** and **t** are joined from the top of the **c** to the headstroke of the **t** [Figure 17, lines 3, 7, 11, 18; Figure 18, lines 11, 13].

The work of anonymous Nun-Scribe B is found in three manuscripts: Vorau MS 193 (ff. 207r–208v), Admont MS 651 (ff. 124r–128r and 155r–186v), and Admont MS 682 (ff. 1v–17v and 26r–29v). The curved stroke of her abbreviation for *-us* ending of the dative and ablative plurals floats just above or slightly to the side of the lobe of the **b**. Occasionally the curved stroke is attached to the lobe of the **b** [Figure 19, lines 1, 12, 16, 24; Figure 20, lines 10, 17]. When **c** and **t** appear in sequence, the headstroke of the **t** extends only from the right side of the shaft. In these cases, the shaft of the **t** is always the same height as the ascenders of the **b**, **d**, **h**, and **l** [Figure 19, lines 1, 25; Figure 20, lines 9, 10]. The foot of her ampersand rests on the text line while its lobe sits slightly above the text line tipping it to the right. A closed loop is attached to the top right of the character's lobe. Scribe B's abbreviation for *-orum* is similar to that used by Regilind [Figure 19, lines 7 and 9].

### *Vorau, Stiftsbibliothek MS 193*

Vorau MS 193 is a composite manuscript composed of a series of individual units of varying length (see Table 3.3). In common with other related manuscripts produced at Admont, the scribes used single leaves to lengthen a gathering if space ran short, rather than having the text extend into the next gathering. Likewise, they used shortened gatherings of two bifolia if that was all the space required to finish a text or to copy a shorter text. The next text was copied into a separate quire.

This composite manuscript can be divided into three main sections. The first section, folios 3 through 80 (quires 1–11), is the work of one scribe, here identified as Scribe 1. This is the only hand at work in this portion of the manuscript, which contains anonymous sermons. Each folio was ruled for twenty-two long lines, and this ruling pattern distinguishes this segment from the others in the manuscript, which were ruled for twenty-seven lines of text. The frequent hand changes in sections two and three also set them apart from this first part in which one scribe writes for eighty folios. This hand appears in no other section of the manuscript. These differences in the preparation of materials and in the pattern of collaboration imply that section one was copied at a different time, or perhaps in a different scriptorium, from sections two and three, and there is nothing within to link it with nun-scribes.

Section two contains the work of five scribes, here identified as Scribes 2–6. This segment extends from folios 81–156 (quires 12–23), and these five hands appear only in this section. All of the texts here are anonymous biblical commentaries, but it is impossible to say whether the scribes were monks or nuns. The third section (folios 157 through 214, quires 24–29) contains Irimbert's commentaries on Ruth and Judges. These folios measure 190 by 100 mm, with a text area of 140 by 70 mm.[100] Four scribes, here identified as Scribes 7–10, copied these pages, and it is within this section and to these scribes that we must look to identify the hands of Regilind and Irmingart. In the commentary on Judges, the principal scribe

[100] See ruling pattern 1 on p. 146.

Table 3.3 *Vorau, Stiftsbibliothek MS 193*

| Scribe | Location | Text | Comments |
|---|---|---|---|
| 1 | 3r–80r<br>Quires 1 to 11–II, IV, V* | Anonymous, *Sermons* | |
| 2 | 81r–83v<br>Quire 12–III | Anonymous, *Sermons* | |
| 3 | 84r–91v<br>Quire 13–III<br>Quire 14–II | Anonymous, *Sermon for Palm Sunday* | |
| 2 | 93r–102r<br>Quire 15–IV<br>Quire 16–II | Anonymous, *Sermons* | |
| 4 | 102v–104v<br>Quire 16–II | Anonymous, *Sermons* | |
| 5 | 105r–120v<br>Quire 17–IV<br>Quire 18–IV | Anonymous, *Sermons* | |
| 6 | 121r–156r<br>Quire 19–IV<br>Quire 20–IV<br>Quire 21–IV<br>Quire 22–IV<br>Quire 23–II | Anonymous, *Sermons* | |
| 7 = Regilind | 157r–167r<br>Quire 24–IV<br>Quire 25–V | Irimbert of Admont, Commentary on Judges 19–21 | |
| 8 = Anon. Nun-Scribe A | 167v–170r, line 23<br>Quire 25–V | — | 164v contains correction by Irmingart<br>Irmingart also copied the last 13 lines on f. 169v |
| 9 = Irmingart | 170v, lines 23–174v<br>Quire 25–V | — | |
| 7 = Regilind | 175r–182v<br>Quire 26–IV | — | |
| 8 = Anon. Nun-Scribe A | 183r–185r<br>Quire 27a–II | — | |
| 9 = Irmingart | 186r–196v<br>Quire 27b–IV | Irimbert of Admont, Commentary on Ruth | |
| 8 = Anon. Nun-Scribe A | 197r–206v<br>Quire 28–IV | — | |
| 10 = Anon. Nun-Scribe B | 207r–208v<br>Quire 29–IV | — | |
| 8 = Anon. Nun-Scribe A | 209r–210v<br>Quire 29–IV | — | |
| 9 = Irmingart | 211r–214v<br>Quire 29–IV | — | |

* Roman numerals given in the Location column in these tables indicate quire structure; the numeral refers to the number of bifolia. Where more than one roman numeral is given, the segment contains more than one type of gathering.

(Scribe 7) began the text, copying ten folios. A second scribe (Scribe 8) took over on folio 167v and continued until 170v. A third hand (Scribe 9) copied the text on folios 170v to 174v. Scribe 7 returned on folio 175r and continued copying as far as folio 182v. Scribe 8 returned from 183r to 185r.

Three scribes also copied Irimbert's Ruth commentary. Two of these scribes (Scribe 8 and Scribe 9) also copied portions of the work on Judges. The primary hand was Scribe 9, who copied the beginning and the end of the text. Scribe 9 began the commentary on 186r and continued through 196v. Scribe 8 copied folios 197r to 206v. Scribe 10, in his or her only contribution to the manuscript, copied a short piece of the text on folios 207r to 208v. Scribe 8 worked again from folios 209r to 210v. Scribe 9 returned to copy the last section (folios 211r through 214v). If we accept that Scribes 7 and 9 were nuns, then Scribes 8 and 10, who worked intimately with them, were also nuns. For the sake of clarity in the present discussion, Scribes 8 and 10 will be referred to as anonymous Nun-Scribes A and B respectively. We can thus identify four female scribes in Vorau MS 193. It is possible that one or more of the other six scribes in the manuscript were also nuns. If so, they must remain unidentified since we lack sufficient evidence to place them in the women's scriptorium.

## *Admont, Stiftsbibliothek MS 650*

Admont MS 650, like Vorau MS 193, is a composite manuscript.[101] Folios 1r through 25v (quires 1–3) contain a copy of Irimbert's commentary on Ruth (see Table 3.4). Folios 26r through 55r (quires 4–6) contain his commentary on Judges 19–21. The last quire (folios 56r through 64r) contains an anonymous commentary on the book of Exodus. This manuscript closely resembles Vorau MS 193. The parchment is the same size (190 by 100 mm) and of roughly the same quality.[102] The text area in both measures 140 by 70 mm and is ruled for twenty-seven long lines, and their ruling patterns are identical.[103] These similarities suggest that the parchment for both manuscripts was prepared and ruled in the same place.

An analysis of the two hands at work in Admont MS 650 reveals that the primary scribes of their exemplar, Vorau MS 193, copied the texts (Scribes 7 and 9). The Ruth text was copied by the scribe identified as Irmingart in Vorau MS 193. Hers is the only hand at work in the manuscript's first three quires, which contain the entire commentary. Two single leaves were added to the third quire to create enough

[101] The restorer E. Klee divided the manuscript into two parts in the 1950s. The two units have different paleographical and codicological features and Klee evidently felt that they did not belong together in a single manuscript. The resulting two manuscripts are now designated MS 650a and MS 650b. 650a is the manuscript here under discussion.

[102] See the Summary of Codicological Features on p. 140

[103] Both were ruled according to pattern 1. See p. 146.

Table 3.4 *Admont, Stiftsbibliothek MS 650*

| Scribe | Location | Text | Comments |
|---|---|---|---|
| 1 = Irmingart | 1v–25r<br>Quire 1–III+1<br>Quire 2–IV<br>Quire 3–IV+2 | Irimbert of Admont, Commentary on Ruth | |
| 2 = Regilind | 26r–47v<br>Quire 4–IV<br>Quire 5–IV<br>Quire 6–IV | Irimbert of Admont, Commentary on Judges 19–21 | |
| 1 = Irmingart | 48r–49v<br>Quire 6–IV | — | |
| 2 = Regilind | 50r–55r<br>Quire 7–II+2 | — | |
| 1 = Irmingart | 56r–64r<br>Quire 8–IV+1 | Anonymous, Commentary on Exodus | |

space for Irmingart to complete the text. This scribe, the primary copyist of the two earliest versions of the text, played a continuing role in the copying of the text of Ruth. The same scribe who copied this text in the exemplar (Vorau MS 193), identified as Regilind, copied the commentary on Judges in Admont MS 650. She too seems to have followed the production of the text from Ur-text to this intermediate recension of the Judges commentary.

## *Admont, Stiftsbibliothek MS 682*

Admont MS 682 is a composite manuscript identical in format to Vorau MS 193 and Admont MS 650.[104] The parchment for this manuscript, ruled for twenty-seven long lines, was probably produced in the same workshop that produced the parchment for Vorau MS 193 and Admont MS 650.

Table 3.5 outlines the hand changes within the manuscript. Scribe 1, anonymous Nun-Scribe B, copied the first seventeen folios of the commentary on Ruth (ff. 1v–17v, quires 1 and 2). This is the main scribe of the text, identified as a co-worker of Irmingart and Regilind in Vorau MS 193 (Scribe 10). Irmingart took over from Scribe 1 on folio 18r, copying the entire third quire (ff. 18r–25v.). Nun-Scribe B returned to copy quire 4 (ff. 26r–29v). Quires 5 through 9 (ff. 30r–68v) contain a single hand, that of Nun-Scribe A, who also worked alongside Regilind and Irmingart in Vorau MS 193 (Scribe 8). Regilind's is the sole hand in the next quire,

[104] See ruling pattern 1 on p. 146.

Table 3.5 *Admont, Stiftsbibliothek MS 682*

| Scribe | Location | Text | Comments |
|---|---|---|---|
| 1 = Anon. Nun-Scribe B | 1v –17v Quire 1–IV+1 Quire 2–IV | Irimbert of Admont, Commentary on Ruth | |
| 2 = Irmingart | 18r–25v Quire 3–IV | — | |
| 1 = Anon. Nun-Scribe B | 26r–29v Quire 4–II | — | |
| 3 = Anon. Nun-Scribe A | 30r–68v Quire 5–IV Quire 6–IV Quire 7–IV Quire 8–IV Quire 9–III+1 | Irimbert of Admont, Commentary on Judges 19–21 Anonymous, Commentary on Exodus | |
| 4 = Regilind | 69r–82v Quire 10–VI+2 | Irimbert of Admont, Commentary on 1 Kings 9: 1–10, 8 | |
| 5 | 83r–90r Quire 11–IV | Irimbert of Admont, Commentary on 1 Kings 21: 1–9 | |
| 2 = Irmingart | 91r Quire 12–III | Anonymous, Commentary on Isaiah 9: 6 | |
| 6 = Anon. Nun-Scribe D | 91r–93r Quire 12–III | — Anonymous, Commentary on Song of Songs 5: 1 | |
| 7 = Anon. Nun-Scribe E | 93v–95v Quire 12–III | — | |
| 8 = Anon. Nun-Scribe C | 96r–96v Quire 12–III | Irimbert of Admont, Commentary on Song of Songs 5: 1 and 5: 2–3. | |
| 7 = Anon. Nun-Scribe E | 97r–98v Quire 13–IV | — | [Except few lines on 97v] |
| 9 = Anon. Nun-Scribe F | 99r–111r Quire 13–IV Quire 14–IV | — | |
| 10 = Anon. Nun-Scribe G | 111r–112v Quire 14–IV | Anonymous, *Sermon for the Assumption of the Virgin Mary* (Song of Songs 2: 13–14). | |
| 11 | 113r –113v Quire 15–I | — | |

Table 3.5 (*cont.*)

| Scribe | Location | Text | Comments |
|---|---|---|---|
| 9 = Anon. Nun-Scribe F | 114r–121r Quire 16–IV | Anonymous, Commentary on Song of Songs 5: 2–6 | |
| 4 = Regilind | 122r–137v Quire 17–IV Quire 18–IV+1 | Irimbert of Admont, Commentary on 4 Kings 6: 24–27, 17 | |
| 10(?) | 138r Quire 18 (stub)–IV+1 | — | |
| 3 = Anon. Nun-Scribe A | 139r Quire 19–II | — | |
| Several hands: 8 = Anon. Nun-Scribe C (and others?) | 139v–164v Quire 19–II [Quire 20–II+3 Quire 21–IV] Quire 22–II+3 | Anonymous, Commentary on Proverbs Anonymous, Commentary on Isaiah 9: 6 Anonymous, Commentary on Song of Songs 7: 1–6 | [significant water damage] |

which was composed of six bifolia and two single leaves and contains Irimbert's commentary on 1 Kings 9: 1–10.[105]

A group of at least four scribes copied folios 83r–121r (quires 12–16), which contain a series of anonymous commentaries on the Song of Songs, a sermon on the assumption of the Virgin Mary, and a sermon on the birth of Christ. Irmingart wrote the first few lines of text on folio 91r, perhaps setting the scale of handwriting for the scribes whose work follows. Table 3.5 outlines the frequent hand changes in this section of the manuscript. Paleographical analysis of this portion of the manuscript is complicated by the almost complete illegibility of the text on some folios resulting from water damage (especially to quires 20 and 21). If we apply the criteria presented above for identifying nun-scribes by their collaboration within quires with previously identified female scribes, then Scribes 6 through 9 can be taken to be nuns. Scribe 6 completed folio 91r, of which Irmingart had written the first few lines. Scribes 6–10 alternated within quires 12 through 14. The identification of these four scribes as nuns from this evidence alone is not certain – Irmingart may possibly have written the first lines of the text and then sent the quire out of the enclosure for scribes in the monks' scriptorium to complete, but this seems unlikely.

105 This is a good example of the adjustment of quire length to suit the needs of the text being copied.

The identification of Scribes 6–10 as nuns is supported by an analysis of quires 17–22. Regilind copied part of Irimbert's commentary on 4 Kings (quires 17 and 18). Scribe 10 then copied one side of the following folio, which is a single folio and may have been appended later to the end of the text. Anonymous Nun-Scribe A returned on folio 139r (quire 19). Within this same quire, Scribe 8 began to copy an anonymous commentary on the book of Proverbs (f. 139v), suggesting that this was a nun who worked closely with Nun-Scribe A. Scribe 8 later copied two anonymous commentaries on the Song of Songs in the last two quires of the manuscript (ff. 139v–164v, quires 19–22). It seems likely that this scribe was a nun, since she appears to have worked alongside anonymous Nun-Scribe A in quire 19. This scribe (identified in Table 3.5 with the letter C), worked with two more scribes within quires 13 and 14 (ff. 97r–104v and ff. 105r–112v), who were thus probably nuns. They are identified in Table 3.5 as anonymous Nun-Scribes D (ff. 91r–93r) and E (ff. 111r–112v). Nun-Scribe D also worked in quire 12 (ff. 91r–96v), which Irmingart had begun. Scribe E worked within quire 13 with two copyists, identified as Nun-Scribes F and G. As suggested by the inconsistencies in their work, it is possible that anonymous Nun-Scribes C, D, E, F, and G were less experienced scribes in the nuns' scriptorium. Nine of the eleven copyists whose work is represented in Admont MS 682 (including Irmingart and Regilind) were probably nuns. Only Scribes 5 (quire 11) and 11 (who copied only a stub, quire 15, f. 138r) had no discernible ties to the nuns' scriptorium.

### *Admont, Stiftsbibliothek MS 17*

Admont MS 17 contains Irimbert's commentaries on Joshua, Judges 19–21, and Ruth. The larger format (400 by 275 mm), historiated initials, and careful script reflect its status as the final redaction of these texts. The work is arranged in two columns, each with thirty-seven lines.[106] According to Braun, the texts of Judges and Ruth were copied both from Admont MS 650 and from MS 682.[107]

The difference in overall quality between Admont MS 17 and its three precursors is easily explained by the place of each in the evolution of the commentaries on Ruth and Judges. While the small-format commentary manuscripts represent several stages in the editing of these texts, Admont MS 17 was probably intended to be a definitive version from which subsequent copies would be made (although we lack any such later copies). The quire structure of MS 17 was more regular. This was not a composite manuscript, but one copied as a unit (see Table 3.6).

Three main scribes, probably including Irmingart and Regilind, alternated throughout the manuscript, with these two scribes collaborating only within quire 10. Scribe 3 worked alongside Irmingart in quire 12, and Scribe 5 worked with her

[106] See ruling pattern 2 on p. 146. [107] Braun, "Überlieferung," pp. 95 and 107.

Table 3.6 *Admont, Stiftsbibliothek MS 17*

| Scribe | Location | Text | Comments |
|---|---|---|---|
| 1 = Regilind | pp. 1–35<br>Quires 1 and 2 | Irimbert of Admont, Commentary on Joshua | |
| 2 = Irmingart | pp. 36–71<br>Quires 3 and 4 | — | |
| 1 = Regilind | pp. 72–149<br>Quires 5–10<br>Q10 = III | — | |
| 2 = Irmingart | pp. 149–195<br>Quires 10–12 | — | |
| 3 = Anon. Nun-Scribe H(?) | pp. 196–199<br>Quire 12 | — | |
| 2 = Irmingart | pp. 201–215<br>Quire 13 | — | |
| 4 | pp. 216–218<br>Quires 13–14<br>Q12 = V | — | Pages 216/217 comprise a single leaf. First three lines on 218 written on erasure. Probably added later. |
| 2 = Irmingart | pp. 218–386<br>Quires 14–24<br>Q24 = V | Irimbert of Admont, Commentary on Ruth | |
| 5 = Anon. Nun-Scribe I(?) | pp. 387–442<br>Quires 24–27 | Irimbert of Admont, Commentary on Judges 19–21 | |

in quire 24, suggesting that these two unidentified scribes might have been nuns (identified in Table 3.6 as Nun-Scribes H and I). Scribe 4's work was inserted into the gathering on a single folio (pp. 216/217) and continued for three lines on page 218, which were written over an erasure. The date of the manuscript is uncertain, but it must have been begun after 1153, when Irimbert completed his commentary on Joshua. Since Regilind was probably one of the scribes, the volume (or at least the sections she copied) was likely completed prior to her departure to reform Bergen in 1159.

## OTHER COMMENTARY MANUSCRIPTS OF THE ADMONT SCHOOL

### *Admont, Stiftsbibliothek MS 16*

Admont MS 16, which was kept in the women's library, contains Irimbert's complete cycle of sermon-commentaries on Kings, preached to the nuns of

Table 3.7 *Admont, Stiftsbibliothek MS 16*

| Scribe | Location (paginated) | Text | Comments |
|---|---|---|---|
| 1 = Regilind | 1–164<br>Quire 1–IV+1 Quire 2–10 = IV | Irimbert of Admont, Commentary on 1 Kings | Preached to the nuns of St. George on Langsee in 1151. |
| 2 = Irmingart | 165–326<br>Quires 11–19 = IV<br>Quire 20 = IV+1 | Irimbert of Admont, Commentary on 2 Kings | Preached to the nuns of St. George on Langsee in 1151. Prologue written at Admont after 1152. |
| 3 = Anon. Nun-Scribe A | 327–524<br>Quires Q21–31 = IV<br>Quire 32 = V+1 | Irimbert of Admont, Commentary on 3 Kings | Preached to the nuns of Admont in 1152. |
| 1 = Regilind | 525–534 col. 2, line 32<br>Quire 33 = IV | Irimbert of Admont, Commentary on 4 Kings | Preached to the nuns of Admont in 1152. |
| 3 = Anon. Nun-Scribe A | 534 col. 2, line 32–684<br>Quires 33–42 = IV | — | |

St. George on the Langsee (1 and 2 Kings) and Admont (3 and 4 Kings) in 1151 and 1152. Irimbert tells us that the fire of 6 April 1152 delayed the completion of this long work, which fills the 684 pages in this final recension.

An examination of this and two earlier versions of these commentaries reveals what is probably the hand of a single scribe throughout the project. In the early recensions, this scribe, whom I have identified as Regilind, copied Irimbert's sermon-commentaries on 1 Kings 9: 1–10 and 4 Kings 6: 24–27 (Admont MS 682), and 3 Kings 18: 42–45 (Admont MS 651). Regilind possibly also copied the first 164 pages of the final recension of the series, MS 16.

The second nun-assistant is harder to identify because four other scribes helped with the copying. One candidate is Nun-Scribe B, whom we see in Admont MS 651 copying commentaries on 4 Kings 2: 1–18, 3 Kings 22: 1–38, 4 Kings 13: 14–21, and 4 Kings 6: 1–7 (Admont MS 651). Another possibility is Scribe 5 in MS 682/3 in MS 651, who copied Irimbert's explanation of 1 Kings 9: 1–10. The sex of this third scribe cannot be determined. The third possibility is Irmingart, who copied the entire 2 Kings commentary in MS 16. Finally, there is Nun-Scribe A, who copied the 3 Kings commentary and the bulk of the 4 Kings commentary in this same volume.

In the small-format volumes containing the earlier versions of the texts, Regilind copied the commentary on 3 Kings and the bulk of the commentary on 4 Kings.

When we look at the hands at work in Admont MS 16, the final version, we again see a scribe that may possibly be Regilind. Here she collaborated with Irmingart and Nun-Scribe A. Regilind and Irmingart copied roughly equal portions (173 and 161 pages respectively), but A, who copied 347 pages, dominates the work. The dominance of both Regilind and A in the Kings manuscript group suggests that they were the two primary assistants whom Irimbert thanked.

The commentary on each book was copied by a single scribe who was given just enough parchment to complete her portion. Irmingart, for example, used ten standard gatherings of four bifolia plus an eleventh gathering with an extra leaf (IV+1) to accommodate the prologue and commentary on 2 Kings. Nun-Scribe A filled ten standard quaternions and a quinion with one added leaf (V+1) for 3 Kings. This distribution of quires among three scribes allows for the possibility that they worked simultaneously, each copying her assigned piece independently of the other two.

## *Admont MS 651*

Admont MS 651 contains a group of biblical sermons, most of which were probably delivered to the Admont nuns by Irimbert in the 1140s. The codex contains the work of nine scribes (see Table 3.8). The ruling pattern is identical to that in Vorau MS 193, and Admont MS 650 and MS 682.[108] Scribe 1 copied the first quire (ff. 1r–7r). Scribe 2 and Scribe 3 both worked within the second quire (ff. 8r–14v). Scribe 1 returned to copy the fourth quire and the first part of the fifth (ff. 21r–36r). Scribes 1 and 3 then alternate within quires up to the end of quire 11 (ff. 36v–86r). These three scribes were almost certainly workers in the same scriptorium. Scribe 3's hand is familiar from Admont MS 682 (Scribe 5, p. 95). Unfortunately this is not one of the hands linked thus far to the nuns' scriptorium. Three other scribes were probably nuns: Scribe 4 was Regilind, Scribe 5 was Irmingart, and Scribe 6 was anonymous Nun-Scribe B.

## PATTERNS OF SCRIBAL COLLABORATION

There are frequent hand changes in Vorau MS 193, Admont MS 650, and Admont MS 682, and the scribes often appear to have been writing quickly. Both the script and pattern of collaboration in these volumes implies that speed of execution was of central concern; copyists working cooperatively could produce faster results. Practical considerations apparently took precedence over aesthetics, although an effort was made to use a uniform book hand and parchment with the same characteristics

108 See ruling pattern 1 on p. 146.

Table 3.8 *Admont, Stiftsbibliothek MS 651*

| Scribe | Location | Commentary on text | Comments |
|---|---|---|---|
| 1 | 1r–7r<br>Quire 1–III+1 | Matthew 21: 1–9<br>Psalm 117: 26 | |
| 2 | 8r–14v<br>Quire 2–IV | Matthew 20: 1–16 | |
| 3 | 14v–20v<br>Quire 2–IV<br>Quire 3–I+3 | Matthew 15: 21–28 | |
| 1 | 21r–36r<br>Quire 4–IV<br>Quire 5–IV | John 10: 11–15 | |
| 3 | 36v–38r<br>Quire 5–IV<br>Quire 6–IV | John 16: 16–22 | |
| 1 | 38r–71r<br>Quire 6–IV<br>Quire 7–III+2<br>Quire 8–III+2<br>Quire 9–IV+1 | Luke 6: 36–42<br>Luke 5: 1–11<br>Mark 7: 31–37<br>Matthew 6: 24–33 | |
| 3 | 72r–77v<br>Quire 10–III+2 | Luke 10: 38–41 | |
| 1 | 77v<br>Quire 10–III+2 | — | |
| 3 | 78r–86r<br>Quire 10–III+2<br>Quire 11–II+3 | Luke 22: 24–30 | |
| 4 = Regilind | 87r–116r<br>Quire 12–IV<br>Quire 13–IV<br>Quire 14–IV+1<br>Quire 15–I+3 | John 13: 1–15<br>Matthew 28: 1–7<br>Luke 24: 13–35<br>Luke 24: 36–47<br>John 20: 19–31<br>John 16: 23–30<br>Ephesians 4: 7–13 | |
| 5 = Irmingart | 117r–124r<br>Quire 16–IV | Matthew 11: 25–30 | |
| 6 = Anon. Nun-Scribe B | 124r–128r<br>Quire 16–IV | Luke 11: 14–28 | |
| 5 = Irmingart | 129r–143r<br>Quire 17–IV<br>Quire 18–III+1 | Isaiah 21: 1–10<br>Judges 11: 1–2 and 28–40 | |
| 4 = Regilind | 144r–154v<br>Quire 18–III+1<br>Quire 19–IV<br>Quire 20–I+1 | Daniel 5: 1–7 and 25–28<br>3 Kings 18: 42–45 | |

Table 3.8 (*cont.*)

| Scribe | Location | Commentary on text | Comments |
|---|---|---|---|
| 6 = Anon. Nun-Scribe B | 155r–186v<br>Quire 21–IV<br>Quire 22–IV<br>Quire 23–IV+1<br>Quire 24–III+1 | 4 Kings 2: 1–18<br>3 Kings 22: 1–38<br>4 Kings 13: 14–21<br>4 Kings 6: 1–7 | |
| 7 | 187r–197r<br>Quire 25–IV<br>Quire 26–III+1 | Nehemiah 8: 1–10 | |
| 8 | 197r–200 *bis* v<br>Quire 26–III+1 | Luke 1: 57–68 | |
| 3 | 201r–209r<br>Quire 27–III+2 | Deuteronomy 26: 1–10 | |

throughout. Significant modifications were made to the texts from recension to recension, indicating that the commentary was still a work-in-progress.[109] Each of these volumes is composed of irregular gatherings (i.e. other than the common gathering of four bifolia, or a quaternion) tailored to suit the text contained.[110] For example, if a text required six folios, a three-bifolia gathering was constructed.[111] If this same six-folio text had been copied into uniform quaternions, two bifolia at the end of the gathering would have been left blank. In order to conserve parchment, those two bifolia would be used for the beginning of another text. Similarly, a text requiring nine folios could be copied into a gathering of four bifolia plus one single leaf, rather than into two gatherings of four, leaving seven folios in the second blank.[112] The use of irregular quires eliminated the need for coordinating space for texts within gatherings, and was thus ideal for accommodating the rapidly growing group of sermons and commentaries that was being produced in two separate scriptoria; as new texts were written, they could be added to the manuscript. These sub-units must be treated individually when attempting to determine their origin, as they may have been copied in different places. Codicological features such as ruling patterns and parchment quality are not reliable indicators of origin, since the nuns' and monks' scriptoria may have shared a common source of

[109] A collation of the various manuscripts and an analysis of the textual changes made, while clearly beyond the scope of the present study, would likely yield interesting information about the genesis of both works.

[110] P. R. Robinson, "The 'Booklet': A Self-Contained Unit in Composite Manuscripts," *Codicologica* 2 (Leiden, 1978), pp. 46–69.

[111] For example, see Table 3.3, p. 92, quire 12. This gathering, constructed of three bifolia (indicated here by the roman numeral III), contains a complete sermon.

[112] See Table 3.4 on p. 94. Quire 8 was made up of four bifolia (IV) plus one single leaf (+1) at the end of the quire to provide exactly enough space for the commentary.

parchment and employed similar ruling practices. A more elegant script, uniform quaternions, illuminated initials, and a larger format distinguish the manuscript containing the final recension of the texts (Admont, Stiftsbibliothek MS 17) from the earlier recensions, a fact consistent with the hypothesis that its producers now viewed its contents as fixed.

The close proximity of Admont's male and female communities may have facilitated collaborative copying, and the composite approach to producing manuscripts would have been especially useful when scribes of various sections worked independently. For example, a nun could copy a commentary in one sub-unit made up of one or more quires. A monk could copy another text, which was later added to the others. Coordination to avoid excess or insufficient space for text at the end of quires was not necessary when manuscripts were constructed in this manner, and the use of parchment from a common source would minimize visual differences between the sections.

* * *

Admont's book collections represent a collective achievement – the result of close cooperation among scribes of both sexes who strove to employ a uniform script and who shared the work – and their surviving books thus reflect their strong sense of community and common purpose.[113] The libraries in both the women's and the men's houses provided the basic tools for the reformed spirituality that characterized the monastery in the twelfth century. At Admont, as at other twelfth-century monasteries associated with the Hirsau reform, learning and piety were deeply connected. Literacy was a key to participation in one of the most basic practices of spiritual life in these reformed communities: the *lectio divina*.

It is particularly significant, then, that Admont's twelfth-century nuns participated in the intellectual revival at the monastery at all levels – as scribes, readers, preachers, and biblical commentators. The ability of some of the women to take dictation and to copy books enabled them to play a critical role both in building a library that could support active and serious study of the Bible, and in constructing the monastery's exegetical voice. The books they owned and copied are a window on their spiritual, intellectual, and material participation in reformed monastic life. Through that window we see a twelfth-century religious community that took seriously the intellectual and spiritual abilities and accomplishments of its women. Although strictly enclosed, these women were certainly not marginal to the most fundamental aspects of the reformed life that the community embraced. Their ability to participate fully in central aspects of religious life at Admont may not have been atypical among contemporary dual-sex communities connected with the Hirsau reform.

113 On collaborative copying as an expression of community, see David Ganz, "The Preconditions for Caroline Minuscule," *Viator* 18 (1987): 32.

# 4

## *Unlikely allies in the scriptorium: the female scribes of Schäftlarn*

In 1140, Bishop Otto of Freising (d. 1158) came upon a small and declining chapter of secular canons situated beside the Isar River in his diocese. This community, Schäftlarn, had a tumultuous past. The priest Waltrich first founded it as a house of Benedictine monks in 760, but this was in ruins by 932, devastated by the Magyar invasions and the appropriation of its property by Arnulf, duke of Bavaria (d. 937). Arnulf financed an army in part through the secularization of a number of Bavarian churches and monasteries, including Schäftlarn. Religious life was restored at Schäftlarn late in the tenth century when the chapter of secular canons was established.[1] Otto seized the opportunity to transform this struggling house into a new type of community spreading rapidly in German lands – a Premonstratensian monastery dedicated to the pursuit of the *vita apostolica*.[2] Otto, who was himself a Cistercian, was a zealous champion of clerical reform,[3] a cause he advanced within his territory by converting houses like Schäftlarn into houses of regular canons – Premonstratensian and Augustinian – and

[1] For a history of Schäftlarn, see Leo Abstreiter, *Geschichte der Abtei Schäftlarn* (Schäftlarn, 1916); Sigisbert Mitterer, ed., *1200 Jahre Kloster Schäftlarn* (Schäftlarn, 1962); Josef Hemmerle, *Die Benediktinerklöster in Bayern*, Bayerische Heimatsforschung 4 (Munich, 1951), pp. 115–116. See S. Tyroller, "Zu den Säkularisationen des Herzog Arnulf," *StM* 65 (1953): 303–312, and The Historical Commission of the Bavarian Academy of Science, *Neue deutsche Biographie* 1 (Berlin, 1953), pp. 396–397. After 1140, Schäftlarn remained Premonstratensian until the secularization of 1803. King Ludwig I of Bavaria re-founded the monastery and restored the observance of the Benedictine Rule in 1866, and it remains a functioning community today.

[2] As the new order spread to Germany, Bavaria became its main center of activity. For an outline history of the Premonstratensians in Bavaria, see Romuald Bauerreiss, *Kirchengeschichte Bayerns*, 7 vols. (Munich, 1949–1970), vol. III, pp. 39–42.

[3] On Otto's career and literary work, see Cornelia Kirchner-Feyerabend, *Otto von Freising als Diözesan- und Reichsbischof* (Frankfurt-am-Main, 1990); Hans-Werner Goetz, *Das Geschichtsbild Ottos von Freising*, Beihefte zum Archiv für Kulturgeschichte 19 (Cologne and Vienna, 1984); Adolf Hofmeister, "Studien über Otto von Freising," *Neues Archiv* 37 (1912): 99–161; Justus Hashagen, *Otto von Freising als Geschichtsphilosoph und Kirchenpolitiker* (Leipzig, 1900).

populating them with individuals from previously established reformed communities.[4]

Schäfltarn's new residents, colonists from the Premonstratensian double monastery of Ursberg in Swabia, took stock of their books almost immediately. As experienced Premonstratensians, they were no doubt accustomed to a library larger than the one they found in their new home.[5] Schäftlarn's past inhabitants had left them only a small collection of texts, produced mainly in the workshop that supplied books for the library of the bishops of Freising.[6] The library's earliest books, dated on palaeographical grounds to the time of Bishops Arbeo (d. 784) and Hitto (d. 836), are largely known to us through fragments discovered in fifteenth-century bindings.[7] A fragment of the *Dialogues* of Gregory the Great (Clm 17162), originally part of a ninth-century southern German or Swiss manuscript, has also been recovered from a late medieval binding, a discovery that points to origins beyond Freising for some of the library's earliest holdings.

It is clear that the library that the newly arrived Premonstratensians found was inadequate for the monastery's central work of training priests. To correct this deficit, the community immediately set up a scriptorium, the first ever at Schäftlarn. A booklist written around 1164 reflects the growth of the monastery's book collections during the community's first twenty-four years (1140 to 1164) and suggests the most urgent needs of the growing library.[8] The list includes a number of liturgical books: five missals, two *libri matutinales* for travelers, two "old" *matutinales*, a *plenarium*, a homiliary. There were also a number of Patristic and Carolingian theological works and commentaries: Augustine's *De trinitate* and his *Enchiridion*, and *De quadragesima*, Jerome's commentary on Daniel, Gregory the Great's *Moralia in Job*, *Dialogues*, and commentary on Ezekiel, Origen's commentary on Leviticus, Bede's commentary on the Acts of the Apostles and commentary on the Song of Songs, the *Hierarchia coelestis* of Pseudo-Dionysius, Rhabanus Maurus' Commentary

[4] Otto's second Premonstratensian foundation was Neustift, also reorganized in 1140 and colonized, like Schäftlarn, with individuals from Ursberg. His Augustinian foundations were Schliersee (1140), Schlehdorf (a former Benedictine abbey, converted in the 1140s), and St. Zeno/Isen (date unrecorded). See Kirchner-Feyerabend, *Otto von Freising*, pp. 145–146 and 161–162.

[5] Ursberg had joined the Premonstratensian Order fourteen years earlier, in 1126.

[6] Paul Ruf, "Die Handschriften des Klosters Schäftlarn," in *1200 Jahre Kloster Schäftlarn, 762–1962*, ed. Sigisbert Mitterer (Schäftlarn, 1962), p. 29.

[7] Paul Ruf, "Handschriften," pp. 29–39. The use of outdated or unneeded texts as reinforcement in bookbinding was common, and modern conservation projects continue to yield such fragments from numerous centers. Pieces of parchment were used either as paste-downs for the front or back cover, or to stiffen the spine.

[8] The list appears on folio 186r of Clm 17078. For a photograph, see Ruf, "Handschriften," p. 55. An edition of the list is found in MBKr, 726. The list does not include manuscripts received as gifts, copied prior to 1140, or books copied under Prior Henry. For an interpretation of the dating and purpose of this list, see Ruf, "Handschriften," p. 48.

on Kings, Haimo of Auxerre's commentary on the Apocalypse, and Paschasius Radbertus' *De corpore et sanguine Domini.* Anselm of Canterbury's *De processione spiritus sancti*, and Hugh of Fouilloy's *De claustra animae* are the only contemporary or near contemporary writings on the list, and Philo (whose text is not specified) is the sole non-Christian author.[9]

We know that the monastery produced a large number of books under Prior Henry (1164–1200). The primary source of information about the activity of the scriptorium during his priorate is the large number of colophons written by contemporary scribes that either name him or specify a date of production between 1164 and 1200. The wording of these colophons – many of which were written in the form of prayers – leaves little doubt that these were canon- and canoness-scribes. Of the professed status of Irmingart, who calls herself "sister" there is no doubt. The male Adalbertus referred to himself as "martirum Christi ultimus servus."[10]

From the number and variety of texts thus identified, and from texts dated on paleographical grounds to this period, we can conclude that Henry undertook a campaign to expand Schäftlarn's library. The book collection seems at this point to have evolved from a more general collection of theological and exegetical works into one that more clearly reflected the needs of this community of monk-priests and priests-in-training. Notable are the numerous works of pastoral theology including Ambrose of Milan's *De officiis ministrorum*, Gregory the Great's *De cura pastorali*, Bernard of Clairvaux's *De consideratione*, Rupert of Deutz's *De divinis officiis*, and John Beleth's *Summa de ecclesiasticis officiis.*[11] But the growth of the library points also to the continuing pull of the contemplative side of Premonstratensian spirituality, with interest in monastic *lectio*, and perhaps even newer intellectual approaches to the study of the Bible. New to the collection, for example, were Augustine's *Enarrationes in Psalmos* and commentary on the Gospel of John, Haimo of Auxerre's commentary on the Letters of Paul, commentaries on the Song of Songs by Rupert of Deutz and Honorius *Augustodunensis*, and also Peter Comestor's *Historia scholastica.* Hagiographical works added to the collection under Henry included the Life of Saint Norbert, the Life of Saint Martin by Sulpicius Severus, the Life of Saint Corbinian by Arbeo,[12] and the Life of Saint Thomas of Canterbury. Textual links between several Schäftlarn manuscripts and manuscripts from Tegernsee, Benediktbeuren, and Herrenchiemsee suggest that

[9] Ruf attempted to match surviving manuscripts with titles from this inventory, and he tentatively identified thirty of the forty-six books named with extant manuscripts now housed at the Bayerische Staatsbibliothek in Munich. See Ruf, "Handschriften," p. 49.

[10] Ruf, "Handscrhriften," pp. 40–47.

[11] On Rupert of Deutz and the interest of his *De divinis officiis* to those trying to balance monastic contemplation and priestly duties, see John Van Engen, *Rupert of Deutz* (Berkeley, 1983), pp. 58–67.

[12] d. 784

these communities exchanged books for reading and copying. The library of the diocese of Freising may have also been a source of exemplars.[13]

Schäftlarn enjoyed considerable prosperity during the twelfth century, and a significant portion of the wealth generated by various forms of patronage must have been channeled into the library. Donations were made at a relatively constant rate under the first four Premonstratensian priors (1140–1200).[14] Noble men and women and *ministeriales* were the monastery's most enthusiastic patrons, and their gifts included landed estates, vineyards, saltworks, and mills, as well as unfree servants, although donations were also made by a number of non-aristocratic patrons. In addition to the proceeds of this patronage, *tributales* or *censuales*, individuals who were obliged to pay an annual sum to the monastery in exchange for protection, provided an important source of community income. A number of Schäftlarn's *tributales* may have been former serfs who also gained through this relationship freedom from forced labor services.[15] Others were sons and daughters of the noble and ministerial classes, and it seems likely that some of these higher-born women were either paying guests of the monastery, or those admitted *ad succurrendum*, that is, men or women who paid to receive care in sickness or old age.[16]

Patronage also came in the form of book donations. By 1162, the priest Arbo of Herbertshausen had donated a number of books to the library: a precious one-volume missal with lectionary and evangeliary, several *libri matutinales*, a glossed copy of the Pauline Epistles (perhaps Clm 17042), and Ivo of Chartres' *Panormia*.[17]

[13] Ruf, "Handschriften," p. 47.

[14] Donations and dedications of *tributales* were made at a rate of 3 per year under Prior Englehart (1140–1153), 5 per year under Prior Eberhard (1153–1160), 3.5 per year under Prior Arnold (1160–1164), and 5.5 per year under Henry (1164–1200). Since many of the charters reflected in these numbers cannot be dated precisely, the calculated per-year donation rates given are approximations.

[15] For a discussion of the development of this type of arrangement between individuals and ecclesiastical institutions, see J. B. Freed, *Noble Bondsmen: Ministerial Marriages in the Archdiocese of Salzburg, 1100–1343* (Ithaca, NY, 1995) and T. Reuter, *Germany in the Early Middle Ages, 800–1056* (New York, 1991) p. 232. Eight donations made to Schäftlarn by patrons of lower status were recorded. See Alois Weissthanner, ed., *Die Traditionen des Klosters Schäftlarn, 760–1305*, Quellen und Erörterungen zur bayerischen Geschichte, NS 10/1 (Munich, 1953), Tr. 58, 68, 86, 127, 142, 155, 165, and 220.

[16] For a discussion of admittees to female communities *ad succurrendum*, see Penelope D. Johnson, *Equal in Monastic Profession: Religious Women in Medieval France* (Chicago, 1991), pp. 29, 177, and 224. A list compiled between 1140 and 1150 gives the name of sixty-three *tributales*, twenty-five of whom were female. Schäftlarn's *liber traditionum* records the establishment of this type of relationship between the monastery and twenty-nine women between 1140 and 1200. See Weissthanner, *Traditionen*, p. 448.

[17] Weissthanner identified this book as Clm 17000: "Ipsa quoque die domnus Arbo presbiter de Herebrehteshusen tradidit duos bonos libros: missale cum lectionario et evangeliario in uno volumine precioso martiri sancto Dionisio et sancte Iuliane cum tribus talentis ad emenda vineta pro salute anime sue omniumque parentum suorum renovans per hec priorem traditionem bonorum matutinalium et apostoli glosati et canonum Iuonis." (On this same day, lord Arbo, priest of Herbertshausen, gave two good books – a missal with lectionary and an evangelary in one precious volume – to the martyr Saint Dionysius and to Saint Juliana, with three talents for the purchase

In *c.* 1180, the priest Engilbert, *confrater* of St. Castulus in Moosburg, also made a donation of books – Gratian's *Decretum* and a *Summa* on the *Decretum* (probably by Stephen of Tournai).[18] The thanks given the two donor-priests – a daily mass said in their honor for one year after death – reflect the importance that this community placed on books.[19]

Book producers, like book donors, were clearly highly valued by the community. This may account, in part, for the unusual visibility of Schäftlarn's copyists. About one-fifth of Schäftlarn's approximately sixty-six twelfth-century volumes contain the name of a scribe or scribes. Schäftlarn alone accounts for eleven of the thirty-four named scribes who emerge from the Bavarian manuscripts cataloged by Elisabeth Klemm.[20] These statistics reflect a culture in the monastery that permitted, encouraged, or in some cases even required individual scribes to take credit for their work in greater numbers than at other contemporary Bavarian centers. An exceptionally large number of Schäftlarn's scribes identified themselves in subscriptions, both under Henry and his three predecessors. Almost one-fifth of Schäftlarn's approximately sixty-six surviving twelfth-century volumes contain the name of a scribe or scribes, and Schäftlarn alone accounts for eleven of the thirty-four named scribes who emerge from the manuscripts cataloged by Klemm.[21]

That women were a significant component of this highly visible scribal work force makes the case of Schäftlarn still more unusual. At least three women – Adelheid, Sophia, and Irmingart[22] – contributed to book production during the twelfth century. Although we know of Adelheid only through an entry in the monastery's necrology, Sophia and Irmingart recorded their own names. But

of vineyards, for the salvation of his soul and those of all of his relatives, confirming with these his prior gift of good *matutinales*, a glossed copy of the Pauline Epistles, and the canons of Ivo.) Weissthanner, *Traditionen*, pp. 121–122.

18 "quidam venerabilis sacerdos nomine Engilbertus confrater sancti Castuli de Moseburch plebanus ac decanus dedit libros suos: Gratianum et Summam ipsius libri sancto Dionisio Scheftlaren, Sententias autem Petri sancto Petro ad Novam Cellam." (a certain venerable priest by the name of Engilbertus, an affiliate of Saint Castulus in Moosburg, priest and dean, gave his books to Saint Dionysius, Schäftlarn: [The Decretum of] Gratian and the Summa [of Stephan of Tournai], and to Saint Peter, Neustift, the Sentences of Peter [Lombard].) Weissthanner, *Traditionen*, p. 240; "Quidam presbiter et decanus sancti Castuli Moseburg tradidit sancto Dionisio et sancte Juliane hunc codicem et alterum bonum Gratianum pro salute anime sue." (A certain priest and dean of St. Castulus in Moosburg gave to Saint Dionysius and Saint Juliana of Schäftlarn this codex and another good one of Gratian for the salvation of his soul.) Weissthanner, *Traditionen*, p. 239.

19 "His duobus presbiteris hac vita defunctis plenarie fraternitatis communionem nec non per singulos unius anni dies specialem in missa debemus recordítationem." (After the death of these two priests we owe a special commemoration in a daily mass for one year.) Weissthanner, *Traditionen*, p. 122.

20 Elisabeth Klemm, *Die romanischen Handschriften der Bayerischen Staatsbibliothek*, 3 vols. (Wiesbaden, 1980–).

21 Klemm, *Die romanischen Handschriften.*

22 This is the same Irmingart who wrote the cruciform colophon shown on p. 3.

Premonstratensian women were denied access to education and were normally prohibited from reading anything beyond a few Psalms and prayers. How did women in this intellectually restrictive environment find themselves at work in the scriptorium, and to what extent did these women contribute to the wider Premonstratensian reform? To answer these questions, we must turn first to Schäftlarn's female community.

## WOMEN AT SCHÄFTLARN

The traditional date of the decree of the Chapter General of the Order of Prémontré calling for the division of all of its double monasteries into separate communities for men and women is 1140. This was, in the eyes of modern scholars, including the eminent German historian Herbert Grundmann, a critical moment in the Order's effort to "free itself from the participation of women."[23] There followed in 1198 a second general decree – this one ratified by none less than Pope Innocent III – forbidding the further admission of women to any Premonstratensian house.[24] In the early thirteenth century the famous preacher Jacques de Vitry (d. 1240) voiced his approval of the decision to eliminate women from the Order, complaining of violations of claustration at women's communities.[25] In 1240 the Chapter General partially reversed itself, ruling that women might be received only at the French monastery of Bonœil (which had previously been a double community and had received some of the women from Prémontré after its division) with the consent of the abbot, prior, sub-prior, and the senior members, providing that their number remained below twenty. The decree emphasized that the women were to follow the Order's statutes strictly, and placed the new female community under the direction, not of a prioress as before, but of a *magistra*, who was to be obedient in all things to the abbot.[26] Although this ruling, confirmed by Pope Innocent IV in 1247 (*Licet sicut vestra*, 12 December 1247), was then taken as a general decree affecting all

[23] Herbert Grundmann, *Religious Movements in the Middle Ages*, trans. Steven Rowan (Notre Dame, IN, 1995), pp. 77–78.

[24] JL 168.

[25] "Postquam vero fenestras in ostia converterent, et primo fervore tepescente improvida securitas torporem et negligentiam inducere cepit." (After that, indeed, they converted the windows into doors, and the first wave of fervor having cooled, careless security began to allow in torpor and negligence.) AASS 1 June, p. 324. See also A. Erens, "Les soeurs dans l'Ordre de Prémontré," *Analecta Praemonstratensia* 5 (1929): 8, and Hugues Lamy, *L'Abbaye de Tongerloo depuis sa fondation jusqu'en 1263*. Recueil de travaux publiés par les membres des conférences d'histoire et de philologie 44 (Louvain and Paris, 1914), pp. 96–97.

[26] See Charles-Louis Hugo, ed., *Sacri et canonici Ordinis Praemonstratensis annales*, Sacrae antiquitatis monumenta historica, dogmatica, diplomatica, notis illustrata 1 (Nancy, 1725), vol. I, col. 120. For a discussion of the use of the term *magistra* in the context of Benedictine monasticism, see p. 27 and following above.

Premonstratensian houses, some double communities continued to operate into the modern period.[27]

While it would thus seem that Premonstratensian canonesses were condemned to a process of gradual extinction, documents and manuscripts from Schäftlarn tell a different story. There is no evidence that Schäftlarn's women were ever housed in the mandated separate building placed at a distance from the main monastic complex. The monastery's charters show that the monastery continued to accept new female members after the decree of 1198.[28] Charters dated after 1198 show that Schäftlarn accepted women into the community (*in consortium nostrum* and *in communi vita*), using language similar to that of charters drawn up prior to the 1197/1198 decree.[29] After the division, it was expected that the women would continue to be led by a prioress, and the authority of the male community was maintained by a praepositus (prior), who was responsible for monitoring the canonesses' activities and administering the sacraments to them.[30] At Schäftlarn, this prior was the same individual who headed the male community, but it is not clear whether this was commonly the case. In some houses, there may have been one prior for the men and another in charge of the women.[31]

In 1138, Pope Innocent II reminded the male houses of the Order to provide adequately for their female affiliates.[32] Three popes – Celestine II (1143), Eugenius II (1147), and Adrian IV (1155) – found it necessary to remind the canons of their obligations to the women, suggesting an ongoing problem with support in some

[27] One house, the Dutch monastery of Tusschenbeek, for example, maintained a female community until the eighteenth century. See Maur. De Meulemeester, "Les soeurs norbertines de Tusschenbeek," *Analecta Praemonstratensia* 4 (1928): 42–44.

[28] A charter from 1163–1170, which documents the entrance of a brother and sister, seems to refer to a single community: "Notum sit omnibus, quod Isengrim minister Frisingensis et filius eius Rodolf et filia eius Luitkart delegaverunt predium unum et molendinum in villa Basingen situm, cultum et incultum, super altare sancti Dionisii et sancte Iuliane Scheftlaren, ut idem Rodulfus et Luitkart ad communem vitam ibidem susciperentur, quod factum est." (Let it be known to all that Isengrim, a *ministerialis* of Freising, and his son Rodolf and daughter Luitkart, transferred one estate, cultivated and uncultivated, and a mill, situated in the village of Basingen to the altar of Saint Dionysius and Saint Juliana, Schäftlarn, so that the same Rodolph and Luitkart might be admitted there, which was done.) Weissthanner, *Traditionen*, pp. 131–132.

[29] For example, a charter of 1187/1188 records the entry of a woman to the monastery: "Quedam mulier nomine Berhta de Massenhusen delegavit curiam unam apud Naters sitam, ipse et due filie Bertha et Richkart . . . ad ecclesiam sancti Dionisii Sceftlarn, ut filia ipsius Berthe ibidem ad communem reciperetur vitam, quod factum est." (A certain woman named Bertha of Massenhusen, together with her two daughters, Bertha and Richkart, gave one estate situated in Natters to the Church of Saint Dionysius Schäftlarn so that her daughter Bertha might be there received into the common life, which was done.) Weissthanner, *Traditionen*, p. 272. Erens, "Les soeurs," p. 8. Lamy, *Tongerloo*, p. 93.

[30] See, Lamy, *Tongerloo*, p. 94; C. H. Lawrence, *Medieval Monasticism: Forms of Religious Life in Western Europe in the Middle Ages*, second edition (London and New York, 1989), p. 223.

[31] Lamy, *Tongerloo*, p. 93. [32] See JL 7878.

cases.[33] But while other Premonstratensian communities may have neglected their women, records from Schäftlarn show that ample donations were made to the monastery by and on behalf of women, and there is nothing in surviving documents to suggest that the canons failed to meet their financial obligations to their canonesses.

The first documented entrance of women to Schäftlarn was between 1152 and 1154. Gertrude, a noblewoman and the widow of Pilgrim of Pasing, made a donation to the monastery on the occasion of the entrance of her two daughters as lay sisters. This charter indicates that there was a female community at Schäftlarn already under the first or second Premonstratensian prior.[34] Charters dated from *c.* 1152 to 1200 record the entrance of eleven female religious: seven were daughters of the nobility, two from ministerial families, and the social status of the remaining two was not recorded. The monastery's earliest necrology, maintained between 1180 and *c.* 1200, lists the death date of twenty-three female community members. Fifteen of these women were identified as *conversae*, three as *monialis* or *monacha*, and the status of the remaining five was not recorded. A total of ninety-six women are listed, but only these twenty-three are identified as community members. The remaining seventy-three may have been patrons, *tributales*, or full members of the community whose status as such was omitted by the scribe.[35] These documents, though incomplete, reflect at least a modest population of women during the twelfth century. Charters from the same period record the profession of eight men: two noblemen, two *ministeriales*, and four of unrecorded social status. The twelfth-century necrology includes the names of thirty-six men: sixteen *conversi*, six monks (three of whom were listed as both monk and priest or deacon), six priests or deacons, and eight of unstated status.

Two types of religious women lived at Schäftlarn during this period: professed sisters (*sorores* or *moniales*) who took irrevocable monastic vows, and lay sisters (*conversae*) who did not. A donation made in 1152–1154 by Mathilde of Moorenweis, a *conversa* at the time of the gift, reflects the ability of lay sisters, unlike their professed counterparts, to retain private property.[36] Entries in Schäftlarn's

33 See JL 8450 (Celestine II), JL 9050 (Eugenius II), and JL 9972 (Adrian IV); Erens, "Les soeurs," p. 9.

34 Weissthanner, *Traditionen*, p. 85.

35 *Necrologium Scheftlariense*, ed. Franciscus Ludovicus Baumann. MGH, Necrologiae Germaniae 3, pp. 116–133.

36 "Notum sit omnibus Christi fidelibus, quod quedam nobilis femina nomine Mahthilt conversa et filius Odilschalch de Morenwis delegaverunt tria predia: unum in Eglingen situm, aliud in Laimberingen, tercium ad Forhah, super altare sancti Dyonysii pro salute anime sue." (Let it be known to all the faithful of Christ that a certain noblewoman named Mahthilt, *a conversa* and her son, Odilschalk of Moorenweis, transferred three estates – one in Egling, another in Laimering, and a third in Farchach – to the altar of Saint Dionysius for the salvation of her soul.) Weissthanner, *Traditionen*, p. 89.

necrology made between 1180 and *c.* 1200 name fourteen *conversae*, but only two *moniales*, suggesting that lay sisters were more numerous. Professed sisters were strictly cloistered.

This was the intention, at least, of the drafters of the Order's first statutes. These regulations, promulgated around 1134, extended the Rule of Saint Augustine and set the pattern for daily life throughout the Order. This legislation amplified the Rule of Saint Augustine and set down the pattern of daily life for the entire order. While the drafters' primary focus was on the male community, the last nine of the text's eighty chapters specifically concern the sisters. These final chapters address issues of governance, food, dress, claustration, and restrictions on private devotional reading, and represent the ideal pattern held up for the community.[37] One of the few things that the statutes have to say about women is that they should be kept under tight supervision. Outsiders were permitted to enter in groups of two or three, and then only to administer the Eucharist, to perform last rites, and to hear confession.[38] The door to the canonesses' enclosure was to be opened only with two or three mature sisters looking on, and conferences with visiting abbots or other religious persons took place through a window in the canonesses' enclosure in the presence of witnesses.[39] Travel to other religious communities was allowed only to groups of at least ten women.[40] A woman who left the cloister without permission for more than a day or a night was not to be received back into the

[37] Raphael van Waefelghem, "Les premiers statuts de l'Ordre de Prémontré," *Les Analectes de l'Ordre de Prémontré* 11 (1913): 3–74.

[38] "Ad eas nemo ingrediatur, nisi provisor earum si necessitas cogat, cum duobus vel tribus maturis fratribus vel sacerdos cum totidem ad communicandum vel inungendum infirmas, sive, mortua sorore, commendationem faciendam vel earum abbas cum totidem ad faciendum sermonem sive visitandas infirmas vel audiendas confessiones singularum, et tunc removeatur quidem longius ne possint audiri sed tamen in propatulo ut ab illis testibus vel pluribus sororibus plane videantur." (Let no one go in to them except if necessity compels it, their overseer with two or three mature brothers. A priest [may enter] with the same number [of witnesses] to serve communion, to anoint the sick, or for a dead sister to commend her soul. Their abbot [may enter] with the same number to deliver a sermon, to visit the sick, or to hear the confessions of each of them, and on that occasion he should be removed at a distance such that they are not able to be heard, but nevertheless in an open place so that they may be seen clearly by those witnesses or many sisters.) Van Waefelghem, "Les premiers statuts," p. 65.

[39] "Si quis autem alius abbas vel quelibet religiosa persona ad consolandum venerit, per licentiam magistri cum totidem fratribus loquatur uni vel pluribus sive omnibus ad fenestram." (If, however, any other abbot or any religious person shall come to encourage [them], with the permission of their overseer and with the same number of brothers he may speak to one, to many, or to all of them at the window.) Van Waefelghem, "Les premiers statuts," p. 65. "Ad aperiendum vero posticium, ad dandum aliquid accipiendum, non minus quam due vel tres ponantur de maturioribus etate et moribus." (When opening the door for giving or receiving something, no fewer than two or three sisters of mature age and habits ought to be sent.) Van Waefelghem, "Les premiers statuts," p. 66.

[40] "Si qua ecclesia tot habeat [sorores] ut in diversis locis poni necesse sit, non minus quam decem simul ponantur." (If any church shall have so many sisters that it is necessary to send them to different places, let no fewer than ten be sent together.) Van Waefelghem, "Les premiers statuts," p. 66.

community.[41] Because the statutes do not mention lay sisters, we do not know if they were subject to these same regulations.

Whatever her status, a Premonstratensian woman could expect a life dominated by manual labor, primarily in the service of the men. This was the niche that the leaders of the Order prescribed, and one that ensured that women remained marginal to the spiritual life of the community. Throughout the day, work took priority over worship. A sister who needed to speak with the prioress about a work-related matter was permitted to break the rule of silence. The prioress likewise was allowed to speak when needed to distribute work to the sisters.[42] The most common occupations, if the statutes of 1134 are an accurate reflection, were sewing, repairing, and washing clothing for the canons.[43] At Schäftlarn and other houses, however, women also copied books.

The dominance of work over more purely spiritual pursuits extended also to the celebration of the Divine Office. Women were not permitted to stop for communal worship when they were occupied during the day with manual labor. Instead, they attended matins only, and sang Psalms at the other appointed hours while working. When they did attend, women did not assist the men in singing the *opus Dei*, but gathered in silence behind a wall or grille to pray and listen. The canonesses did maintain some spiritual autonomy in the form of a daily chapter of faults, during which the prioress heard confession and assigned penance according to the guidelines established for the men.[44] This spiritual marginality is also reflected in the small number of female Premonstratensian saints from the twelfth century. At Schäftlarn, as in the wider movement, female piety was not frequently celebrated, a fact that complicates the picture of the twelfth century as a time of influence and prestige for religious women. While spiritual equality may have been, as Giles Constable shows, on the mind of Abelard and Rupert of Deutz,[45] Premonstratensian women seem to have confronted – even embraced – a different reality. The first Premonstratensian canoness, Blessed Ricwera (d. 1136), the widow of Count Raymond of Clastres is said to have received the veil from Saint Norbert himself. But Ricwera emerges from her *vita* as little more than an exemplum, a model of Premonstratensian female spirituality who lived in strict accordance with the statutes pertaining to canonesses. She reportedly observed the rule of silence, did

41 "Soror si fugiens extra claustrum per diem aut per noctem moratur, non recipitur." (If a sister, fleeing the cloister remains [without] through a day or a night, she should not be taken back.) Van Waefelghem, "Les premiers statuts," p. 66.

42 "Sorores continuum observabunt silentium, absque signis et nutibus, nisi in loco ad hoc determinato loquantur priorisse de necessitatibus suis, ubi et illa eis disponat de operibus suis." (The sisters shall observe continual silence, except for gestures and nods, unless they speak to the prioress about their needs in a pre-determined place and when she distributes work to them.) Van Waefelghem, "Les premiers statuts," p. 63.

43 Lamy, *Tongerloo*, p. 93.

44 Lamy, *Tongerloo*, p. 94.

45 See Giles Constable, *The Reformation of the Twelfth Century* (Cambridge, 1996), pp. 65–66.

not sing in the church, wore coarse woolen clothes, and never left the monastery enclosure.[46] Her biographer tells us that Ricwera's primary occupation was running a hospital for the poor, and paints her as a hybrid of the biblical sisters Mary and Martha – both contemplative and active, and certainly reflective of core Premonstratensian ideals.[47] Blessed Agnes of Braine (d. 1145 or 1149) is also said to have loved the poor, hiring workers to serve them and working herself when the workers themselves needed rest.[48] Their biographers, more interested in the ideal than the real, praised these women for their piety as it was expressed through acts of charity, service to the poor, and humility – qualities that were encouraged and admired in Premonstratensian canonesses. Neither education and learning, nor even devotional reading, were held up as components of female piety or as evidence of sanctity.

How closely did men and women at Schäftlarn follow the Order's statutes during the twelfth century? Between 1140 and 1153, the monastery made a copy – in fact, the *earliest* surviving copy – of these regulations for their library, so it seems likely that at least some members of the community read them.[49] Perhaps in the first rush of enthusiasm following the conversion Schäftlarn embraced the plan vigorously, but no surviving documents reflect actual practice in the women's enclosure.

Schäftlarn's female community, and others like it, persisted because they satisfied a complex set of spiritual and social needs within the society that supported them. Such institutions provided noble and ministerial families with a suitable place for their daughters, and for lay sisters, admission may not have required the permanent alienation of property. The continued patronage of the laity may have depended, in part, on the maintenance of a community for these women. The admission of women provided needed material resources to the community, and at double monasteries, the canonesses could render further service to the male community through manual labor. Spiritual impulses were also at work: the new forms of religious life that emerged during the twelfth century held various attractions for women, and the pressure to accommodate them was significant.[50]

46 AASS 11 October, 51; Agnes B. C. Dunbar, *A Dictionary of Saintly Women*, 2 vols. (London, 1905), vol. II, p. 187.

47 On medieval interpretations of the biblical sisters Mary and Martha, see Giles Constable, *Three Studies in Medieval Religious and Social Thought* (Cambridge, 1995), pp. 3–141.

48 Jean Le Paige, *Bibliotheca Praemonstratensis ordinis* (Paris, 1633), p. 340 and p. 480; Dunbar, *Saintly Women*, vol. I, p. 31.

49 Van Waefelghem, "Les premiers statuts," pp. 3–74. The codicological features of this manuscript are summarized below in Appendix A, Table A3.

50 The Cistercian order began to permit the establishment of female communities around the end of the twelfth century. See Herbert Grundmann, *Religious Movements*, pp. 91–92. See also Lawrence, *Medieval Monasticism*, pp. 227–230.

## EDUCATION AT SCHÄFTLARN

Because women lacked pastoral duties, and did not, prior to the separation of the double monasteries, participate in the celebration of the *opus Dei*, there was no perceived need for female education. The earliest statutes are silent about schools for women, and knowledge of reading and writing was not required for the performance of the manual tasks to which the women were normally assigned. In fact, devotional reading beyond a few Psalms and prayers was not generally permitted. Female reading, in general, was merely tolerated, with special concessions sometimes made to accommodate those who were better educated. Reading was intentionally restricted in the women's enclosure, with the range of texts available to women strictly limited:

> [A sister] may have a Psalter or individual Psalms, or the prayers or vigils of blessed Mary according to the provision of the abbot, but then she may learn nothing else. If any one shall have greater learning from outside the community, she shall be able to examine some other book on feast days with the permission of the abbot.[51]

The books normally allowed would enable the women to do little more than read, and perhaps memorize the Psalms, which only the canons were permitted to sing in the church. Even the opportunities for reading available to women who had received some education before entering the monastery were limited and subject to the approval of the abbot. The drafters of the statutes assumed that a woman with a more advanced education would have received it outside the monastery (perhaps as a lay person in a Benedictine school for externs, in which such training was not uncommon), a supposition that indicates that internal schools were not the norm in houses of Premonstratensian canonesses. Beyond their ability to copy books, to which we shall turn below, nothing is known of the intellectual abilities or interests of Schäftlarn's women. No evidence survives of an internal school for canonesses, or of individuals being sent there to be educated. It thus seems likely that although some of Schäftlarn's canonesses were able to read, this was not a community in which women sought spiritual growth through devotional reading and intellectual pursuits. This provides a sharp contrast with Admont, where monastic *lectio* was a fundamental expression of female piety. For Admont's nuns, religious life without devotional reading would have been unthinkable, while at Schäftlarn, women's devotional reading was to be carefully restricted.

The educational expectations for canons that emerge from the statutes are, however, quite different. Each house was to establish a school in which male

[51] "Psalteria vel psalmos aliquot vel orationes beate Marie vel vigilias eas habere licebit pro dispensatione abbatis, sed ibi nihil aliud addiscere. Si aliqua exterius amplius didicerit, festivis diebus poterit licentia abbatis in aliquem alium librum inspicere." Van Waefleghem, "Les premiers statuts," p. 66.

members could prepare for ordination and a life of pastoral activity.[52] The men pursued a practical course of study geared toward the pastoral ministry rather than one intended to foster literary productivity.[53] The mandated school structure included the assignment of a *magister* to teach the novices and a schedule for reading and instruction.[54] The brothers were to sit together for a period of silent reading, from which only individuals with pressing duties were excused.[55] The increase in book production that occurred during the long tenure of Prior Henry probably reflects the canons' growing interest in reading. A fifteenth-century chronicler remembered Henry as patron of books, and the number and diversity of books copied in the house scriptorium during his priorate support this image of him as a library-builder [56] Intellectual activity at the house appears to have been limited to reading and copying existing texts, as there is no surviving evidence to suggest that the canons produced any new literary works. This was true, also, of the order as a whole, which lagged far behind the Benedictines in terms of literary productivity.[57]

It was probably at the instigation of the more literate male community and for their use that a number of written records were maintained at Schäftlarn during the twelfth century. Charters and records of donations made by patrons were preserved from the time of the community's founding in the eighth century, but these and current documents were systematically recorded in a *Liber traditionum* between the twelfth century and the fourteenth century, and the originals were not preserved.[58] The so-called *Annales Scheftlarienses maiores*, begun in 1162 and continued into the thirteenth century, record events of both local and universal importance and provide an important source of the early history of nearby Munich.[59] The community began its necrology in c. 1180, and this was maintained into the thirteenth century.

## SCHÄFTLARN'S FEMALE SCRIBES

Women were a significant component of the scribal workforce responsible for producing these books and documents. Of the house's thirteen named scribes,

52 Lamy, *Tongerloo*, p. 288.

53 Lamy described the canons' schools as "véritables séminaires." See Lamy, *Tongerloo*, p. 289.

54 Van Waefelghem, "Les premiers statuts," p. 22.

55 Van Waefelghem, "Les premiers statuts," p. 40.

56 "Item post hec a.D. 1164. dominus Hainricus, vir multe probitatis ac religionis, in prelatum eligitur, et in 36. anno ad Dominum transmigravit 5. Non. Iulii. Hic huic ecclesie multa bona fecit in prediis augmentandis, libris scribendis et bonis omnibus ampliandis." (Likewise after these things, in 1164 AD, Lord Henry, a man of great probity and religion, was chosen for the prelature, and in the thirty-sixth year passed on to the Lord on 5 July. He did many good things for this church by augmenting its estates, copying books, and increasing all good things.) *Catalogus praepositorum Scheftlariensium*, ed. Philipp Jaffé, MGH, Scriptores 17, p. 348.

57 Lamy, *Tongerloo*, p. 289.

58 Weissthanner, *Traditionen.*

59 *Annales Scheftlarienses maiores*, ed. Philipp Jaffé, MGH, Scriptores 17, pp. 334–343.

three were female. Two female copyists are identified in colophons and a third, Adelheid, was identified in the house necrology.[60] Given the restrictions placed on women's reading, the absence of ex-libris annotations indicating that manuscripts belonged to the canonesses, lending lists, or other records of book use by the women, it seems likely that they copied books for the men's community. Since we find no school, and evidence neither of female intellectual activity, nor even of significant devotional reading at the monastery, it is difficult to imagine that canonesses were among the library's regular users. The impact of the house's large book collection on the devotional and intellectual life of the monastery's women was probably small, in spite of their important role in its production.

How, then, did these women come to copy manuscripts? During a period of active book production, new members of both sexes who were competent copyists would have been welcomed into the community and its scriptorium. Recruits with previous scribal training were probably assigned to the scriptorium for their primary manual work. Although none of the texts copied by Schäftlarn's female scribes was, according to the statutes, available for their reading, this was apparently not an impediment to participation in book production. The formula used in Irmingart's two surviving colophons (*obtentu domni Heinrici prepositi*) – a formula also used by the male scribe Altmanus – indicates that the prior's permission was required, at least for some copyists copying some texts. The drive to produce more books for the library probably cleared the way for the female copyists' activity, the products of which may not have been intended for their use, but for the use of the canons. Reading and copying are two distinct activities, and it is possible that appropriately trained women were assigned to copy books without encouragement to explore the content of the materials they reproduced. An intellectual environment was not an essential prerequisite for scribal activity, nor did a scribe need to understand all that he or she wrote.

The manuscripts that the women copied do not, however, show evidence of a low level of Latinity. The overwhelming majority of corrections that Adalbertus made to Sophia's work in Clm 17052 and Clm 17053 reflect scribal omissions of the type that frequently occur when identical words or combinations of words, or words with similar beginning or ending sounds, appear in the text, errors known as *saute du même à même*, or haplography errors. In Clm 17052 (f. 214r), for example, Sophia omitted the words *iam non iniquus* from a sentence that Adalbertus amended to read: "ego iniquus [iam non iniquus] non anime ablato . . ." Sophia's confusion here seems to stem from the repetition of the word *iniquus*, particularly given the proximity of both iterations to the word *non*, rather than from poor Latin skills. Another error of omission on f. 5r shows Sophia leaving out the words *nocte dormiunt* from a sentence that Adalbertus corrected to read: "Qui

60 See p. 119 and following below.

autem dormiunt [nocte dormiunt]." Her confusion here seems to result from the repetition of the *dormiunt* at the end of the sentence. In Clm 17116, Irmingart's principal error was consistently failing to leave enough space for Adalbertus to add the titles, which resulted in their cramping and awkward spilling over into the margins. There are fewer omissions corrected in Irmingart's work, but where they do occur, they are of the same type seen in Sophia's manuscripts. On f. 65r of Clm 17116, for example, *nubis . . . columpna* was omitted from a line that was corrected to read: "ut columpna [nubis. nunc igne sui spiritus accendens ut vere columpna]" – the repetition of the *ut* and *columpna* seems to have been the source of her confusion. It is also possible that these scribal omissions were already present in the exemplar, and that the corrector picked them up while comparing them to a different copy of the text. In any event, the errors that Sophia and Irmingart made are not of the type or magnitude that suggest scribal incompetence or illiteracy.

Schäftlarn was not unique among Premonstratensian houses in putting women to work in the scriptorium. Emo (1204–1237), the first abbot of the double monastery of Wittewerun, noted that some of the community's women were educated and trained as copyists, and claimed that the natural diligence of women made them particularly able scribes.[61] During periods of growth, which many Premonstratensian houses experienced during the late twelfth and early thirteenth centuries, a high demand for liturgical books and texts for devotion and study may have encouraged the appropriation of the labor of all who could contribute. The ability of some women to participate in this and other activities of central importance to the community may account, in part, for their continued admission in spite of persistent opposition from the order's hierarchy.

Still other barriers could fall when a community needed to produce books. Several surviving manuscripts from Schäftlarn contain evidence of collaboration between male and female scribes, indicating that scribes of both sexes worked together, in one case possibly even side by side, to speed the process of copying.[62] The close cooperation between male and female scribes may reflect a somewhat relaxed policy at Schäftlarn regarding the enclosure of lay sisters when scribal work was concerned – a strong contrast with the situation at both Wessobrunn and

[61] "non solum sic in clericis, quos ad scribendum fervide incitabat, et per se ipsum instruebat, verum etiam sedulitatem in femineo sexu considerans, sorores ad hoc habiles sollicite in scribendo informabat." (Thus he educated in writing, not only the clerics, whom he had himself instructed, but also the sisters who were well-suited to this work in view of the assiduity of the female sex.) *Kronijken van Emo en Menko*. Werken Vitgegeven door het Historisch Genootschap, NS4 (Utrecht, 1866), p. 167.

[62] Evidence for this collaboration is presented below in the discussion of the work of Sophia, beginning on p. 120.

Admont, where there was a documented preoccupation with the segregation of the sexes.

Two of Schäftlarn's named female scribes worked under the direction of the head of the men's scriptorium. No standard script was taught or used, and this resulted in the production of some manuscripts with a rather careless appearance. Indeed, the wide variation in scribal hands in evidence in the products of Schäftlarn's scriptorium suggests that these individuals were trained in diverse schools. Thus, again in contrast to Admont, no single book hand can be identified as typical of this workshop.[63]

Schäftlarn's self-identified scribes – female and male – may have followed the example of their master Adalbertus, who himself attached his name to five surviving manuscripts.[64] Where Adalbertus received his own scribal training is unknown, but it may have been a center whose scribes also tended to identify themselves. These scribes also may have seen and imitated scribal colophons in the manuscripts that they borrowed, perhaps from Benediktbeuern (from which one signed manuscript is extant), but particularly from Herrenchiemsee (from which a single signed manuscript also has survived). Herrenchiemsee was a house of regular Augustinian canons, an order known for its strong tradition of commemorating donors and scribes in liturgy and in written record. It may be that some Premonstratensians followed this tradition – particularly those, like Schäftlarn, with close connections to Augustinians.[65]

## *Adelheid*

We know nothing of the career of the *conversa* Adelheid, identified as a scribe in an entry in the necrology on 1 January.[66] Adelheid's name has not been connected with any extant manuscript, and since the year of her death was not recorded, we do not know when she lived. The inclusion of her name in the earliest section of the necrology, however, suggests that she died either in the late twelfth or early thirteenth century. Perhaps examples of her work survive among Schäftlarn's

63 See, for example, the diverse hands at work in Clm 17054, illustrated in Table 4.3 on p. 124.

64 Clm 17075 and 17076 (Gregory the Great, *Moralia in Job*, Books 6–10 and 11–16), Clm 17041 (a theological collection), Clm 17161 (Gratian's *Decretum*), and Clm 17072 (Pseudo-Dionysius the Areopagite and Hugh of St. Victor).

65 Note, for example, the inscriptions in twelfth-century books from Cirencester. See Andrew G. Watson, *Catalogue of Dated and Datable Manuscripts c. 435–1600 in Oxford Libraries* (Oxford, 1984), and the practice of commemoration recorded in the Barnwell Customal (Teresa Webber and Andrew G. Watson, eds., *The Libraries of the Augustinian Canons*, Corpus of British Medieval Library Catalogues 6 (London, 1998), pp. xxv, 26–29.

66 *Necrologium Scheftlariense*, p. 116. 1 January. "Adelhait cv. nra. scriba."

extant manuscripts, but since no subscription naming her exists, it is not possible to identify them.

## *Sophia*

A second female scribe, Sophia, was probably active under Prior Eberhard or Arnold. She may have been active in the scriptorium as early as the 1160s, and it is possible that she was still producing books as late as 1180. Sophia worked closely with the male scribe Adalbertus, who was the master of the workshop under Prior Henry, and possibly earlier. Two lay sisters named Sophia are listed in the necrology, one on 6 January and the other on 7 April, but it is unclear which, if either, was the scribe.[67]

Sophia is identified as a scribe in two contemporary, probably autograph subscriptions, and her hand can be identified in three manuscripts: Clm 17052, Clm 17053, and Clm 17054. Her hand, while not highly consistent, has a clearly recognizable and fluent duct. She used several distinctive letter and abbreviation forms. The **l** and the stems of the **b** and **d** have pronounced serifs that begin well to the left of the letter. The descender of the **q** terminates with distinctive flat serif. This feature is more pronounced (the serif is longer) in Clm 17054. When **c** and **t** appear together, the shaft of the **t** usually curves back down towards the **c** [Figure 21, lines 7, 8, and 11]. The lower lobe of the **g** is usually open, and the shape of the lower lobe ranges from flat and oblong to round. The ampersand consists of an a-shaped lobe, a closed top loop attached to the right top of the lobe, and a short arm that terminates with a small ball. Sophia's abbreviation for *-orum* varies. She seems to have experimented with several forms, the most common of which consists of a closed loop attached to the upper right side of the **o** and two straight strokes, one extending from the **o** down to the right and the other crossing this stroke [Figure 22, line 10]. Her abbreviation for the *-us* ending of the dative and ablative plurals is a **b** followed by a semicolon [Figure 21, lines 4, 5, 6, 12 and 14; Figure 22, line 3]. The **z** is elongated, sometimes equal in height to, or higher than, the tops of the **d**, **b**, **l**, etc. This letter varies in shape: in some places it is shaped like an elongated lower case **h**, and in others like a large lower case **z**.

### Clm 17052 and 17053

Manuscripts Clm 17052 and 17053 are two volumes of what was originally a three-volume set of Augustine's *Enarrationes in Psalmos*. The final volume, which would have contained the commentaries on Psalms 101 through 150, is lost. The 1160–1162 booklist includes a copy of "Augustine's Exposition on the Psalter in Three

[67] *Necrologium Scheftlariense*, p. 116 and p. 122.

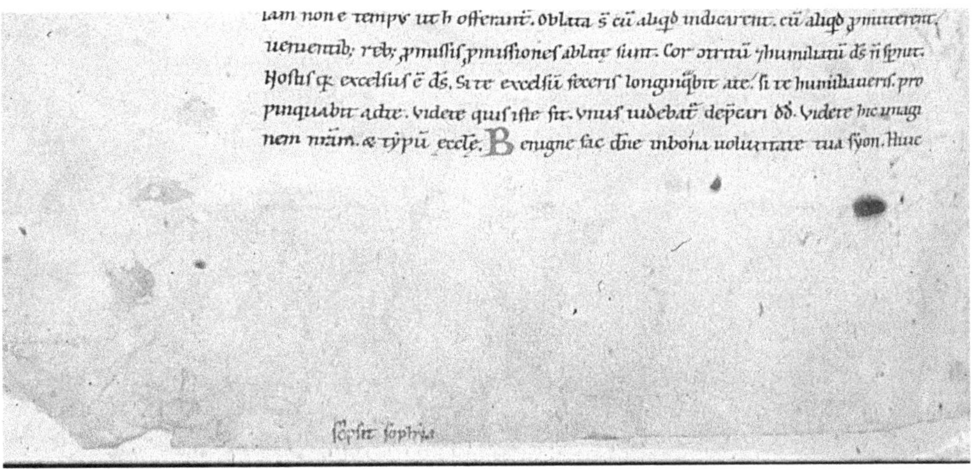

Figure C The signature of the nun Sophya

Fifty-Psalm Parts," probably identical with the two extant Sophia manuscripts.[68] If so, then they must have been completed prior to 1162.[69] Both manuscripts contain a subscription naming Sophia as scribe: Clm 17052 (f. 214v – "scripsit Sophya"; Figure C) and Clm 17053 (f. 108v – "Sophia scripsit"). In each case, the scribe recorded her name close to the bottom edge of the parchment, possibly as a note to the head of the scriptorium, to be trimmed off, perhaps, in the process of binding the volume. On folio 269v of Clm 17053, the name Sophya was cut into the parchment, apparently with a knife or other sharp object. It is impossible to date this scratching or to attribute it to the scribe herself, since the formation of the letters differs from that made by pen and ink.

Clm 17052 and 17053 both contain the work of two copyists, Sophia and Adalbertus, who alternated throughout the text. Adalbertus wrote the titles, portions of the text, and made corrections, but Sophia did the bulk of the copying. Tables 4.1 and 4.2 detail the hand changes in the two volumes, and illustrate the extent to which the two hands worked together, often changing in the middle of a folio, in the middle of a line, or in places even in mid-sentence. How was such close collaboration between a male and female scribe possible? The root of an answer to this question may lie in Sophia's probable status as a lay sister. We have no information about the practice of claustration for *conversae* within the order; the 1134 statutes specified that *sorores* were to be cloistered, but this document makes

[68] MBKg, p. 726; Klemm, *Die romanischen Handschriften* II/1, pp. 97–98.

[69] MBKg, p. 726; Elisabeth Klemm dates the two manuscripts to 1165–1170. This hypothesis requires either the redating of the booklist to a time after 1165, or the rejection of the identification of the three-volume psalm commentary with Clm 17052 and 17053. See Klemm, *Die romanischen Handschriften* I/1, p. 97.

Table 4.1 *Munich, Bayerische Staatsbibliothek Clm 17052*

| Location in manuscript | Scribe | Comments |
|---|---|---|
| ff. 1r–1v (to line 7)<br>Quire 1 | Adalbertus | |
| ff. 1v–41r (to line 10)<br>Quires 1–6 | Sophia | Corrections and titles by scribe 1 (Adalbertus)<br>Example: f. 214v |
| ff. 41r–44v (to line 20)<br>Quire 6 | Adalbertus | |
| ff. 44v–60r (to line 26)<br>Quires 6–8 | Sophia | Corrections and titles by scribe 1 |
| ff. 60r–94r (to line 21)<br>Quires 8–12 | Adalbertus | |
| ff. 94r–129v<br>Quires 12–17 | Sophia | Corrections and titles by scribe 1 |
| ff. 130r–146r (to line 21)<br>Quires 17–19 | Adalbertus | |
| ff. 146r–214v<br>Quires 19–27 | Sophia | Corrections and titles by scribe 1<br>Contemporary subscription (214v), probably written by Sophia = *Scripsit Sophya* |

no specific mention of lay sisters and no documents of practice have survived that mention the status of lay sisters in this regard. Although the claustration of these women may have been the ideal, it is possible that they were not subject to the standards for professed sisters, and under certain circumstances, especially when matters of work were concerned, limited interaction between the sexes may have been permitted. Perhaps lay sisters were allowed access to a shared scriptorium, or alternatively, Adalbertus may have been given permission to enter the residence of the *conversae* to oversee book production there. A third, less likely possibility is that there was no direct interaction between Sophia and Adalbertus, in which case the manuscript would have passed between two scriptoria seven times for Clm 17052, and six times for Clm 17053 (see Tables 4.1 and 4.2).

## Clm 17054

Sophia was probably also the main scribe of Clm 17054, a copy of Augustine's commentary on the Gospel of John. Although this manuscript contains no scribal subscription, there are strong similarities between the main hand of this and Clm 17052 and 17053. This volume was mistakenly identified by Ruf as the third volume of the set of Augustine's *Enarrationes on the Psalms* (Clm 17052 and 17053), an error

Table 4.2 *Munich, Bayerische Staatsbibliothek Clm 17053*

| Location in manuscript | Scribe | Comments |
|---|---|---|
| ff. 1r–28v<br>Quires 1–4 | Sophia | Corrections and titles by scribe 1 (Adalbertus) |
| ff. 29r–35r (to line 11)<br>Quires 4–5 | Adalbertus | Hand change in middle of line 11 |
| ff. 35r–115r<br>Quires 5–15 | Sophia | Corrections and titles by scribe 1<br>Contemporary subscription (f. 108v), probably written by Sophia = *Sophia scripsit.* |
| ff. 115v–139r<br>Quires 15–18 | Adalbertus | |
| ff. 139v–150r (to line 31)<br>Quires 18–19 | Sophia | Corrections and titles by scribe 1 |
| ff. 150r–176v<br>Quires 19–22 | Adalbertus | |
| ff. 177r–277r<br>Quires 22–35 | Sophia | Corrections and titles by scribe 1<br>"*SOPHYA*" scratched into parchment on f. 269v |

that led him to date the manuscript to the time of either Prior Eberhard or Arnold. Klemm rejected this dating on the basis of the style of its decorative initials, and placed it later than the two-volume *Enarrationes.*

Three hands can be seen at work in Clm 17054. As in Clm 17052 and 17053, Adalbertus executed the beginning of the text, titles, and made corrections. Because his hand does not reappear in the body of the text, it seems that Adalbertus did not participate in a joint copying effort such as that seen in the *Enarrationes* manuscripts, but acted as director for the work. He copied the prologue to the commentary on folio 1r, and a second male scribe, Marchwardus, copied the next section of the text, ending his work on the last folio of the first quire (f. 8v). Sophia's hand appears at the beginning of the second quire, and continues through the end of the text. At no point did the two male scribes and Sophia collaborate within a quire, with the exception of the titles and corrections added after the main text was copied. This pattern of collaboration differs from that seen in Clm 17052 and 17053, volumes characterized by frequent alternation between Sophia and Adalbertus. Clm 17052 and 17053 may have been written earlier, when Sophia was less experienced. As she gained more experience, she may have required less supervision and she may have been able to work faster, which could have led to her being given a job to complete herself. It is also possible that claustration was tightened after the

Table 4.3 *Munich, Bayerische Staatsbibliothek Clm 17054*

| Location in manuscript | Scribe | Comments |
|---|---|---|
| f. 1r | Adalbertus | |
| Quire 1<br>ff. 1v–8v | Marchwardus | |
| Quire 1<br>ff. 9r–200v<br>Quires 2–25 | Sophia | f. 31v, col.1 contains an 11-line correction made by Marchwardus,<br>Other corrections and titles by Adalbertus |

Table 4.4 *Munich, Bayerische Staatsbibliothek Clm 17087*

| Location in manuscript | Scribe | Comments |
|---|---|---|
| f. 1r<br>Column 1<br>Quire 1 | Adalbertus | |
| ff. 1r (col. 2)–223v<br>Quires 1–28 | Irmingart | Example: ff. 4r and 185r<br>Corrections and titles by Adalbertus |

completion of the earlier volumes – the manuscripts were probably copied under different priors – preventing the type of collaboration between men and women that was possible earlier. See Table 4.3.

### *Irmingart*

Irmingart, a professed sister at Schäftlarn, is identified as a scribe at Schäftlarn both in the necrology and in two colophons, and as many as four examples of her work are extant. We know of her status as a professed sister both from the wording of her two surviving colophons and from the necrology. She identified herself as one of the scribes of Clm 17087, a copy of homilies on the epistles and Gospels, in a cruciform colophon on folio 223v (see Figure A, p. 3). The scribe Adalbertus copied the first column of text, perhaps to establish a pattern for Irmingart to follow after the parchment was passed into the enclosure for her to complete. He also made corrections and wrote the titles, suggesting that he directed the production of the volume (see Table 4.4). Irmingart was the sole scribe of Clm 17116, a copy of Rupert of Deutz's *De divinis officiis*, which contains a colophon written by a second hand on folio 129v. The wording of both colophons, "This book, written by sister Irmingart with the permission of Prior Henry, belongs to Saint Dionysius, Schäftlarn," suggests that the record of her name might have acted as a form of authorization for her copying.[70] Because she identified Prior Henry as her superior, we know that she was active in the scriptorium between 1164 and 1200. Irmingart apparently worked alone; there is no evidence that she participated in team copying. She may have been prevented from close collaboration by the requirements of claustration, since she was a professed sister and subject to the strict regulations outlined in the statutes. It is possible that she worked under Adalbertus' direction without any face to face contact with him, as suggested by scribal patterns in Clm 17087.

Examples of Irmingart's work are found in two manuscripts: Clm 17087 (f. 1r, cols. 2 – 223v) and Clm 17116 (entire). Like Sophia, Irmingart was not entirely consistent in the formation of some characters. Her abbreviation for *-orum* is a curved, sometimes almost z-shaped stroke extending down from the top right of the **o** with a cross stroke made diagonally. The curved stroke varies from rounded to angular [Figure 24, line 4]. Her abbreviation for the *-us* ending of the dative and ablative plurals is usually the letter **b** followed by a semicolon [Figure 23, line 13; Figure 24, lines 8 and 15], although she also occasionally uses a **b** with a curved stroke extending from the middle of the right side of the stem [Figure 23, line 11; Figure 24, lines 8 and 15]. The lower lobe of the **g** is generally, but not always, closed and rectangular. The abbreviation for *pro-* is a **p** with an s-shaped stroke attached to the left side of the descender. In places in Clm 17116, the stroke forms a loop. The **c** and **t** are consistently joined from the top of the **c** and the left side of the headstroke of the **t** [Figure 23, line 1; Figure 24, line 3]. The ampersand consists of an a-shaped lobe, a closed top loop attached to the right top of the lobe, and a long, curved arm that terminates with a small ball, although she frequently used the tironian note for *et* in place of an ampersand. When two **p**s appear together (as in the abbreviation for *propter*), the letters are conjoined [Figure 24, line 1]. The **z** resembles an **h** and has a short, sometimes z-shaped, stroke extending from the top left of the ascender [Figure 23, line 7].

There is no codicological evidence to suggest the operation of two scriptoria at Schäftlarn. On the contrary, an analysis of manuscripts signed by male scribes, and their comparison with volumes with female contributions reveals a high degree of similarity between the two groups in terms of codicological features, quality of parchment, and decoration – similarities that imply the existence of a single source for parchment, assembly, and illumination. This hypothesis is consistent with

70 "Iste liber pertinet ad sanctum Dyonisium Sceftlaren quem scripsit soror Irmingart obtentu Domni Hainrici prepositi." Clm 17087; "Iste liber pertinet ad sanctum dyonisium sceftlaren quem scripsit soror Irmengart obtentu domni Hainrici prepositi." Clm 17116.

and supported by the evidence of the extensive collaboration between men and women.

The Summary of Codicological Features on page 141 shows that all but two of the manuscripts examined followed Gregory's Rule. Only in Clm 17036 and 17037 (copied by Adalbertus), and Clm 17151 (copied by Irmingart) was this rule occasionally not observed. Ruling pattern B (see p. 147) was used in all of the manuscripts copied by or with the help of Sophia and Irmingart (except Clm 17052 and 17053, which follow pattern A), as well as those copied by Adalbertus alone, and it should be noted that patterns A, B, and C consist of double bounding lines at the top and side margins – they differ only in the addition of a center column guide (B) or guide (C). Similarly, the quires in the manuscripts with known female contributions are marked on the bottom center of the last folio with a roman numeral flanked by a pair of dots, a technique seen also in Clm 17036, the first of a three-volume Bible copied by Adalbertus. The remaining two volumes of this set, also copied by Adalbertus, contain no quire marks, although it is possible that similar marks were used and later were trimmed off during binding. Another of Adalbertus' manuscripts, Clm 17161, contains quire marks of this same style, but they were placed at the bottom center of the first folio of each quire.

There is no evidence that the women were given materials of inferior quality with which to work (which is not surprising, as all of the books were intended for the monks' own library). The quality of the parchment used in these manuscripts, rather, is related to the size of the page, not the sex of the scribe. The smallest manuscripts tend to contain the highest quality parchment. The parchment quality also seems unrelated to the richness of a book's illuminations. For example, 39 percent of the folios in Clm 17050 and 59 percent of those in Clm 17053, neither of which contain elaborate decoration, contain no significant flaws, but only 27 percent of the folios used in Clm 17161, a beautifully and copiously illustrated volume, are unflawed.

* * *

Schäftlarn's female scribes copied books, not for their own use, but for the use of the men of their community. In view of this important difference between Schäftlarn and Admont, where women participated fully in Benedictine devotional observance, enjoyed a rich intellectual life, and used the books they copied, we must conclude that female involvement in the scriptorium does not necessarily reflect an interest in, or the presence of, intellectual opportunities for women.

The community's twelfth-century manuscripts supplement the charters and necrologies that enable us to imagine Schäftlarn's history. These books speak – unselfconsciously – of the creation of a scribal community that defied limits established by the leaders of the Premonstratensian Order. While certainly aware of the various restrictions placed on women and their activities, the canons at Schäftlarn appear to have been ready to bend the rules in order to take advantage of the labor the women could provide. The case of Schäftlarn demonstrates that there were diverse institutional arrangements for segregating men and women and varying degrees of tolerance for contact between the sexes – regardless of what official regulations dictated. When necessity demanded, barriers could fall – both the physical barriers of the cloister and the intellectual barriers that discouraged female literacy. While the manuscripts clearly cannot reveal who read them, they do show women taking an active role, though one still defined and controlled by the men and certainly marginal, in one of the central activities of the wider community: the creation of a library for training priests.

Far from seeking to jettison its female population, the men recognized that there was within the female community a source of labor for book production. This may, in fact, be one explanation for the persistence of Schäftlarn as a double monastery: women were integral members of the community, contributing significantly to its central mission. Though we tend to undervalue domestic labor, we should also not discount the contributions made by the women at Schäftlarn and elsewhere, who cooked, wove, sewed, and washed for the men. We miss an important part of the story of the development of the Premonstratensian Order when we assume too readily that women and unwanted burden were synonymous.

Even as Chapters General and church leaders concerned themselves with establishing broad rules and regulations, individual houses were faced with the day-to-day business of creating and maintaining communities that served the needs both of converts and of the local population. The former established the ideal, and the latter wrestled with squaring that ideal with the exigencies of the real. Schäftlarn's surviving books show us men and women plotting their own course between ideal and reality as they worked together to create and maintain a living religious community during the second half of the twelfth century.

# 5

# *Conclusion*

By the time Diemut of Wessobrunn began copying manuscripts in the first years of the twelfth century, religious women in Germany had participated in book production for over four hundred years. This tradition of female involvement in German scriptoria had begun in the eighth century with the arrival of women from the monasteries of Anglo-Saxon England, who introduced to their new communities a tradition of education in the liberal arts and an interest in biblical study. The emphasis that these new religious houses placed on reading, and the demand for liturgical texts generated by the missionaries with whom they were affiliated, created a need for books, and women were among the earliest frontier scribes. As producers of books, their way had been prepared by earlier generations of religious women on the Continent and in England, and after them, Ottonian and early Salian monasteries for women continued the tradition. Several tenth- and early-eleventh-century female communities commissioned deluxe, illuminated manuscripts, and there were active scriptoria at Essen, Gandersheim, and Niedermünster in Regensburg.

As monastic reform movements and new religious orders spread across Bavaria in the eleventh and twelfth centuries, women continued to play a role in book production. The reforms of both Gorze and Hirsau tended to encourage copying, as both called for a return to a strict adherence to the Benedictine Rule and renewed attention to the study of the Bible. The latter required not only biblical texts, but also patristic and contemporary commentaries to serve as intellectual and spiritual guides. At Wessobrunn, under the successive influence of both of these movements, women and men worked to expand the library, which had been limited to biblical and liturgical texts during the eleventh century and thus was inadequate for biblical study. The advent of the Hirsau reform at Admont brought similarly increased intellectual activity, but here it encompassed both monastic *lectio divina* and written biblical exegesis, which was the motive behind the production of books. At Schäftlarn, as at most contemporary Premonstratensian communities, men were trained for the priesthood, and both men and women worked to meet the demand for books geared toward both pastoral life and biblical study. All three houses thus had an urgent need to produce books, and women with book-related skills were naturally put to the task.

It is important to consider that the female scribes of Wessobrunn, Admont, and Schäftlarn were but a few of the many women who contributed to the resurgence of book production that both grew out of and fueled monastic reform in south Germany during the twelfth century. Religious women also worked as scribes in at least two other contemporary Bavarian monasteries: Niedermünster, where Idung of Prüfening sent his *Dialogue between Two Monks* with a request that the sisters make a legible and carefully corrected copy,[1] and its daughter house Mallersdorf, where the Irish nun Leukardis copied a number of books – all of which are now lost.[2] Beyond Bavaria, the necrology of Zwiefalten records the death of Mahtilt of Nifen, a *conversa* who copied many books at the monastery.[3] Guda, a woman at an unidentified monastery in the middle Rhine region, copied and illuminated a collection of homilies. Her book contains both a colophon in her own hand ("Guda, a sinful woman, copied and painted this book"), and a self-portrait.[4] Nuns at Lamspringe in Lower Saxony received materials and instructions for making books from the monks of Reinhardsbrunn.[5] In 1154, Guta, a nun-scribe of Schwarzenthann (in upper Alsace), and Sintram, a monk-illuminator of neighboring Marbach, together completed a one-volume calendar, necrology, and martyrology.[6] And Hildegard of Bingen and Herrad of Hohenbourg were known for, among other things, overseeing the production of extraordinary manuscripts within their communities. When considered individually, these examples can be dismissed as anomalous or insignificant. Taken together, however, they reveal a pattern of female involvement

[1] See R. B. C. Huygens, *Le moine Idung et ses deux ouvrages: "Argumentum super quatuor questionibus," et "Dialogus duorum monachorum,"* Studi Medievali 13 (Spoleto, 1972), pp. 32 and 91; Jeremiah F. O'Sullivan, Joseph Lehey, and Grace Perrigo, trans., *Cistercians and Cluniacs: The Case for Cîteaux. A Dialogue between Two Monks and an Argument on Four Questions by Idung of Prüfening*, Cistercian Fathers Series 33 (Kalamazoo, MI, 1977), pp. 21–23; Wilhelm Wattenbach, *Schriftwesen im Mittelalter*, third edition (Leipzig, 1896), pp. 444–446.

[2] *Monumenta Mallerstorfensia*, Monumenta Boica 15 (Munich, 1786), p. 249. "quas inter eminebat Leukardis, de gente, ut ajunt, Scotorum, quatuor linguarum, patriae suae, graecae, latinae, & theotiseae gnara, quae plures sua manu Codices in Membrana exaravit, hodie subtractos." Wattenbach, *Scriftwesen*, pp. 449–450. Mallersdorf was dependent upon Niedermünster from 1109 until 1129. The monastery joined the Hirsau reform in 1122; Mallersdorf was one of several monasteries that came under Irish (called Scottish at the time) influence during the twelfth century. Leukardis may have joined the community as a part of an influx of religious women and men from Ireland.

[3] Constant J. Mews, "Monastic Educational Culture Revisited: The Witness of Zwiefalten and the Hirsau Reform," in *Medieval Monastic Education*, ed. George Ferzoco and Carolyn Muessig (London, 2000), pp. 185–186. See also Herrad Spilling, "Reinhard von Munderkingen als Schreiber und Lehrer," in *900 Jahre Benediktinerabtei Zwiefalten*, ed. Josef Pretsch (Ulm, 1989), pp. 73–100.

[4] "Guda peccatrix mulier scripsit quae pinxit hunc librum." Frankfurt-am-Main, Stadt- und Universitätsbibliothek, MS Barth. 42.

[5] *Collectio Reinheresbrunnensis*, ed. Friedel Peeck, MGH Epistolae Selecta 5 (Munich, 1978), pp. 80–81.

[6] Strasbourg, Bibliothèque du Grand Séminaire, Cod. 78.

in book production in a variety of institutional and intellectual contexts in German lands.

As early as the eighth century, and with the arrival of nun-missionaries from England, women emerged as religious leaders in Germanic lands. Lioba, for example, embraced the role of spiritual leader, filling a need within her local community for a "holy man" to control the danger and chaos. When a storm threatened, it was to her that the people of the village fled seeking protection – and she delivered it – quieting the tempest and calming the crowd.[7] Nobody in the story, as her hagiographer told it, seemed concerned at all that Lioba was a woman rather than a man.

Perhaps the upheaval that resulted from the struggle for institutional reform, whether associated with Gorze, Hirsau, or Prémontré, precipitated a crisis in the life of some religious communities – a time of more rapid change during which the immediate needs of the group overshadowed conventional divisions between monks and nuns, or between women's and men's work.[8] When those needs were intellectual, as they often were, books could be needed urgently and barriers to female participation in producing them could fall. These falling and lowered barriers allowed women remarkable access to the literate sphere of the dual-sex reform monastery, a spiritual and intellectual context in which they could take a place alongside men as scribes, readers, preachers, authors, and editors.

Another factor may have been the persistence of the monastery as a center of spiritual and intellectual life in twelfth-century Germanic lands, a role shared in the tenth and eleventh centuries with German cathedral schools.[9] Monastic schools, however, particularly in south Germany, Austria, and Switzerland, continued to build their libraries while the cathedral schools do not seem to have kept pace.[10] Thus, while monastic schools were losing their central importance on the spiritual and intellectual landscape of England, France, and Italy, Germany's religious houses retained their position as the vanguard of learning.[11] While elsewhere the great cathedrals were being built and the schools associated with them were flourishing, and as the scholastic method was taking shape and finding expression in

[7] See Rudolph of Fulda, *Vita Leobae abbatissae biscofesheimensis auctore Rudolpho*, ed. Georg Waitz, MGH, Scriptores 15, p. 128.

[8] Giles Constable describes the eleventh and twelfth centuries generally, particularly 1040 to 1160 as "a period of intense, rapid, and to a high degree self-conscious change in almost all aspects of human thought and activity." See Giles Constable, *The Reformation of the Twelfth Century* (Cambridge, 1996), p. 4.

[9] Julia Barrow, "Education and the Recruitment of Cathedral Canons in England and Germany 1100–1225," *Viator* 20 (1989): 120.

[10] Barrow, "Education and Recruitment," p. 124.

[11] Alfred Haverkamp, *Medieval Germany, 1056–1273*, second edition, trans. Helga Braun and Richard Mortimer (Oxford, 1992), pp. 198–199. On the education of canons in German cathedrals, see Barrow, "Education and Recruitment," pp. 117–137.

the work of such famous scholars as Peter Lombard, Hugh of Saint Victor, and Peter Abelard, Germany's intellectuals remained primarily monastic. This is not to say that German religious were not interested in developments in the schools. On the contrary, both Admont's and Schäftlarn's twelfth-century libraries suggest that readers at both centers had access to a remarkably wide range of texts and authors.

The shape and variety of German monastic reform is mirrored in the libraries that survive from these communities. The library that Diemut copied for Wessobrunn, for example, was clearly shaped and limited by the conservative intellectual tradition associated with the Gorze reformers. If the lists of Diemut's books are a reasonable reflection of the spiritual and intellectual interests of her community, then we have evidence at Wessobrunn, at least during the first half of the twelfth century, of an approach to biblical study that was clearly conservative – one that emphasized monastic *lectio*, with particular interest in the exegetical writings of Gregory the Great, and to the exclusion of more intricate theological treatises and more contemporary works.

Admont's twelfth-century library, which can be documented even more fully than Wessobrunn's, tells a more complex story, and one that further complicates the picture painted by Jean Leclercq of a clean divide between the spiritual and intellectual world of the monastery on the one hand, and the school on the other. While Leclercq argued that this split was pronounced in twelfth-century France, this seems not to have been the case in German lands.[12] Constant Mews has shown, through an analysis of Zwiefalten's twelfth-century library catalogue, that Leclercq's paradigm does not work for this double monastery of the Hirsau reform.[13] Zwiefalten's library, rather, suggests a wide range of intellectual interests among the community's monks and nuns, and reflects an educational culture that was not limited to the writings of "monastic theologians."[14] The same can be said of Admont, where the contemporary writings of Honorius *Augustodunensis*, Hugh of St. Victor, Rupert of Deutz, and even Peter Abelard took their place in the *armariae* alongside the commentaries and homilies of Origen, Jerome, Gregory, and other patristic authors. Readers in these two Hirsau communities were interested, it seems, in a

12 For Leclercq's definition of monastic theology, see Jean Leclercq, *The Love of Learning and the Desire for God: A Study of Monastic Culture* (New York, 1961), pp. 191–235. For a critique of Leclercq's analysis see John Van Engen, *Rupert of Deutz* (Berkeley, 1983), pp. 9–10; for a critique based on evidence from Germany in the context of the Hirsau reform, see Mews, "Monastic Educational Culture Revisited," pp. 183 and 193–195.

13 Mews, "Monastic Educational Culture Revisited," p. 185. On the surviving manuscripts from Zwiefalten, see Sigrid von Borries-Schulten's contribution (Vol. I: *Provenienz Zwiefalten*) in the *Katalog der illuminierten Handschriften der Württembergischen Landesbibliothek Stuttgart* (Stuttgart, 1987).

14 Mews, "Monastic Educational Culture Revisited," p. 194.

wide range of authors, and not exclusively those of a traditionally monastic sort.

Germany's monastic readers could encounter contemporary writings of non-monastic origin with a mixture of interest and resistance, an uneasy ambivalence that they shared with regional theologians, such as Rupert of Deutz, whom John Van Engen characterized as, "deeply rooted in the old order struggling alternately to keep up with and to resist the new."[15] Perhaps it was the tension between old and new in Rupert's work that struck a chord with Admont's readers and exegetes, as their twelfth-century library contained one of the largest known collections of his writings. A certain wariness is visible in the margins of the monks' twelfth-century copy of Abelard's *Liber Sententiarum*, in which the more "dangerous" parts were cordoned off with marginal lines and warnings to the reader to exercise caution in their reading.[16] Excursions beyond the boundaries of the monastic world evidently had their limits.

A clear tendency to resist the new is evidenced in the hand written in the monasteries of south Germany. Throughout the twelfth century we see Bavarian scribes, including the women of Admont, Wessobrunn, and Schäftlarn, writing a distinctive form of script that was slow to change to reflect the new "Gothic" hands that were gaining popularity elsewhere. This conservatism in writing reflects a strong sense of connection to south German regional tradition – a connection that coexisted with interest in the writings emerging from the schools to the north. Out of this desire to preserve the traditional while engaging the new was born a twelfth-century renaissance of a distinctly German and defiantly monastic sort.

That the *physical* locus of intellectual life in German lands remained the monastery had important consequences for women, particularly women in dual-sex communities, which were more common in German lands than elsewhere in Europe in the twelfth century. It is difficult to say whether a historically positive evaluation of women's potential in Germanic lands motivated the formation of these double houses, or whether the women simply provided a convenient and legitimate opportunity for the *cura monialium* – a venue in which men could combine both the contemplative life and the active life, an elusive combination and one highly sought after by twelfth-century reformers. With an adjacent community of women who needed preachers, confessors, and teachers, a monk did not have to go far beyond his own library to add active engagement to a life otherwise dominated by study and contemplation.

[15] Van Engen, *Rupert of Deutz*, p. 3.

[16] Originally Admont MS 729, the manuscript is now Princeton University, Garrett MS 169. The marginal notes and warnings seem to focus particularly upon Abelard's Trinitarian opinions.

Monasteries connected with Hirsau, in particular, not only used the services of resident female scribes, but also provided a setting in which women could participate fully in the central activities of their reformed communities, and this meant access to libraries and teachers. So much of what was going on intellectually and spiritually in England, France, and Italy was tied to schools, and later, to universities – places to which women (except in exceptional cases like that of Heloise) were forbidden access. But while women remained active participants in various forms of religious life in Germany, and literacy enabled many to take part in associated spiritual and intellectual activities, neither a German context nor life in a dual-sex monastic community guaranteed women a central place in that sphere. Women were consciously excluded from the intellectual dimension of Schäftlarn's spiritual life. There, and at other Premonstratensian houses, women were rather assigned the part of Martha – tending to the washing, sewing, and mending, as well as book copying: Mary was evidently a Benedictine.

Why should Hirsau and Prémontré have emerged so differently with respect to women? This difference reflects the centrality at houses such as Schäftlarn of the ideal of apostolic preaching – an ideal from which women were entirely excluded. Perhaps also, as a recent French import, the structure and values of these newly established houses reflected a non-German cultural tradition with respect to the evaluation of the spiritual strengths of women. Schäftlarn's failure to comply with the Chapter General's demand that double monasteries be divided into separate houses, however, does seem to reflect a readiness to adjust practice to the local context. In any case, the more interesting question may be why contemporary women were drawn in large numbers to an order that restricted them so sharply in their intellectual lives. A life of consecrated manual labor may simply have met the spiritual needs of some women more closely than one focused on study and contemplation. This distinction highlights the variety of forms of religious life open to women and to men during the twelfth century, and selecting one order and one community involved, no doubt, a complex set of spiritual, intellectual, social, economic, geographic, and personal factors.

The religious houses of south Germany reflect a series of creative responses to the call for reform that swept across Western Europe in the twelfth century. Renewed interest in biblical study could result – as was the case at Wessobrunn – in a revival of interest in patristic forms of biblical scholarship to the exclusion of intellectual and spiritual engagement beyond the traditional monastic *lectio*. At other centers, particularly those like Admont that were reformed according to the customs of Hirsau, interest in traditional *lectio* and commentary was coupled with interest in new forms of biblical interpretation and theology. And at Premonstratensian Schäftlarn, male readers could choose between monastic and scholastic texts both for devotional reading and for preparation for the pastoral duties of the priesthood.

Each of these three centers mounted a different response to a shared sense of the need for reform. Each of these three centers responded differently to the pull of monastic and German traditions on the one hand, and influences more modern and foreign on the other. All three provided – for different reasons and to different extents – settings in which women could thrive, not only as scribes, but also as shapers of and participants in the monastic reformation of the twelfth century.

# Appendix A

## *Codicological tables*

## EXPLANATION OF CODICOLOGICAL TABLE HEADINGS

**Manuscript** = Shelfmark
**Date** = Approximate date of manuscript completion
**Text** = General contents of manuscript (see individual manuscript descriptions for a precise list of titles)
**Scribe** = Name of any identified scribe or scribes
**Ff.** = Number of folios in the manuscript
**Parch. size / Ruled area** = Parchment dimensions in millimeters (P)
Ruled area in millimeters (R)
**Parch.** = Parchment quality expressed as the percentage of folios in the manuscript without significant flaws (holes, repairs, etc.)
**G.R.** = Is Gregory's Rule followed – that is, does the hairside of each folio face the hairside of the facing folio, and fleshside face fleshside? Y indicates that Gregory's Rule is consistently followed. Y* indicates that Gregory's Rule is usually followed, although with numerous exceptions. N indicates that hair and flesh routinely face one another in the manuscript.
**Quire** = Quire structure expressed in Roman numerals. IV indicates the use of four-bifolia quires. IV* indicates that four-bifolia gatherings are generally used, although with a significant number of exceptions.
**Quire marks** = Numbering of quires on either the first recto or the last verso. N indicates that no quire marks are present. Y indicates the presence of quire marks within the manuscript.
**Ruling pattern** = Ruling pattern code (see pp. 145–147 for diagrams)
**Lines** = Number of lines of text per page. LL indicates the use of long lines and 2C indicates the use of two columns of text.

Table A1 *Codicological features of Wessobrunn manuscripts*

| Manuscript | Date | Scribe | Text | Ff. | Parch. size (P) / Ruled area (R) | G.R. | Quire | Quire marks | Ruling pattern | Lines | Parch. (%) |
|---|---|---|---|---|---|---|---|---|---|---|---|
| Clm 22002 | $xii^{med}$ | Diemut<br>Nun-Scribe 1<br>Nun-Scribe 2 | Homiliary (vol. I) | 215 | 460 × 310 (P)<br>345–355 × 215 (R) | Y | IV* | Y | B | 41<br>2C* | 36 |
| Clm 22003 | $xii^{med}$ | Diemut<br>Nun-Scribe 2<br>Scribe 3<br>Scribe 4 | Homiliary (vol. II) | 243 | 465 × 310 (P)<br>345–355 × 215 (R) | Y | IV* | Y | $C_1$ | 41<br>2C* | (fire damage) |
| Clm 22004 | $xii^4$ | Lodevicus | Flavius Josephus, *The Jewish War* | 174 | 475 × 320 (P)<br>320–345 × 205–215 (R) | Y | IV | Y | D | 36/37<br>2C | 25.5 |
| Clm 22005 | $xii^{med}$ | Diemut<br>Nun-Scribe 2 | Bible (vol. I) | 155 | 450 × 305 (P)<br>335–345 × 210–220 (R) | Y | IV* | Y | B | 41<br>2C | 38 |
| Clm 22006 | $xii^{med}$ | Diemut<br>Nun-Scribe 1<br>Scribe 5 | Bible (vol. II) | 271 | 465 × 310 (P)<br>345–350 × 215 (R) | Y | IV* | N | B | 40–44<br>2C | (fire damage) |
| Clm 22007 | $xii^{in}$ | Diemut | Augustine, Commentary on the Psalms (Ps. 51–100) | 341 | 385 × 255 (P)<br>280 × 170 (R) | Y | IV | N | A | 33<br>LL | 43.4 |
| Clm 22008 | $xii^{in}$ | Diemut | Gregory the Great, *Homilies on Ezechiel* | 178 | 340 × 245 (P)<br>255 × 150 (R) | Y | IV | N | $A_1$ | 28<br>LL | 54.5 |

(*cont.*)

Table A1 (*cont.*)

| Manuscript | Date | Scribe | Text | Ff. | Parch. size (P)/ Ruled area (R) | G.R. | Quire | Quire marks | Ruling pattern | Lines | Parch. (%) |
|---|---|---|---|---|---|---|---|---|---|---|---|
| Clm 22009 | $xii^{in}$ | Diemut | Gregory the Great, *Moral Expositions on the Book of Job* (6–10) | 131 | 350 × 245 (P) 260 × 150 (R) | Y | IV | N | A | 28/40 LL | fire damage |
| Clm 22010 | $xii^{in}$ | Diemut | Gregory the Great, *Moral Expositions on the Book of Job* (17–22) | 198 | 340 × 220 (P) 240 × 135 (R) | Y | IV | N | $A_2$ | 26 LL | 40 |
| Clm 22011 | $xii^{in}$ | Diemut | Gregory the Great, *Moral Expositions on the Book of Job* (23–27) | 153 | 340 × 220 (P) 235–240 × 123–130 (R) | Y | IV | N | A | 26 LL | 39 |
| Clm 22012 | $xii^{in}$ | Diemut | Gregory the Great, *Moral Expositions on the Book of Job* (28–35) | 270 | 335 × 230 (P) 230–235 × 140–150 (R) | Y | IV | N | A | 24–27 LL | 49 |

| | | | | | | | | | | | |
|---|---|---|---|---|---|---|---|---|---|---|---|
| Clm 22014 | $xii^2$ | Diemut | Eusebius, *Ecclesiastical History* | 133 | 340 × 230 (P)<br>270 × 165 (R) | Y | IV | N | D | 40<br>2C | 48 |
| Clm 22015 | $xii^2$ | Diemut | Cassiodorus, *Tripartite Ecclesiastical History* | 167 | 345 × 230 (P)<br>265–270 × 165 (R) | Y | IV* | Y | $D_1$ | 40<br>2C | 32 |
| Clm 22016 | $xii^2$ | Diemut | Theological Collection | 159 | 345 × 230 (P)<br>260–270 × 165–175 (R) | Y | IV* | Y | C | 38–40<br>2C | 24 |
| Clm 22034 | $xii^{ex}$ | Lodevicus | Jerome, *Lives of Illustrious Men* | 61 | 235 × 160 (P)<br>150–155 × 90–99 (R) | Y | IV | Y | A | 20<br>LL | 54 |
| Clm 22040 | $xii^{in}$ | Nun-Scribe 2 | Ritual | 133 | 245 × 160 (P)<br>160 × 100 (R) | Y | IV | N | $A/A_2$ | 17<br>LL | 65 |
| Clm 22044 | $xii^{in}$ | Diemut<br>Nun-Scribe 2 | Gospels | 270 | 250 × 174 (P)<br>195 × 100–110 (R) | Y | IV* | N | A (?) | 23<br>LL | — |
| Clm 23411 | $xii^{med}$ | Nun-Scribe 2 and 2 or 3 unidentified scribes | Lives of the Saints | 83 | 230 × 165 (P)<br>165–175 × 110 (R) | Y | IV | N | A | 24 or 23<br>LL | 71 |

Table A2 *Codicological features of Admont manuscripts*

| Manuscript | Date | Scribe | Text | Ff. | Parch. size / Ruled area | Parch. (%) | G.R. | Quire | Quire marks | Ruling | Lines |
|---|---|---|---|---|---|---|---|---|---|---|---|
| Vorau MS 193 | s.xii$^{med}$ | Anonymous (1–6)<br>Irmingart Regilind<br>Nun-Scribe A<br>Nun-Scribe B | Irimbert of Admont, Commentaries<br>Anonymous, Commentaries | 214 | 190 × 100 mm (P)<br>140 × 70 mm (R) | — | Y* | IV* | N | 1 | 22 LL<br>27 LL |
| Admont MS 650 | s.xii$^{med}$ | Irmingart Regilind<br>Nun-Scribes A–G | Irimbert of Admont, Commentaries<br>Anonymous, Commentaries | 105 | 190 × 100 mm (P)<br>140 × 70 mm (R) | 76 | Y* | IV* | N | 1 | 27 LL |
| Admont MS 651 | s.xii$^{med}$ | Anonymous (1–3, 7–8)<br>Irimgart Regilind<br>Nun-Scribe B | Irimbert of Admont, Commentaries | 209 | 185 × 100 mm (P)<br>140 × 70 mm (R) | 62 | Y* | IV* | N | 1 | 27 LL |
| Admont MS 682 | s.xii$^{med}$ | Irmingart Regilind | Irimbert of Admont, Commentaries | 164 | 190 × 105 mm (P)<br>140 × 70 mm (R) | 56 | Y* | IV* | N | 1 | 27 LL |
| Admont MS 16 | s.xii$^{2}$ | Irmingart Regilind<br>Nun-Scribe A | Irimbert of Admont, Commentaries on 4 Books of Kings | 342 | 305 × 95 mm (P) | | Y | IV* | | 6 | 40 2C |
| Admont MS 17 | s.xii$^{med}$ | Irmingart Regilind<br>Nun-Scribe H(?) and I(I) | Irimbert of Admont, Commentaries | 221 | 400 × 273 mm (P) | 20 | Y | IV* | N | 3 | 37 2C |
| Admont 18 | s.xii$^{ex}$ | Udalricus Johannes | *Liber Matutinalis* | 296 | 390 × 275 mm (P) | 42 | Y | IV | N | 4/5 | 33 2C |
| Admont 58 | s.xii | Female? | Anonymous Admont School, Homilies for Feast Days | 176 | 350 × 240 mm (P)<br>240 × 155 mm (R) | | Y | IV | Y | 3 | 30 LL |
| Admont 62 | s.xii | | Anonymous Admont School, Sermons for Feast Days | | 355 × 244 mm (P)<br>235 × 155 mm (R) | | Y | IV | N | 3 | 30 LL |
| Admont 292 | s.xii$^{ex}$ | Cunradus | Hugh of St. Victor, *Commentary on the Hierarchy of Ps-Dionysis* | 140 | 260 × 180 mm (T)<br>180 × 130 mm (R) | 34 | Y | IV | Y | 2 | 28 2C |

Table A3 *Codicological features of Schäftlarn manuscripts*

| Manuscript | Text | Date | Scribe | Ff. | Parch. size (mm) | Parch. (%) | G.R. | Quire | Quire marks | Ruling pattern | Lines |
|---|---|---|---|---|---|---|---|---|---|---|---|
| Clm 17052 | Augustine, Commentary on the Psalms (1–50) | $xii^{3}$ | Sophia<br>Adalbertus | 215 | 385 × 250 | 39 | Y | IV | Y | A | 37<br>LL |
| Clm 17053 | Augustine, Commentary on the Psalms (51–100) | $xii^{3}$ | Sophia | 278 | 385 × 255 | 58.8 | Y | IV | Y | A | 37<br>LL |
| Clm 17054 | Augustine, Commentary on the Psalms | $xii^{4}$ | Adalbertus<br>Marchwardus<br>Sophia | 200 | 340 × 225 | 32.5 | Y | IV | Y | B/C | 44<br>2C |
| Clm 17116 | Rupert of Deutz, *On the Divine Office* | $xii^{3}$ | Irmingart | 133 | 330 × 220 | 23.5 | Y | IV | Y | B | 40<br>2C |
| Clm 17087 | *Homilies on the Epistles and Gospels (annual arrangement)* | $xii^{3}$ | Irmingart | 223 | 320 × 215 | 44.5 | Y | IV | Y | B | 41<br>2C |
| Clm 17161 | Gratian, *Decretum* | $xii^{3}$ | Adalbertus | 182 | 435 × 295 | 27 | Y | IV | Y | B | 58–64<br>2C |
| Clm 17036 | Bible | $xii^{4}$ | Adalbertus | 212 | 440 × 310 | 50 | Y* | IV* | Y | B | 35<br>2C |
| Clm 17037 | Bible | $xii^{4}$ | Adalbertus | 148 | 435 × 310 | 27.7 | Y* | IV | N | B | 35<br>2C |
| Clm 17040 | Bible | $xii^{4}$ | Adalbertus | 89 | 440 × 315 | 40 | Y | IV | N | B | 35<br>2C |
| Clm 17174 | Premonstratensian Statutes | $xii^{med}$ | Unidentified | 42 | 210 × 145 | 71.4 | Y | IV | N | D | 28/29<br>LL |

# Appendix B

## *Ruling patterns*

## WESSOBRUNN

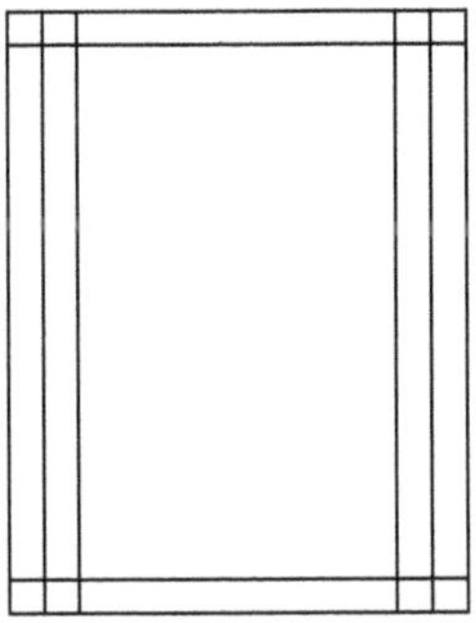

Pattern A

Pattern $A_1$

Pattern $A_2$

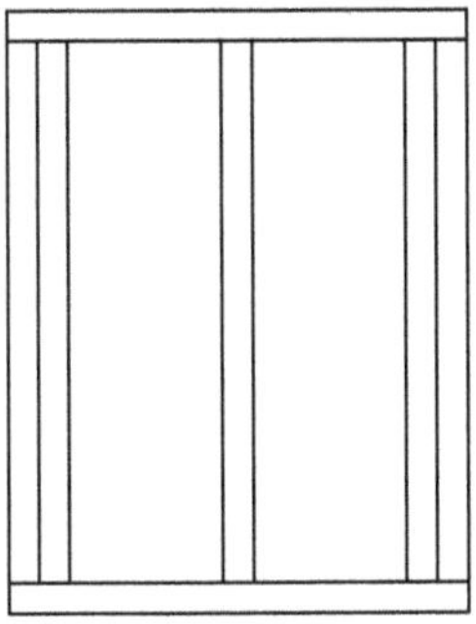

Pattern B

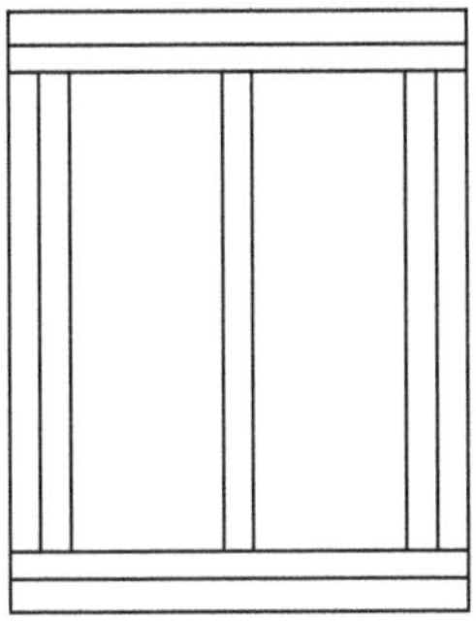

Pattern C

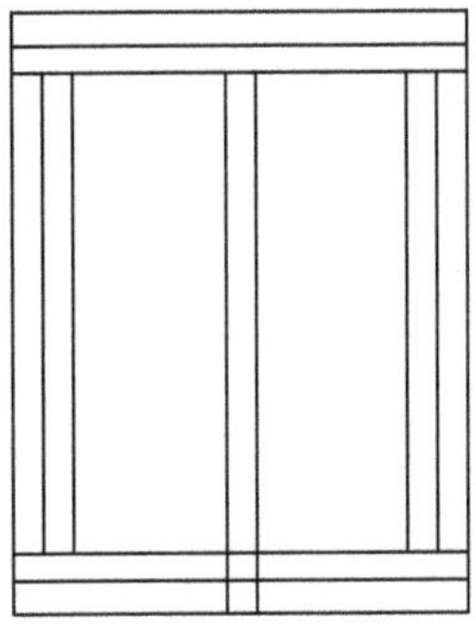

Pattern $C_1$

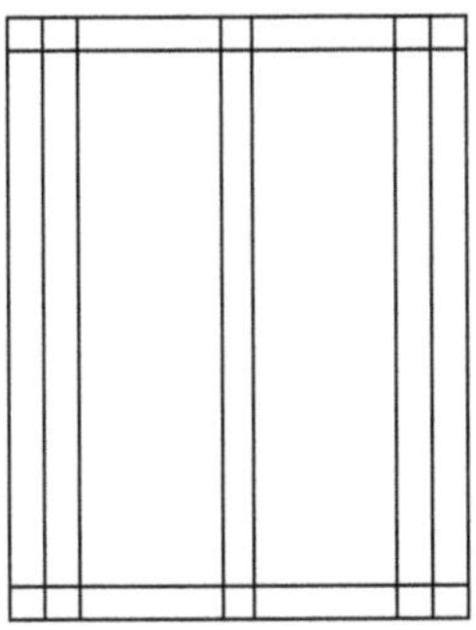

Pattern D

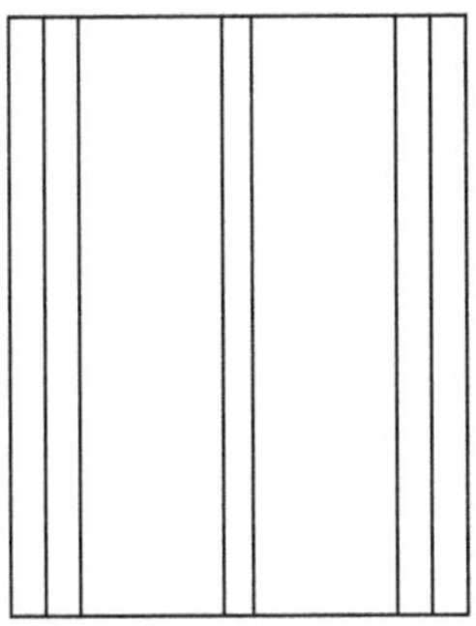

Pattern $D_1$

Pattern E

## ADMONT

Pattern 1

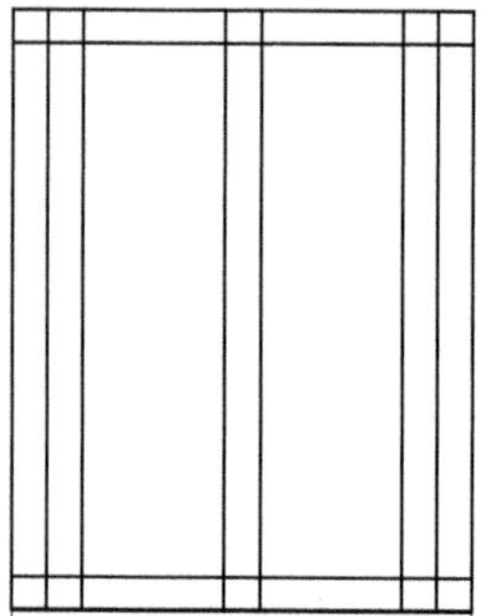

Pattern 2

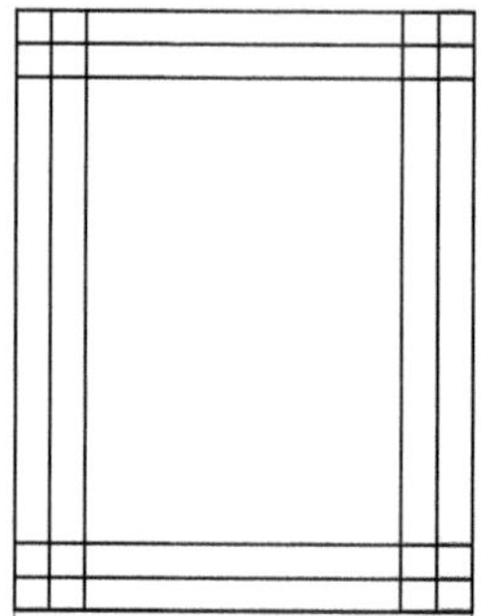

Pattern 3

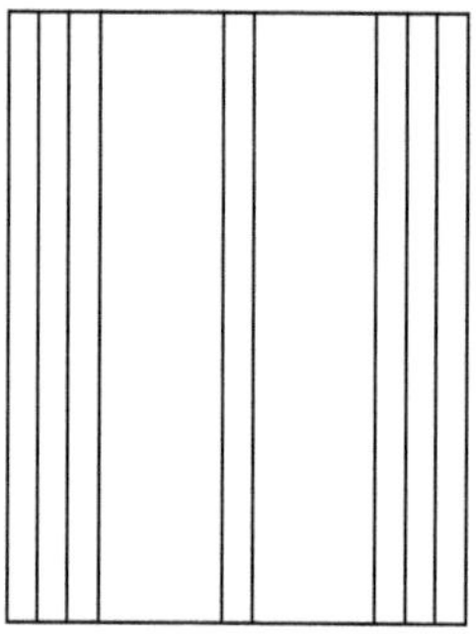

Pattern 4

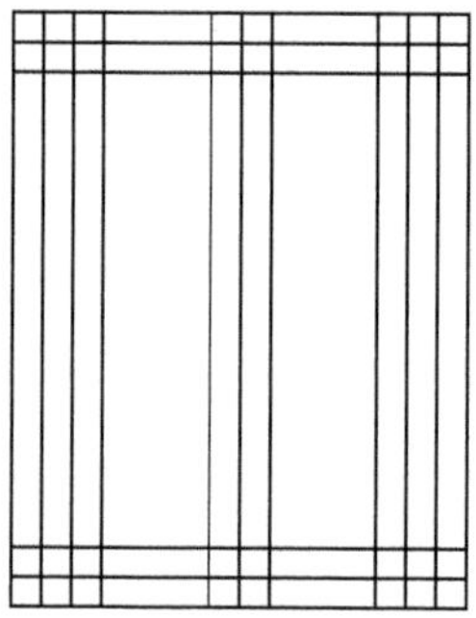

Pattern 5

## SCHÄFTLARN

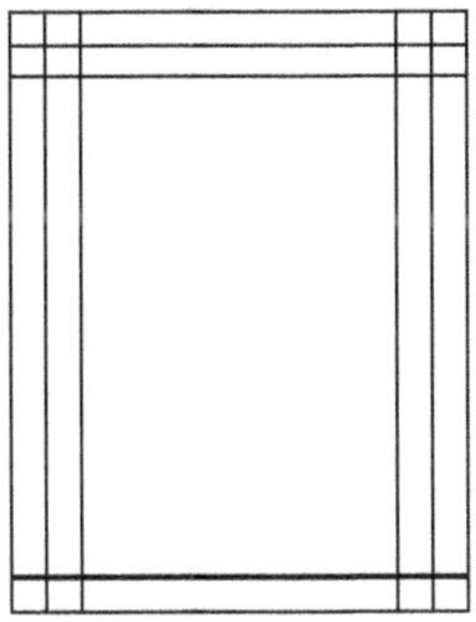

Pattern A

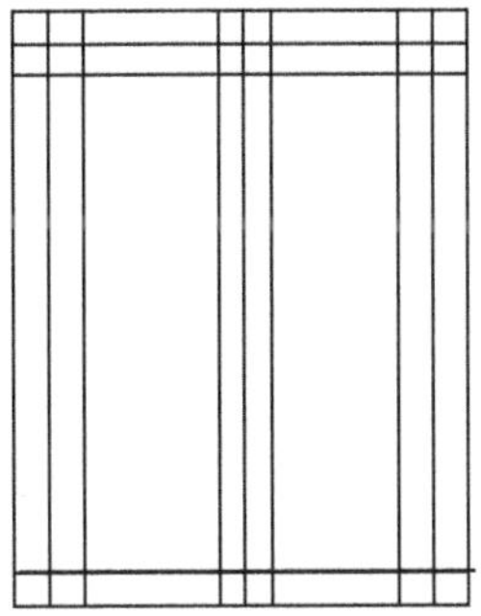

Pattern B

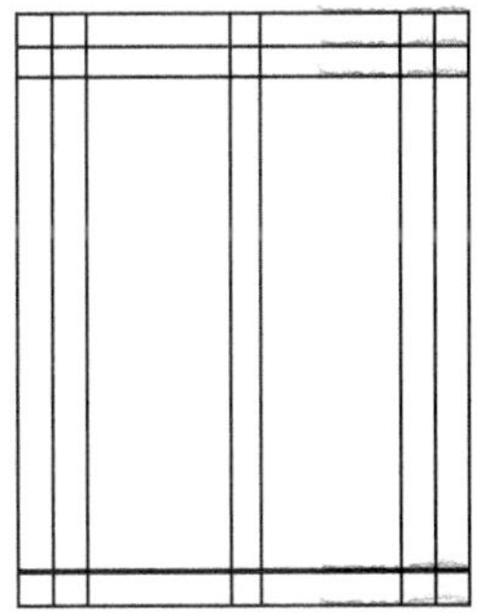

Pattern C

Pattern D

# *Palaeographical figures*

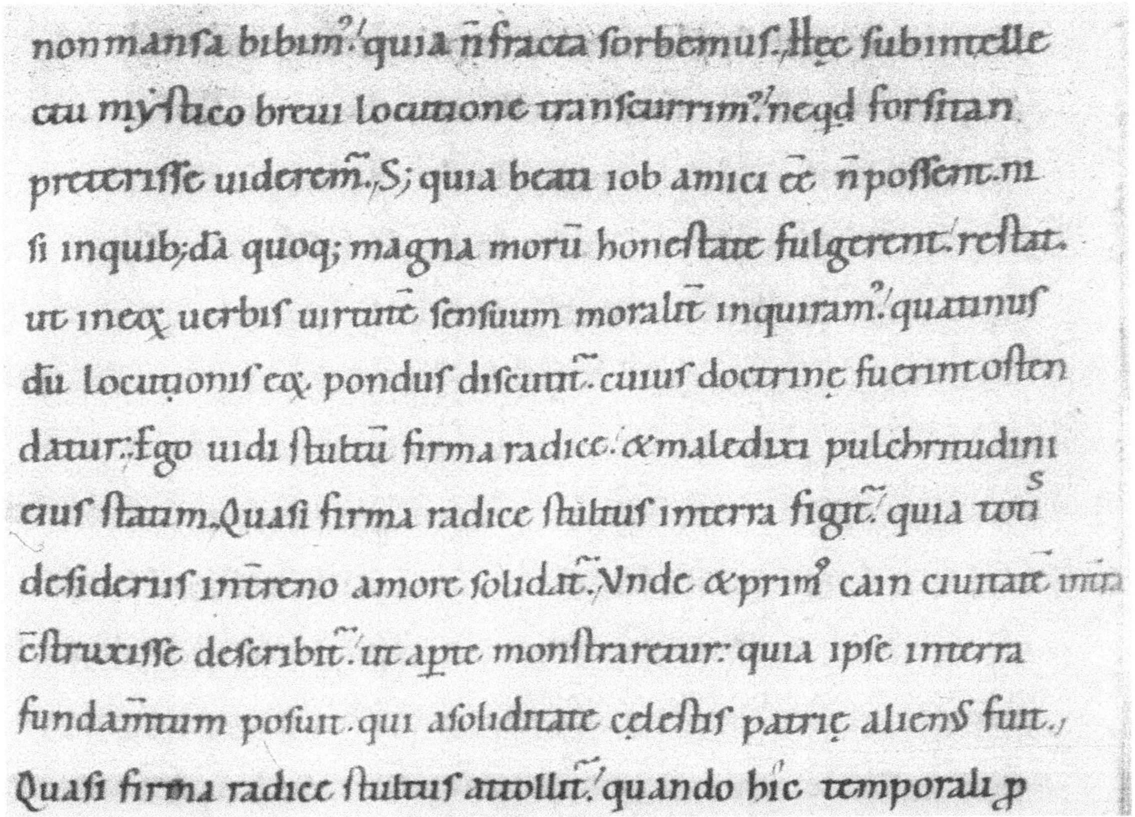
non mansa bibim(us). quia n(on) fracta sorbemus. Hec subintelle
ctu mystico breui locutione transcurrim(us). ne q(uo)d forsitan
preterisse uiderem(ur). S(ed) quia beati iob amici e(ss)e n(on) possent ni
si in quib(us)dam quoq(ue) magna moru(m) honestate fulgerent. restat.
ut in eor(um) uerbis uirtute(m) sensuum moralit(er) inquiram(us). quatinus
du(m) locutionis eor(um) pondus discutit(ur). cuius doctrine fuerint osten
datur. Ego uidi stultu(m) firma radice. et maledixi pulchritudini
eius statim. Quasi firma radice stultus in terra figit(ur). quia tot(us)
desideriis in t(er)reno amore solidat(ur). Vnde et prim(us) cain ciuitate(m) in t(er)ra
(con)struxisse describit(ur). ut apte monstraretur: quia ipse in terra
fundamentum posuit. qui a soliditate celestis patrie alienus fuit.
Quasi firma radice stultus attollit(ur). quando hic temporali p(er)

1 Munich, Bayerische Staatsbibliothek Clm 22009 f. 4v

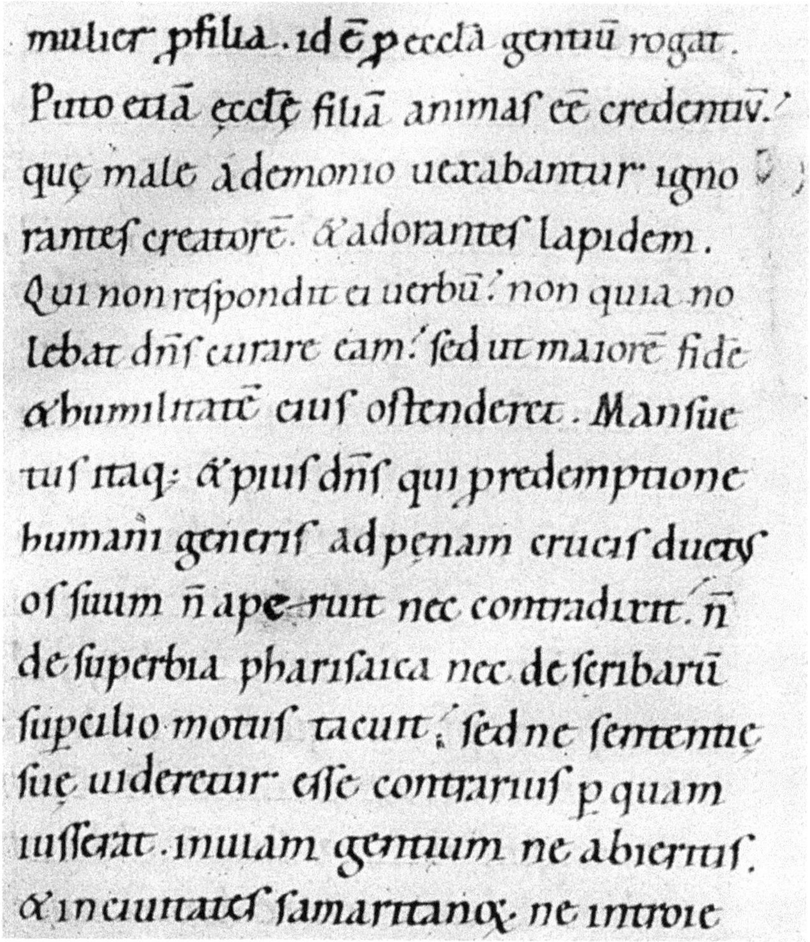

mulier ꝑfilia. id ē ꝓ eccłā gentiū rogat.
Puto etiā ecclę filiā animas ee credentiū.
quę male a demonio uexabantur igno
rantes creatorē. & adorantes lapidem.
Qui non respondit ei uerbū. non quia no
lebat dn̄s curare eam. sed ut maiorē fidē
& humilitatē eius ostenderet. Mansue
tus itaq; & pius dn̄s qui ꝓredemptione
humanī generis ad penam crucis ductus
os suum n̄ aperuit nec contradixit. n̄
de superbia pharisaica nec de scribarū
supcilio motus tacuit. sed ne sententię
suę uideretur esse contrarius ꝑ quam
iusserat. in uiam gentium ne abieritis.
& in ciuitates samaritanoꝝ ne introie

2 Munich, Bayerische Staatsbibliothek Clm 22002 f. 24r

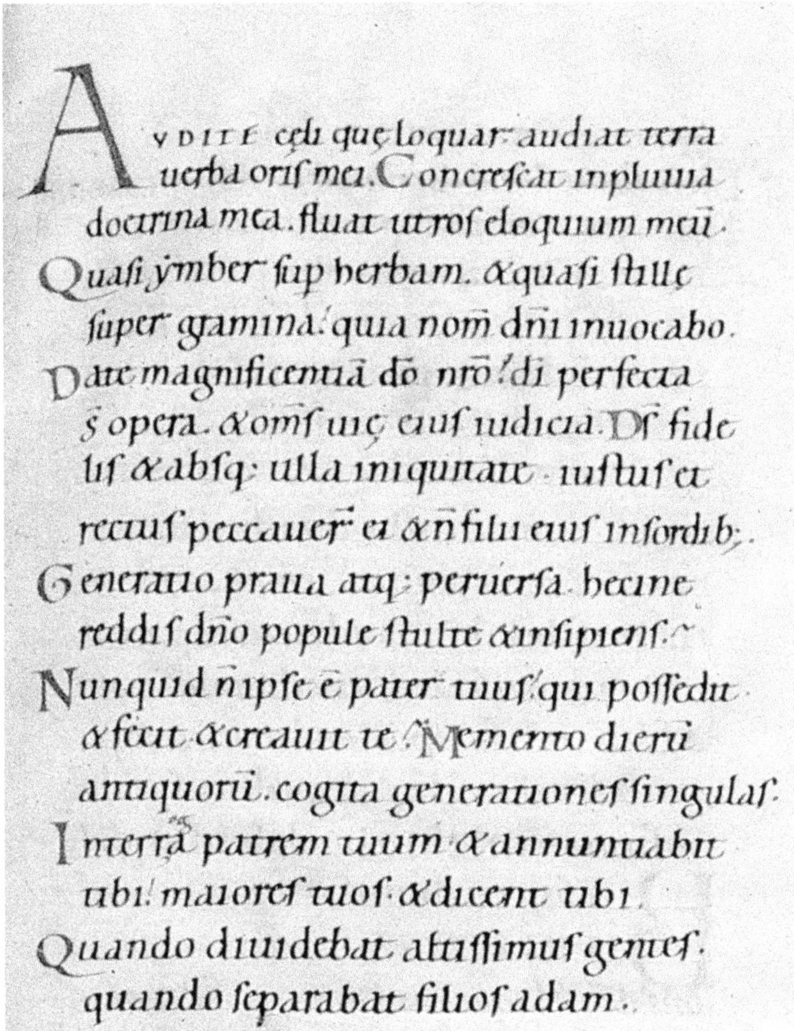
AVDITE celi quę loquar audiat terra
uerba oris mei. Concrescat in pluuia
doctrina mea. fluat ut ros eloquium meū.
Quasi ymber sup herbam. & quasi stillę
super gramina: quia nom̄ dn̄i inuocabo.
Date magnificentiā dō nr̄o: di perfecta
s opera. & omſ uię eius iudicia. Ds fide
lis & absq: ulla iniquitate. iustus et
rectus peccauer̄ ei & n̄ filii eius in sordib;.
Generatio praua atq: peruersa. hecine
reddis dn̄o popule stulte & insipiens.
Nunquid n̄ ipse ē pater tuus. qui possedit
& fecit & creauit te. Memento dierū
antiquorū. cogita generationes singulas.
Interrogā patrem tuum & annuntiabit
tibi: maiores tuos & dicent tibi.
Quando diuidebat altissimus gentes.
quando separabat filios adam.

3 Munich, Bayerische Staatsbibliothek Clm 22005 f. 29r

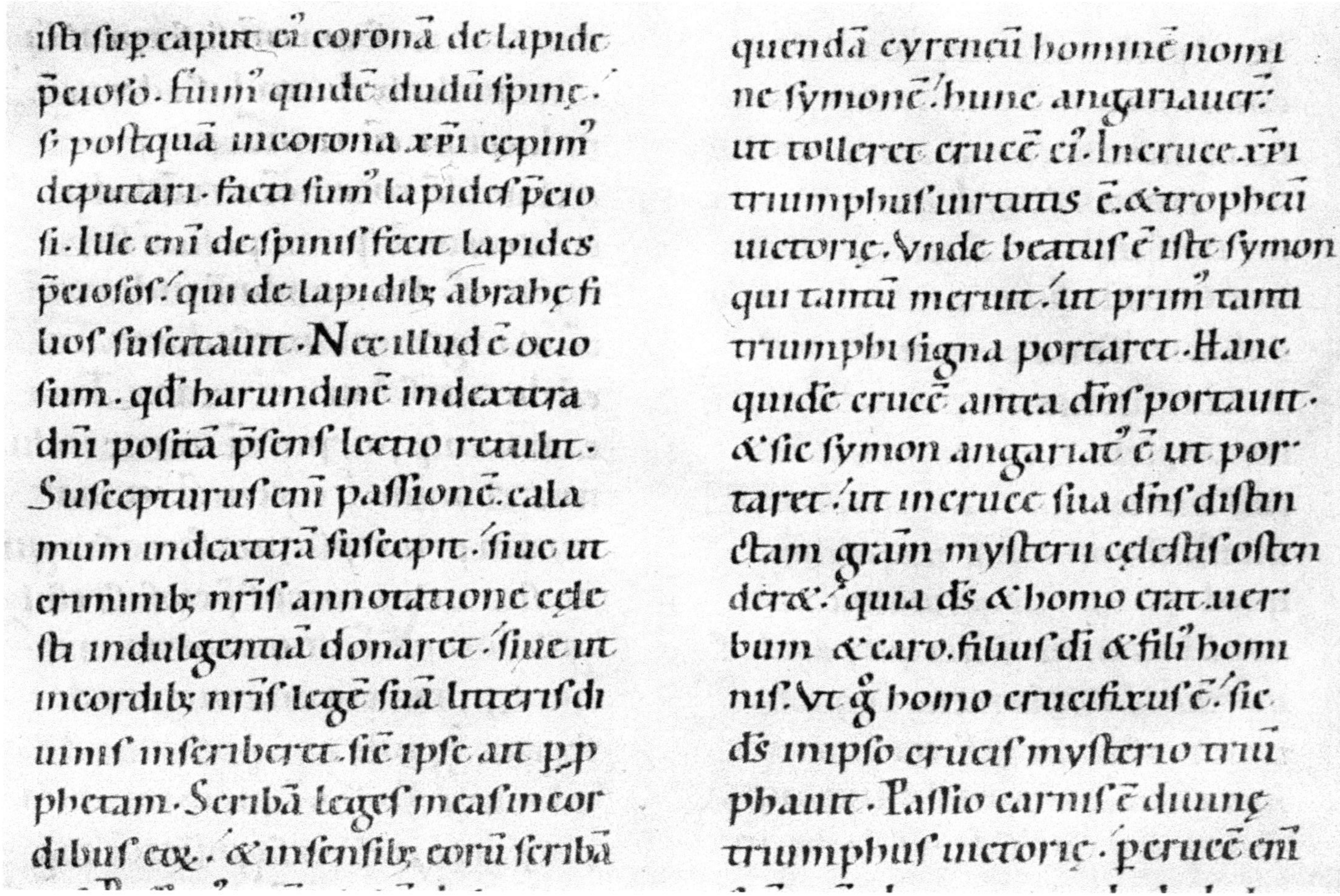

4 Munich, Bayerische Staatsbibliothek Clm 22002 f. 106v (reduced)

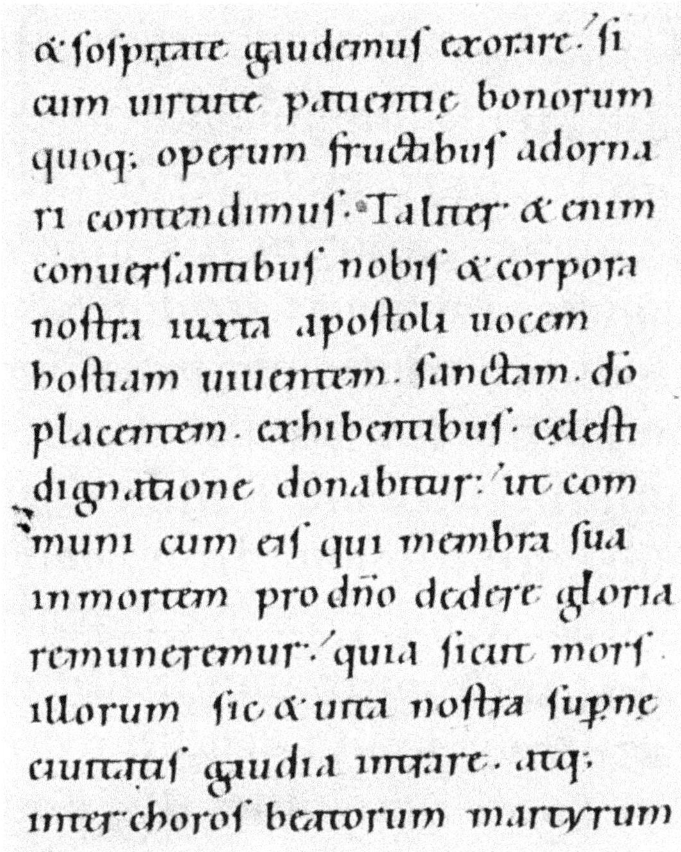

& sospitate gaudemus exorare. si
cum uirtute patientię bonorum
quoq; operum fructibus adorna
ri contendimus. Taliter & enim
conuersantibus nobis & corpora
nostra iuxta apostoli uocem
hostiam uiuentem. sanctam. dō
placentem. exhibentibus. celesti
dignatione donabitur: ut com
muni cum eis qui membra sua
inmortem pro dn̄o dedere gloria
remuneremur. quia sicut mors
illorum sic & uita nostra supne
ciuitatis gaudia intrare. atq;
inter choros beatorum martyrum

5 Munich, Bayerische Staatsbibliothek Clm 22003 f. 54r

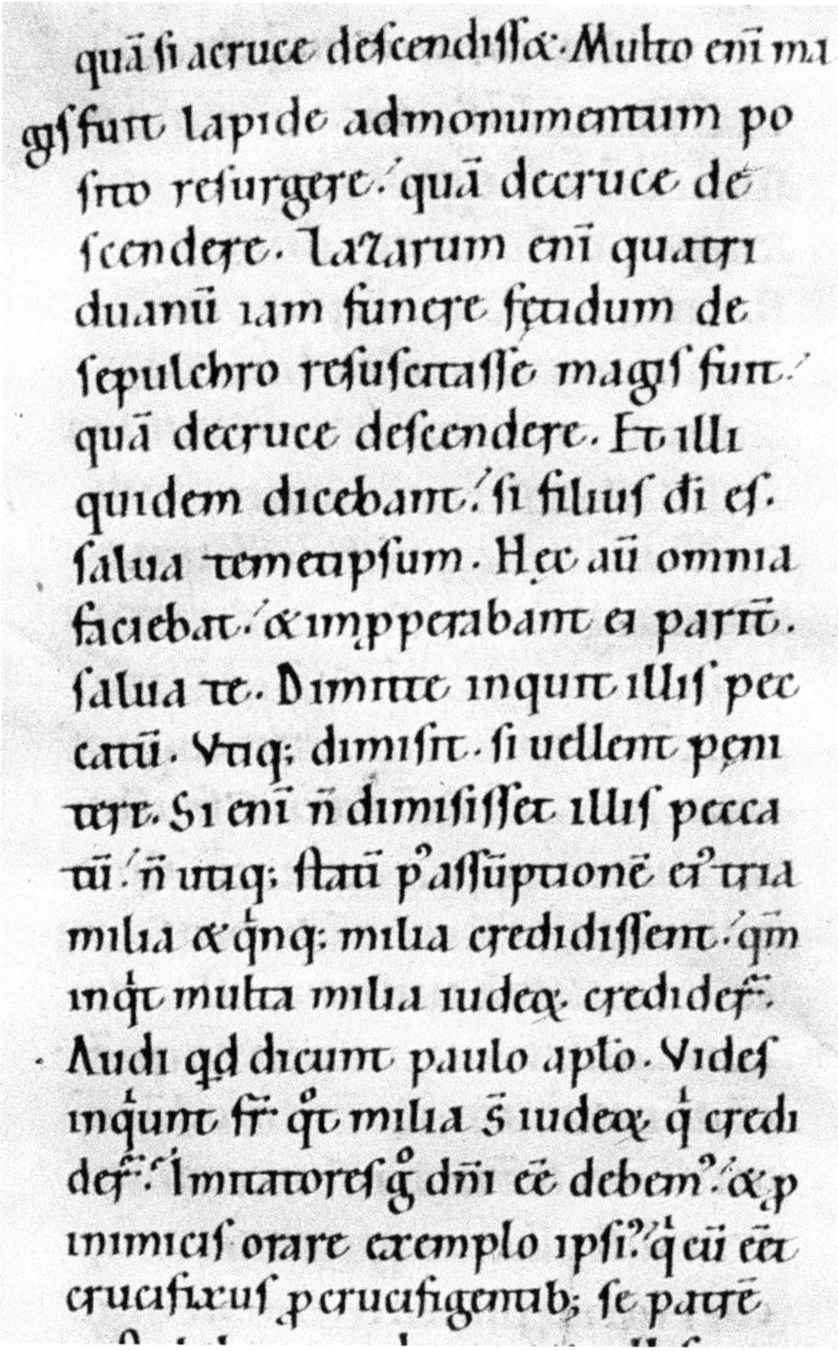

quã si a cruce descendisset. Multo enĩ ma
gis fuit lapide admonumentum po
sito resurgere. quã decruce de
scendere. Lazarum enĩ quatri
duanũ iam funere fetidum de
sepulchro resuscitasse magis fuit.
quã decruce descendere. Et illi
quidem dicebant. si filius di es.
salua temetipsum. Hec aũ omnia
faciebat. & impperabant ei pati.
salua te. Dimitte inquit illis pec
catũ. Utiq; dimisit. si uellent peni
tere. Si enĩ ñ dimisisset illis pecca
tũ. ñ utiq; statĩ p̃ assũptionẽ eĩ tria
milia & qnq; milia credidissent. qm
inqt multa milia iudeorum crediderunt.
Audi qd dicunt paulo aplo. Vides
inquiunt fr̃ qt milia s̃ iudeorum q credi
der. Imitatores g dñi ee debem⁹. & p
inimicis orare exemplo ipsi⁹. q cũ eẽt
crucifixus p crucifigentib; se patrẽ

6 Munich, Bayerische Staatsbibliothek Clm 22002 f. 110v

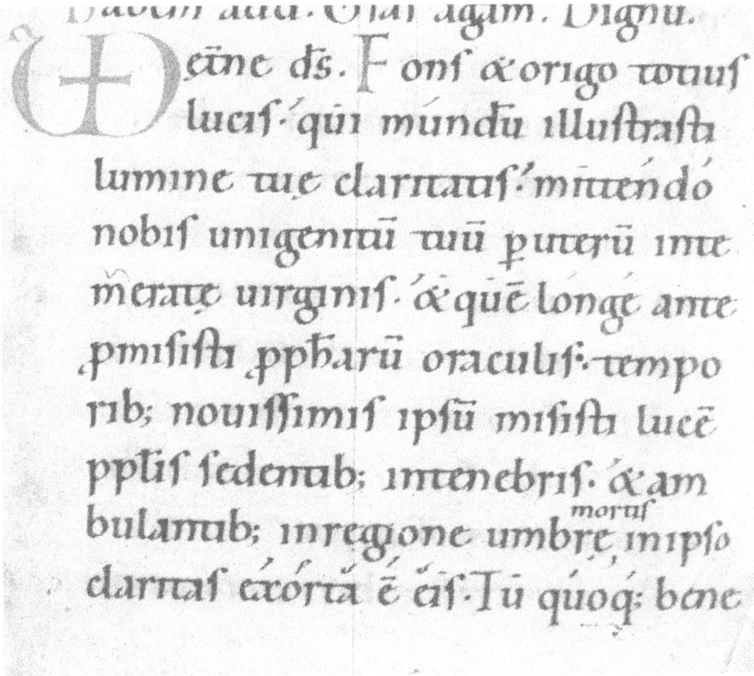

7 Munich, Bayerische Staatsbibliothek Clm 22040 f. 3r

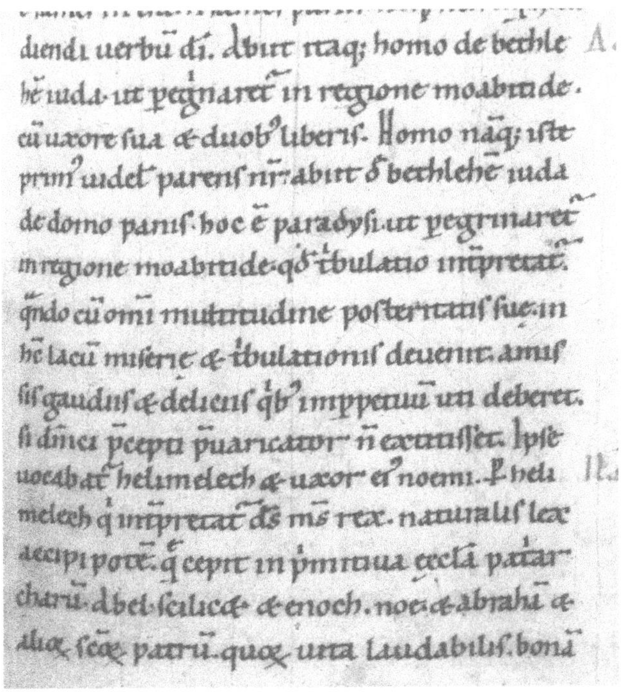

8 Vorau, Stiftsbibliothek MS 193 f. 186r

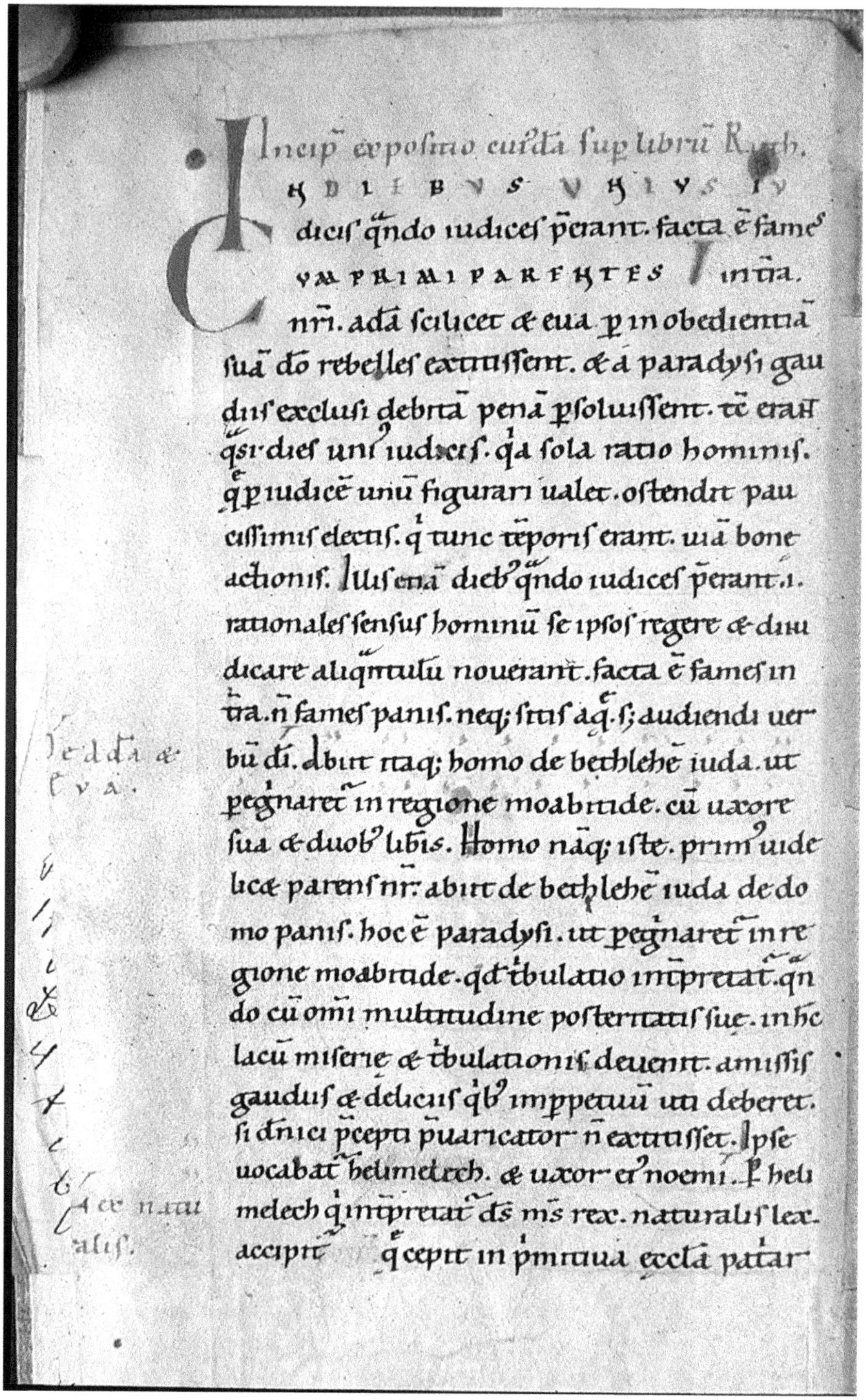

Incip exposicio cuiusda sup libru Ruth.
IN DIEBUS UNIUS IU
dicis qndo iudices perant. facta e fames
CUM PRIMI PARENTES I initia.
nri. ada scilicet et eua p inobedientia
sua do rebelles extitissent. et a paradysi gau
diis exclusi debita pena psoluissent. tc erant
qsi dies unius iudicis. qa sola ratio hominis.
q p iudice unu figurari ualet. ostendit pau
cissimis electis. q tunc tporis erant. uia bone
actionis. Ius etia dieb qndo iudices perant. i.
rationales sensus hominu se ipsos regere et diiu
dicare aliqntulu nouerant. facta e fames in
tra. n fames panis. neq; sitis aq. s; audiendi uer
bu di. Abiit itaq; homo de bethlehe iuda. ut
pegrinaret in regione moabitide. cu uxore
sua et duob libis. Homo naq; iste. prim uide
licet parens nr. abiit de bethlehe iuda de do
mo panis. hoc e paradysi. ut pegrinaret in re
gione moabitide. qd tribulatio interpretat. qn
do cu omi multitudine posteritatis sue. in hc
lacu miserie et tribulationis deuenit. amissis
gaudiis et deliciis qb imppetuu uti deberet.
si dnici pcepti puaricator n extitisset. Ipse
uocabat helimelech. et uxor ei noemi. Heli
melech q interpretat ds ms rex. naturalis lex.
accipit q cepit in pmitiua eccla patar

9 Admont, Stiftsbibliothek MS 650 f. 1v

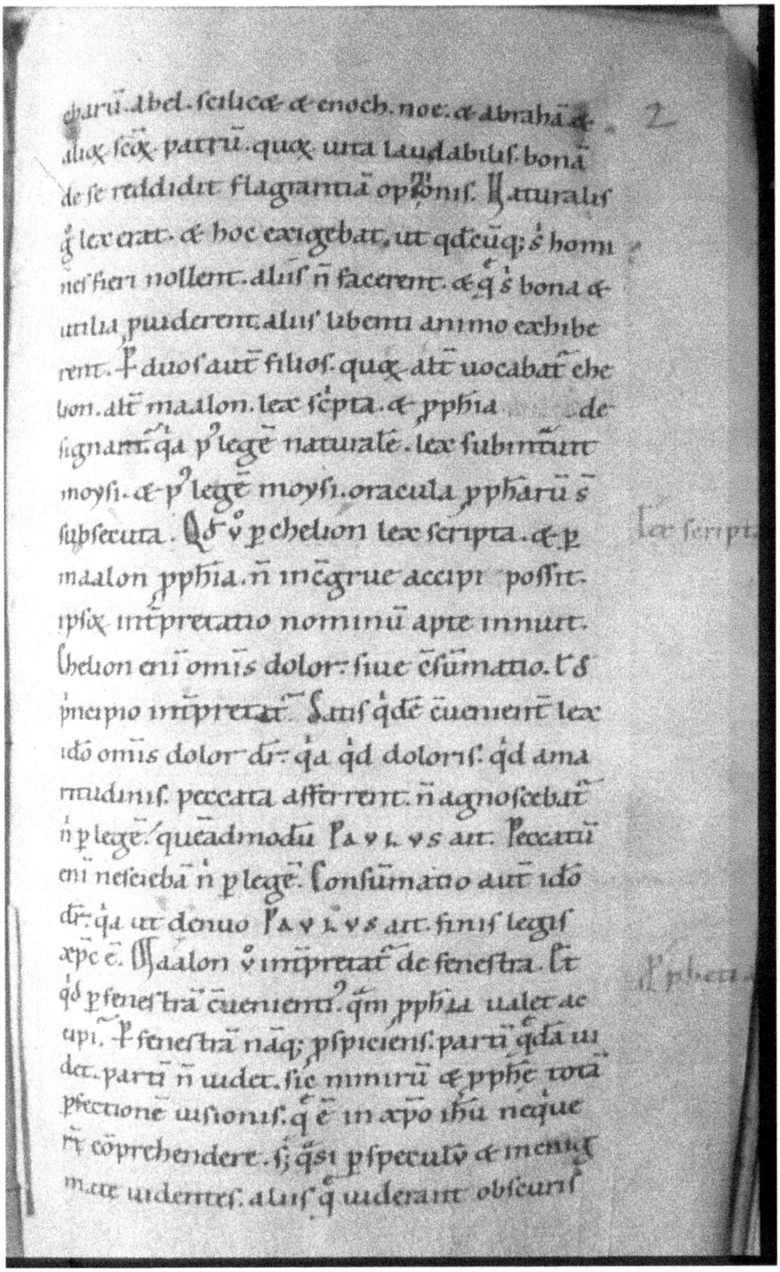
charum abel scilicet et enoch. noe. et abraham et
aliorum sanctorum patrum. quorum uita laudabilis bonam
de se reddidit flagrantiam opinionis. Naturalis
quippe lex erat. et hoc exigebat, ut quodcumque sibi homi
nes fieri nollent. aliis non facerent. et que sibi bona et
utilia prouiderent. aliis libenti animo exhibe
rent. Per duos autem filios. quorum alter uocabatur che
lion. alter maalon. lex scripta et prophetia de
signantur. quia post legem naturalem. lex subintrauit
moysi. et post legem moysi oracula prophetarum sunt
subsecuta. Quod uero per chelion lex scripta. et per
maalon prophetia non incongrue accipi possit.
ipsorum interpretatio nominum apte innuit.
Chelion enim omnis dolor siue consummatio. uel in
principio interpretatur. Satis quidem conuenit lex
ideo omnis dolor dicitur. quia quod doloris. quod ama
ritudinis. peccata afferrent. non agnoscebatur
nisi per legem. quemadmodum PAULUS ait. Peccatum
enim nesciebam nisi per legem. Consummatio autem ideo
dicitur. quia ut denuo PAULUS ait. finis legis
christus est. Maalon uero interpretatur de fenestra. Et
quod per fenestram conuenienter. quoniam prophetia ualet ac
cipi. Per fenestram namque prospiciens. partim quidem ui
det. partim non uidet. sic nimirum et prophete totam
perfectionem uisionis. que est in christo ihesu neque
runt comprehendere. sed quasi per speculum et in enig
mate uidentes. aliis que uiderant obscuris

10 Admont, Stiftsbibliothek MS 650 f. 2r

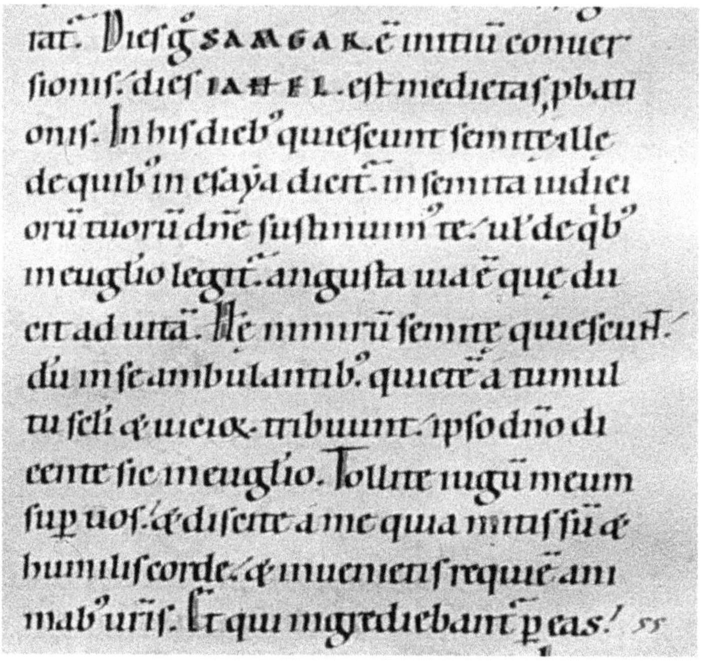

11 Admont, Stiftsbibliothek MS 17 p. 270

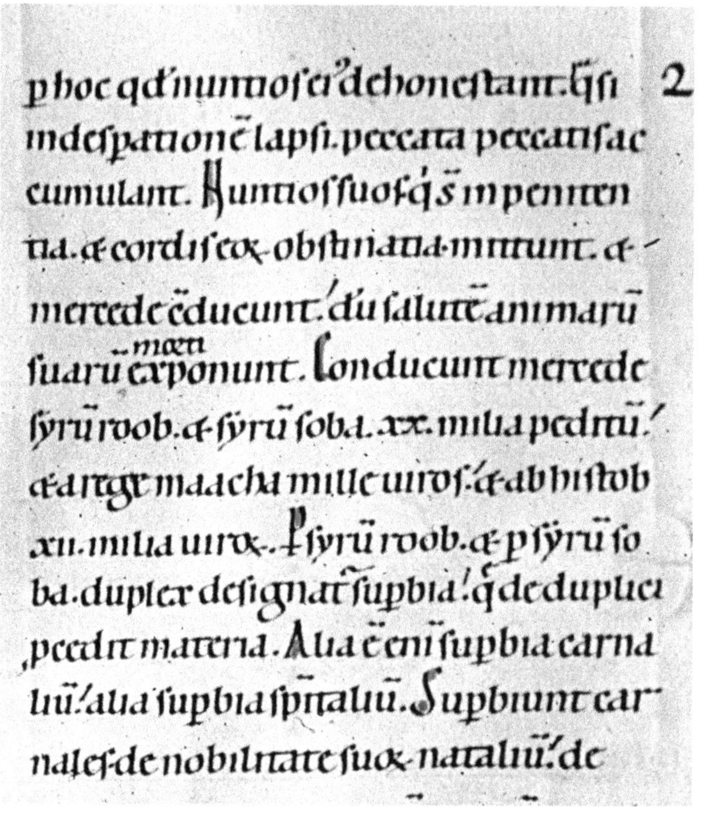

12 Admont, Stiftsbibliothek MS 16 p. 227

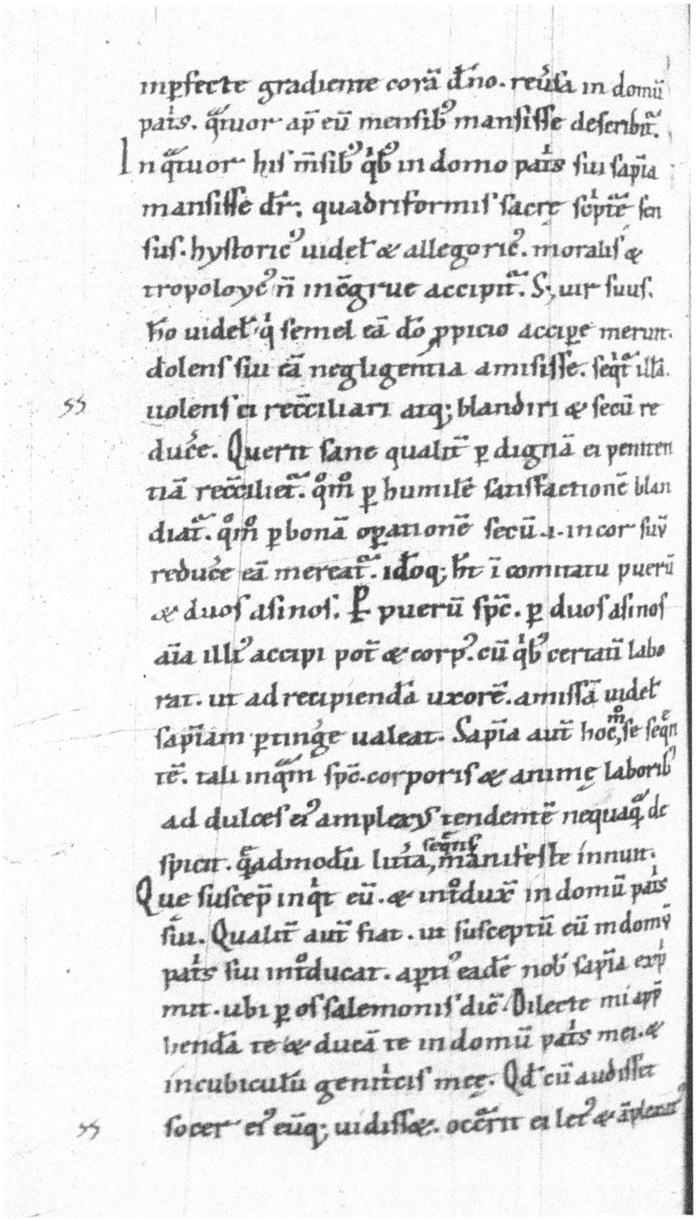

13 Vorau, Stiftsbibliothek MS 193 f. 157v

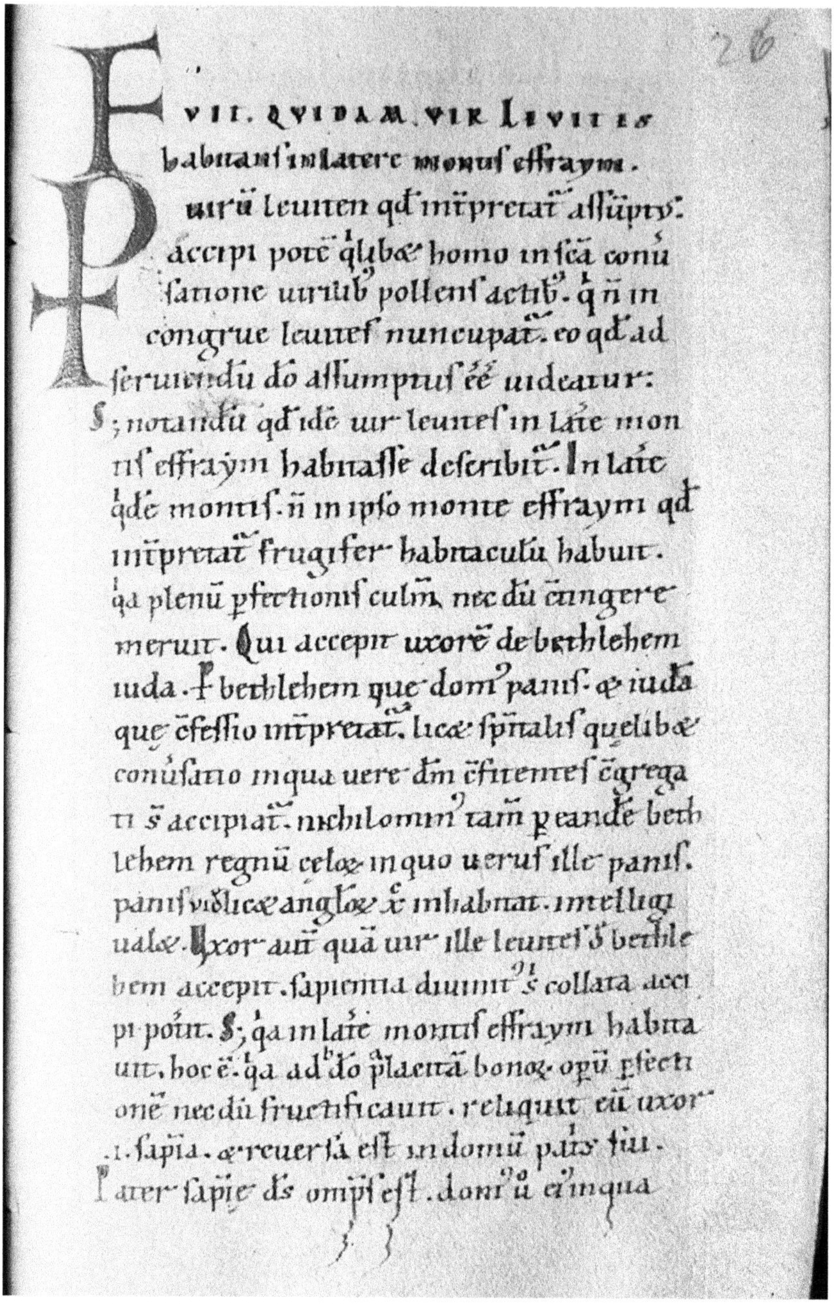
FVIT. QVIDAM. VIR LEVITES
habitans in latere montis effraym.
Virum leuiten quod interpretatur assumptus:
accipi potest quilibet homo in sancta conuer-
satione uirtutibus pollens actibus. Qui non in-
congrue leuites nuncupatur. eo quod ad
seruiendum deo assumptus esse uideatur:
Sed notandum quod idem uir leuites in latere mon-
tis effraym habitasse describitur. In latere
quidem montis. non in ipso monte effraym quod
interpretatur frugifer habitaculum habuit.
quia plenum perfectionis culmen nec dum contingere
meruit. Qui accepit uxorem de bethlehem
iuda. Per bethlehem que domus panis. et iuda
que confessio interpretatur. licet spiritualis quelibet
conuersatio in qua uere deum confitentes egrega-
ti sunt accipiatur. nichilominus tamen per eandem beth-
lehem regnum celorum in quo uerus ille panis.
panis uidelicet angelorum Christus inhabitat. intelligi
ualet. Uxor autem quam uir ille leuites de bethle-
hem accepit. sapientia diuinitus collata acci-
pi potest. Sed quia in latere montis effraym habita-
uit. hoc est. quia ad deo placentam bonorum operum perfecti-
onem necdum fructificauit. reliquit eum uxor
id est sapientia. et reuersa est in domum patris sui.
Pater sapientie deus omnipotens est. domus uero eius in qua

14 Admont, Stiftsbibliothek MS 650 f. 26r

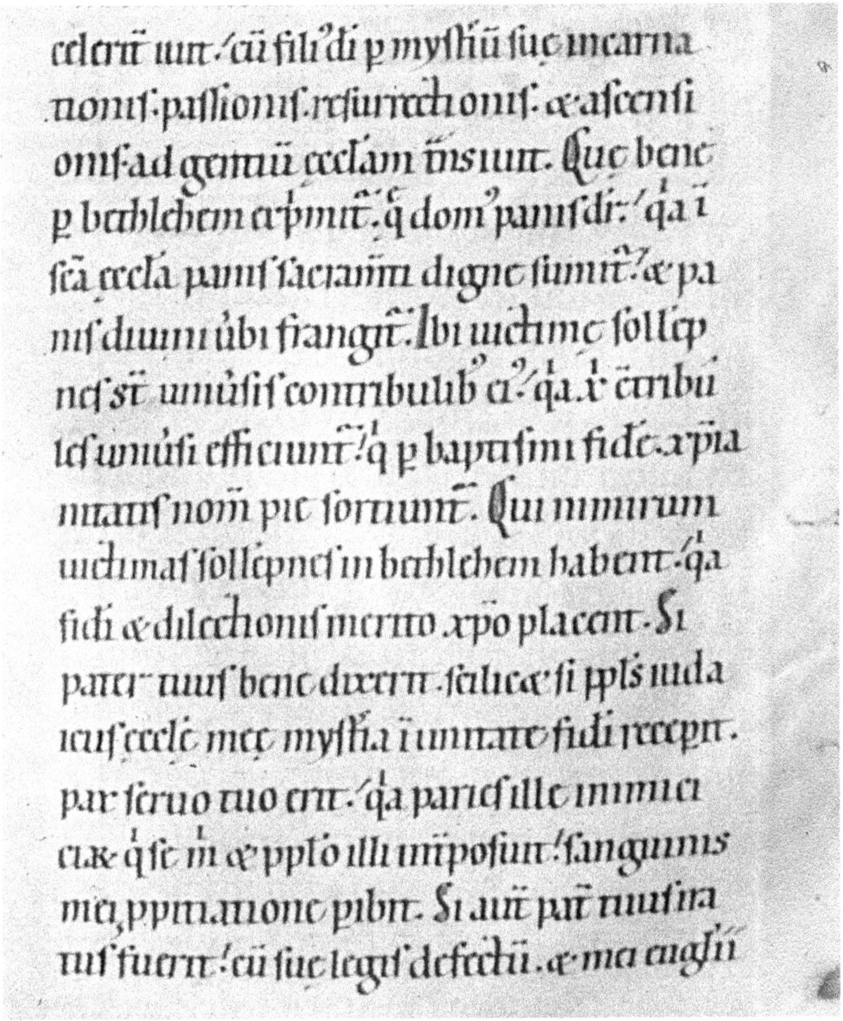

15 Admont, Stiftsbibliothek MS 16 p. 103

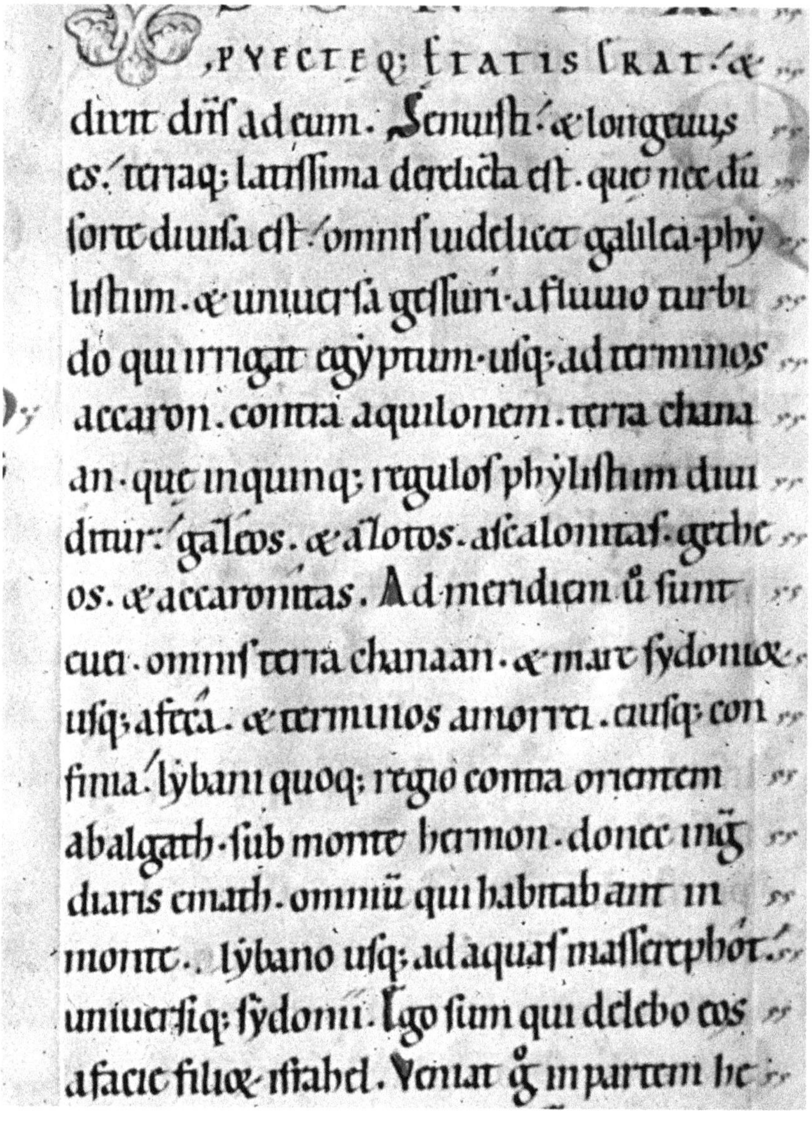
,PYPECTEQ; ETATIS ERAT. &
dixit dns ad eum. Senuisti. & longeuus
es. terraq; latissima derelicta est. que nec du
sorte diuisa est. omnis uidelicet galilea. phy
listhim. & uniuersa gessuri. a fluuio turbi
do qui irrigat egyptum. usq; ad terminos
accaron. contra aquilonem. terra chana
an. que in quinq; regulos phylisthiim diui
ditur. galeos. & azotos. ascalonitas. gethe
os. & accaronitas. Ad meridiem uero sunt
euei. omnis terra chanaan. & mare sydonior(um)
usq; afeca. & terminos amorrei. eiusq; con
finia. lybani quoq; regio contra orientem
a balgath. sub monte hermon. donec ingre
diaris emath. omniu(m) qui habitabant in
monte lybano usq; ad aquas masserephot.
uniuersiq; sydonii. Ego sum qui delebo eos
a facie filior(um) israhel. Veniat ergo in partem he

16 Admont, Stiftsbibliothek MS 17 p. 72

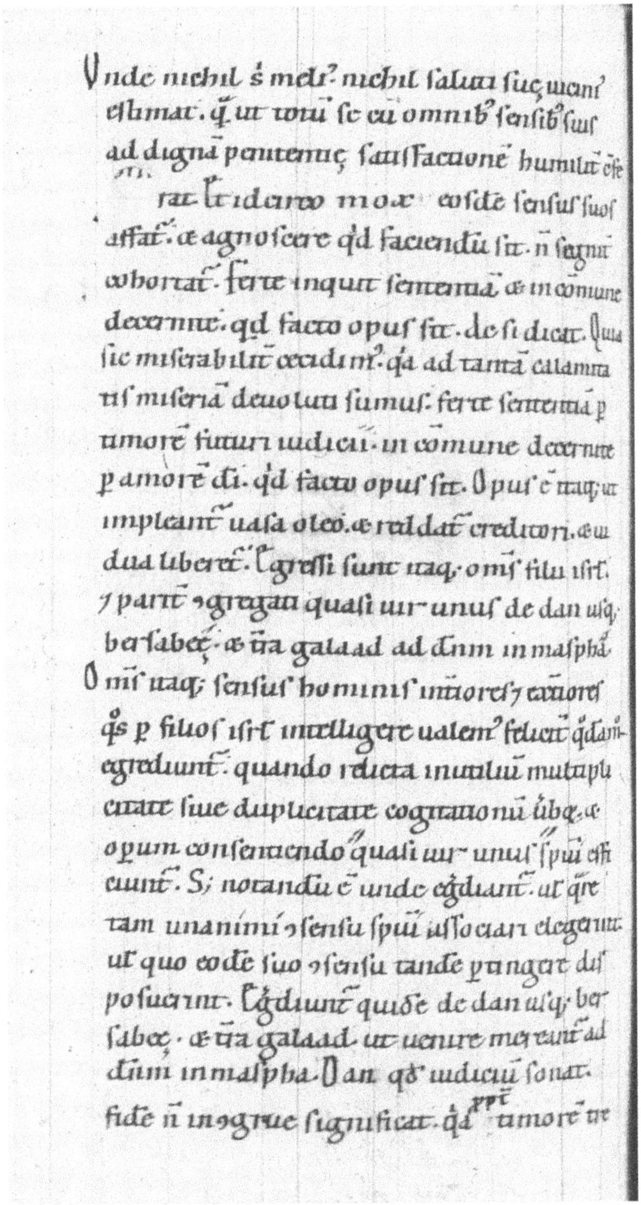

17 Vorau, Stiftsbibliothek MS 193 f. 167v

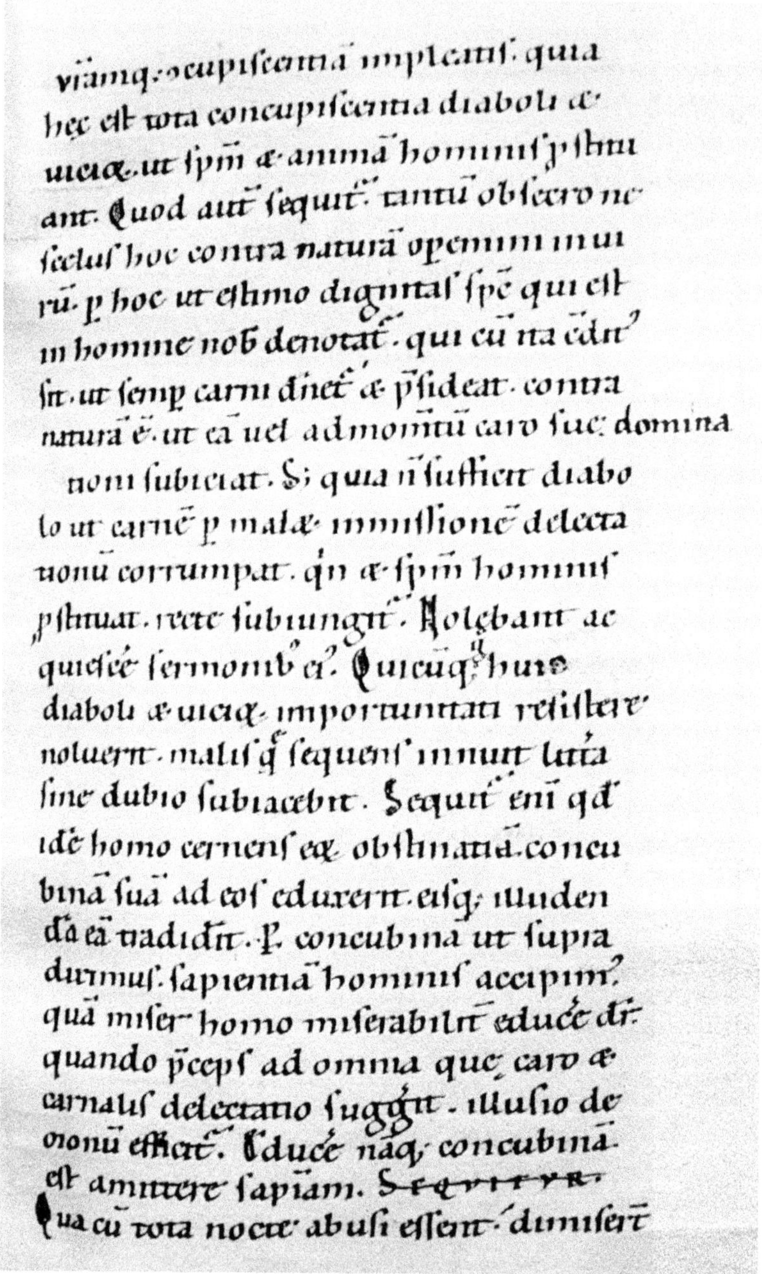

18 Admont, Stiftsbibliothek MS 682 f. 39r

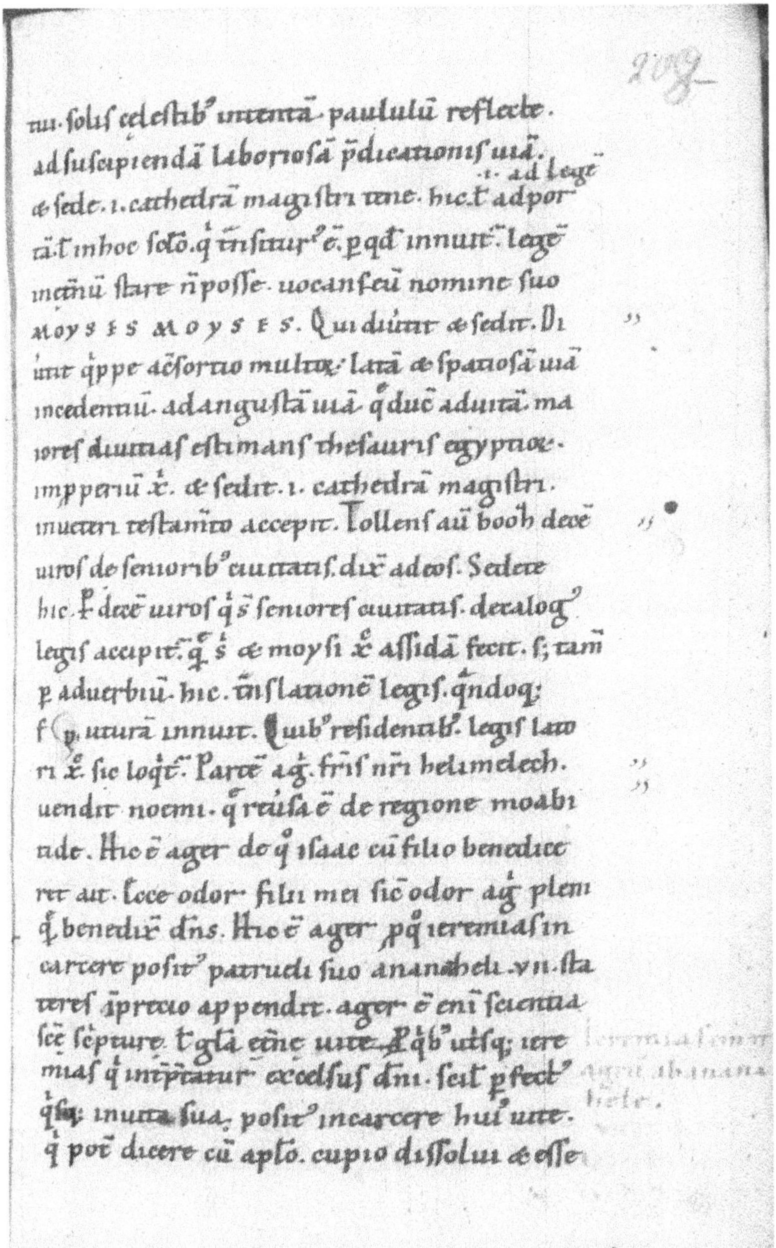

19 Vorau, Stiftsbibliothek MS 193 f. 208r

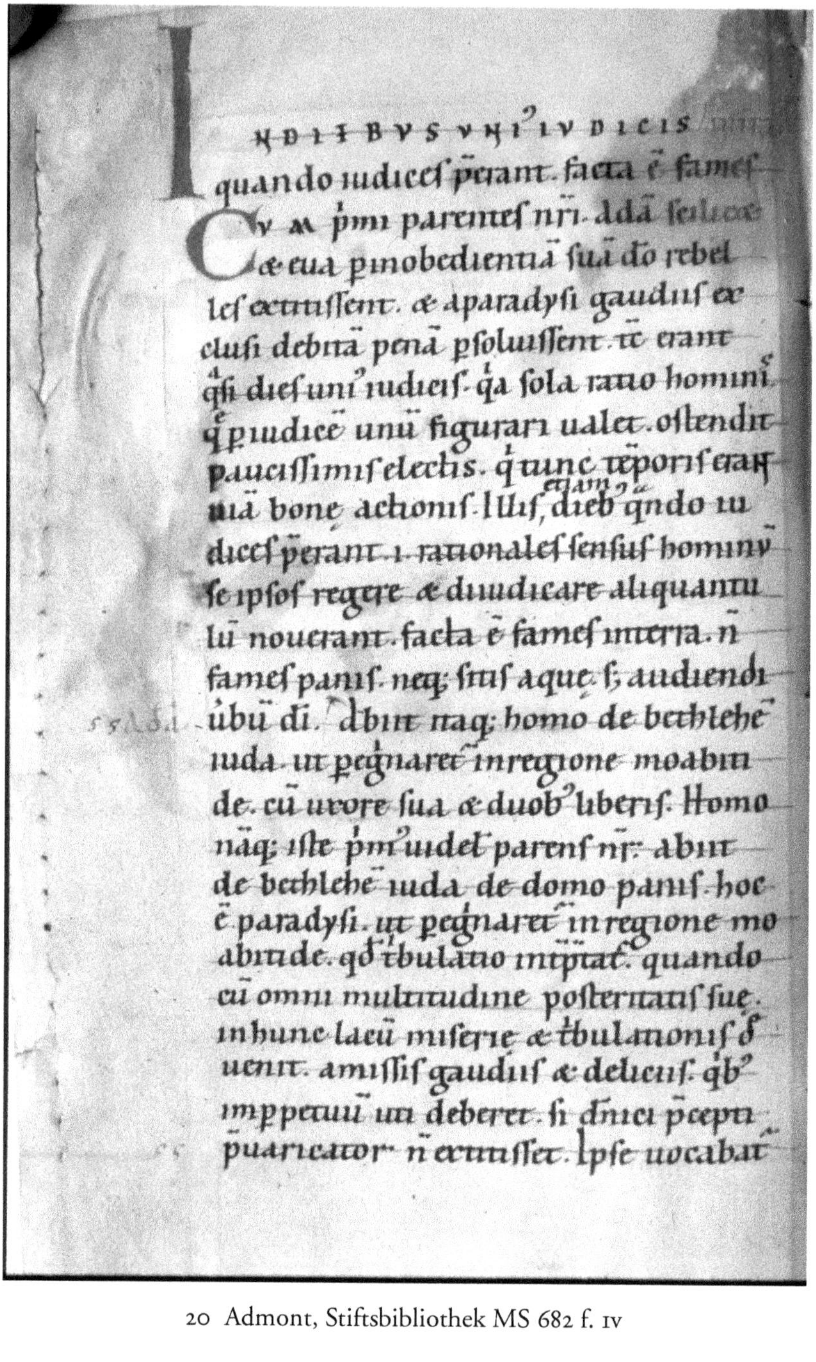

20 Admont, Stiftsbibliothek MS 682 f. 1v

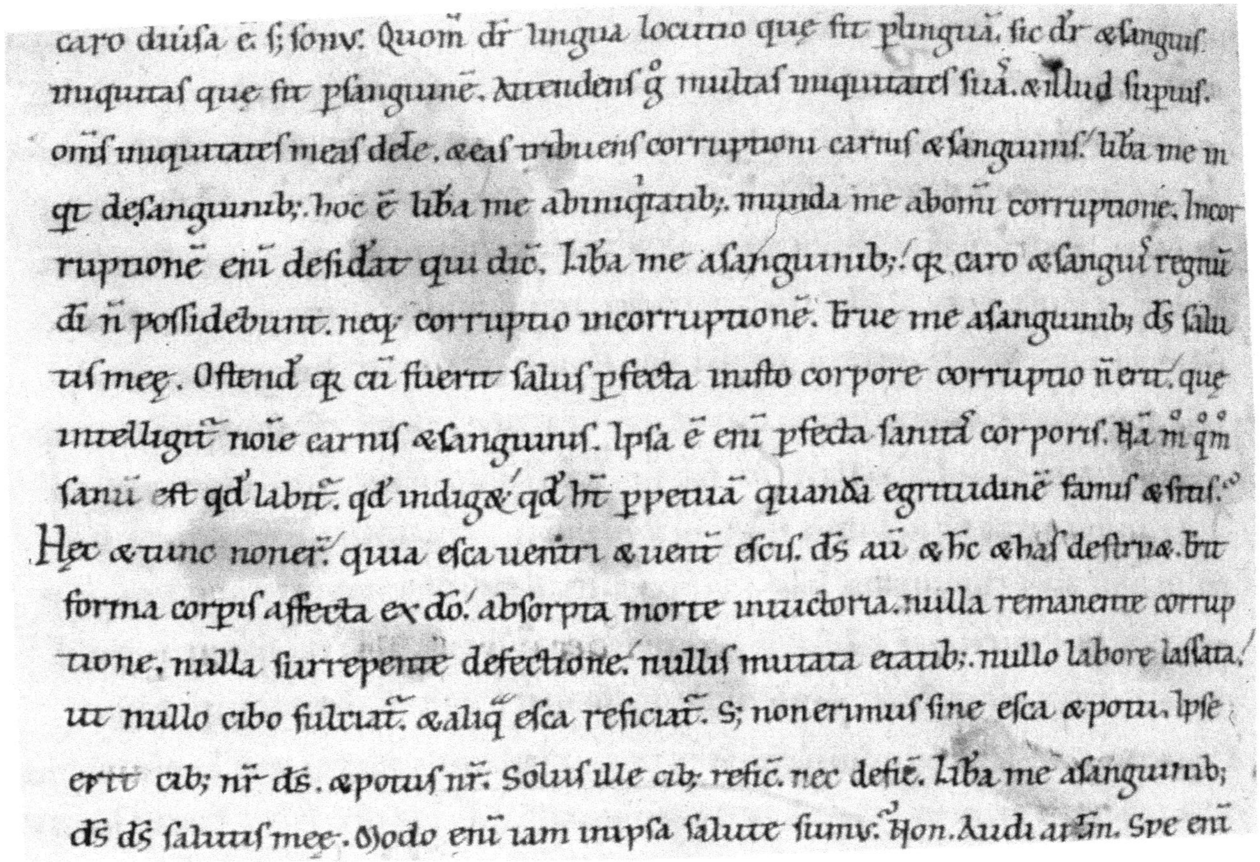

caro diuisa ē. s; sonus. Quom̄ dr̄ lingua locutio quę fit plinguā. sic dr̄ & sanguis
iniquitas quę fit psanguinē. Attendens g̊ multas iniquitates suā. & illud supius.
omīs iniquitates meas dele. & eas tribuens corruptioni carnis & sanguinis. Liba me in
qt de sanguinib;. hoc ē liba me ab iniquitatib;. munda me ab omī corruptione. Incor
ruptionē enī desid'at qui dic̄. Liba me a sanguinib;. qr caro & sanguis regnū
dī n̄ possidebunt. neq; corruptio incorruptionē. Erue me a sanguinib; ds̄ salu
tis meę. Ostend' qr cū fuerit salus pfecta insto corpore corruptio n̄ erit. quę
intelligit̄ noīe carnis & sanguinis. Ipsa ē enī pfecta sanitas corporis. Nā n̄ q̊m
sanū est qd' labit̄. qd' indiget qd' h̄t ppetuā quandā egritudinē famis & sitis.
Hec & tunc non erit. quia esca uentri & uent' escis. ds̄ aū & hc & has destruet. Erit
forma corpis affecta ex dō. absorpta morte in uictoria. nulla remanente corrup
tione. nulla surrepente defectione. nullis mutata etatib;. nullo labore lassata.
ut nullo cibo fulciat̄. & aliq̄ esca reficiat̄. S; non erimus sine esca & potu. Ipse
erit cib; nr̄ ds̄. & potus nr̄. Solus ille cib; refic̄. nec defic̄. Liba me a sanguinib;
ds̄ ds̄ salutis meę. Modo enī iam in ipsa salute sumus. Non. Audi aptm̄. Spe enī

21 Munich, Bayerische Staatsbibliothek Clm 17052 f. 214v

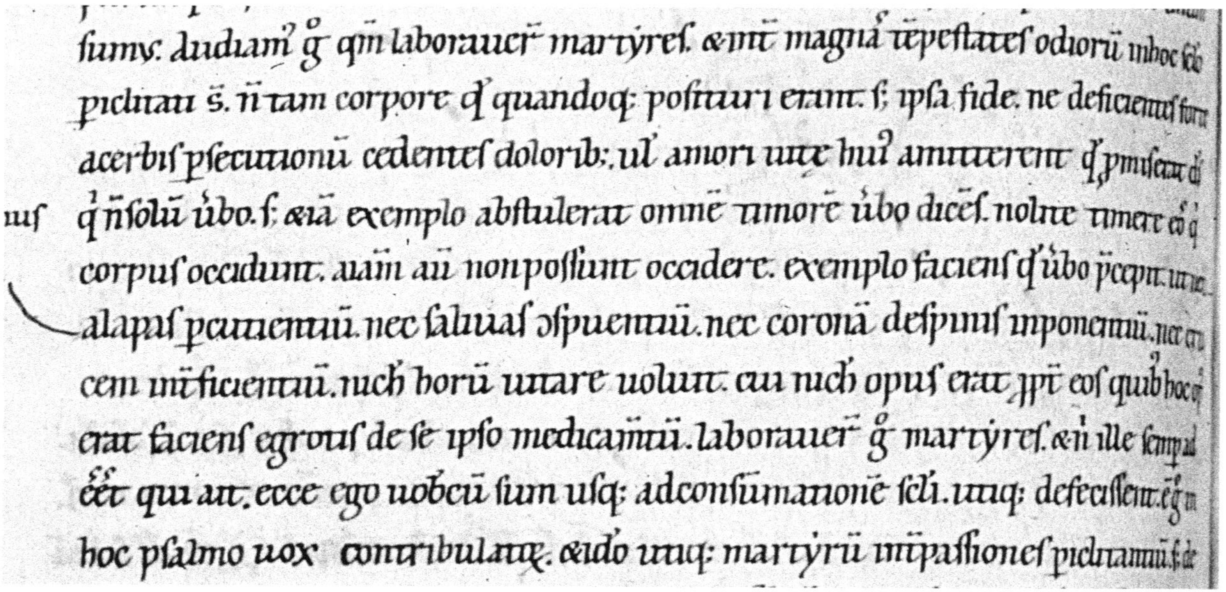

ius

sumus. audiam g qm laborauer martyres. et int magna tepestates odioru in hoc sclo
piclitati s. n tam corpore q quandoq; positi erant. s; ipsa fide. ne deficientes forte
acerbis psecutionu cedentes dolorib;. ul amori uite hui amitterent q pmiserat di
q n solu ubo. s; etia exemplo abstulerat omne timore ubo dices. nolite timere eos q
corpus occidunt. aiam aut non possunt occidere. exemplo faciens q ubo pcepit. ut ne
alapas pcutientiu. nec saliuas cspuentiu. nec corona de spinis inponentiu. nec cru
cem infigentiu. nich horu uitare uoluit. cui nich opus erat. ppt eos quib hoc op
erat faciens egrotis de se ipso medicamtu. laborauer g martyres. et n ille semp ad
eet qui ait. ecce ego uobcu sum usq; ad consumatione scli. utiq; defecissent. eg in
hoc psalmo uox contribulatq. et ido utiq; martyru in passiones piclitantiu s; de

22 Munich, Bayerische Staatsbibliothek Clm 17053 f. 180v

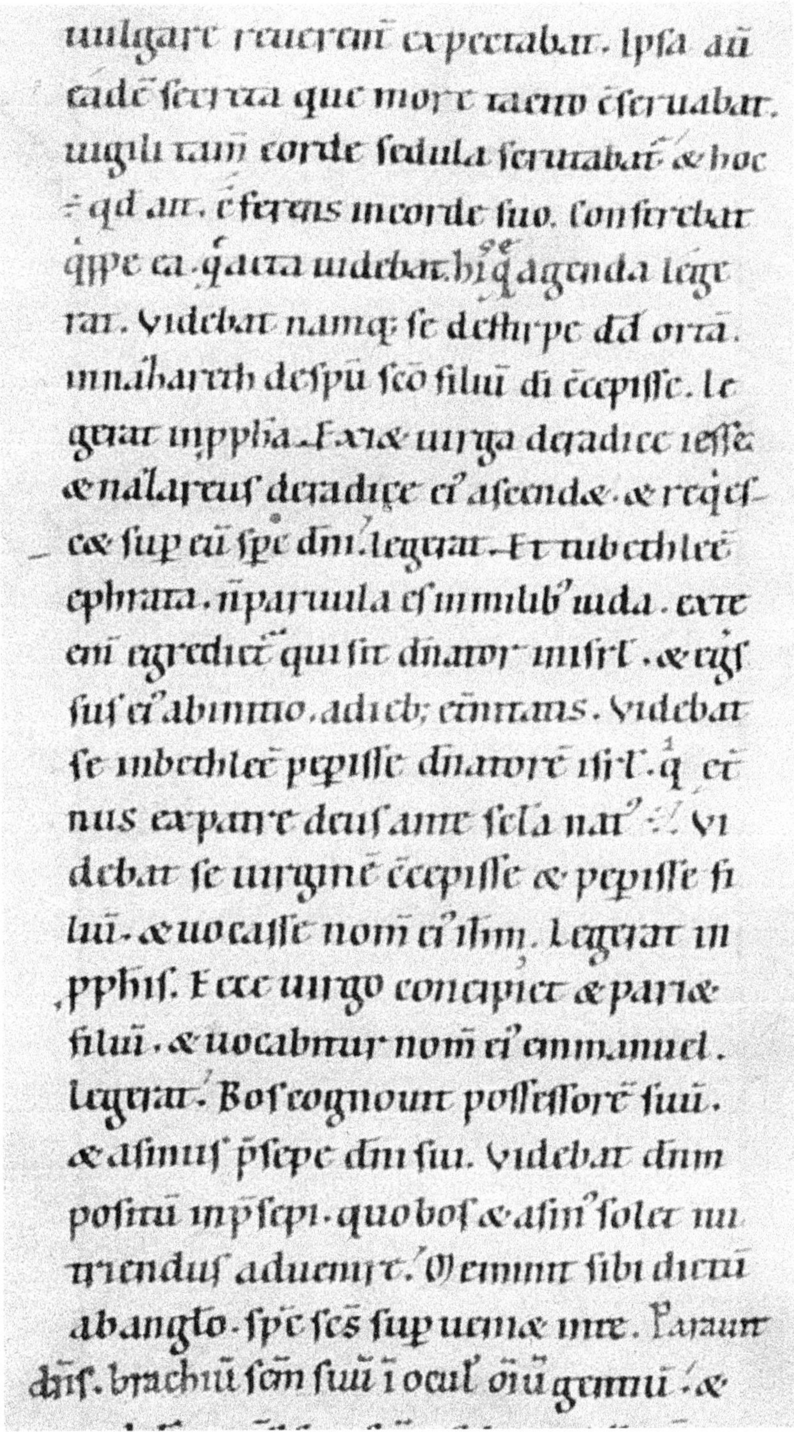

23 Munich, Bayerische Staatsbibliothek Clm 17087 f. 10v

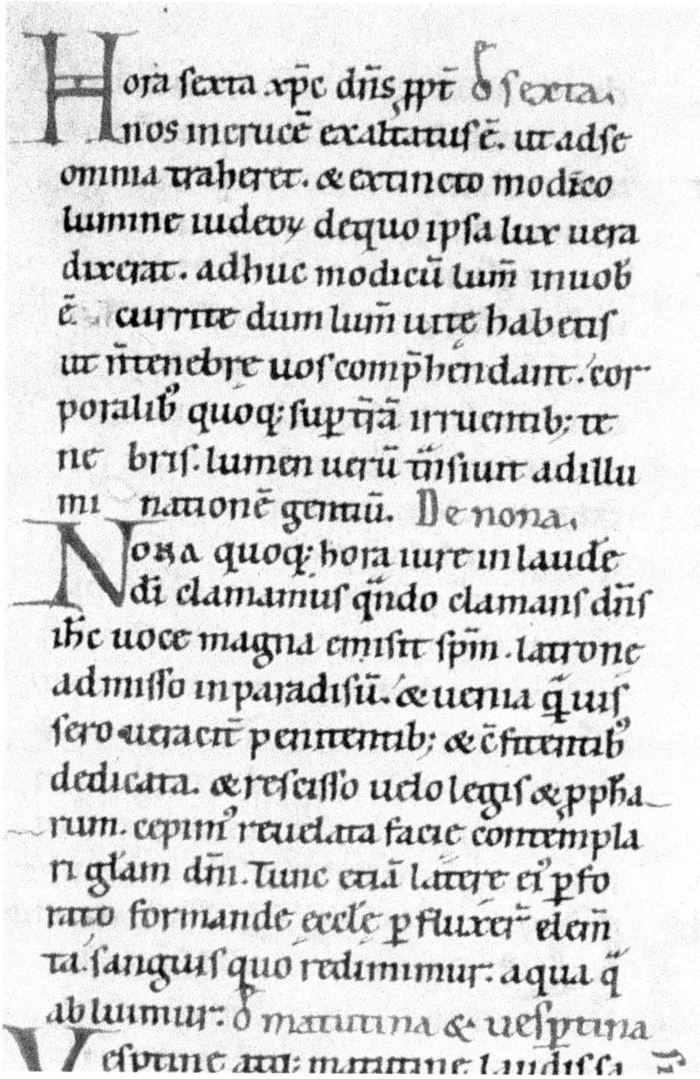

24 Munich, Bayerische Staatsbibliothek Clm 17116 f. 3r

# *Bibliography*

## MANUSCRIPTS

### ADMONT, STIFTSBIBLIOTHEK


MS 16 Irimbert of Admont, Commentaries
MS 17 Irimbert of Admont, Commentaries
MS 18 *Liber Matutinalis*
MS 58 Anonymous, Homilies for Feast Days
MS 62 Anonymous, Homilies for Feast Days
MS 63 Anonymous, Homilies for Sundays
MS 232 Patristic and Medieval Homilies
MS 243 Partial Hebrew Bible
MS 274 Gregory the Great, *Dialogi*
MS 289 Anselm of Canterbury, *Orationes* and *Meditationes*
MS 292 Hugh of Saint Victor, *Commentarius in hierarchiam Pseudo-Dionysii*
MS 376 Passional
MS 579 Honorius *Augustodunensis*, *Hexameron* and *Sigillum sanctae Mariae*; Gerhoch of Reichersberg's letter to the Admont nuns
MS 602 Passional; Gerhoch of Reichersberg's letter to the Admont nuns
MS 638 Miracles of the Blessed Virgin Mary
MS 650 Irimbert of Admont, Commentaries
Anonymous, Commentaries
MS 651 Irimbert of Admont, Commentaries
MS 682 Irimbert of Admont, Commentaries
MS 682 Irimbert of Admont, Commentaries


### MUNICH, BAYERISCHE STAATSBIBLIOTHEK


Clm 17036 Bible
Clm 17037 Bible
Clm 17040 Bible
Clm 17052 Augustine, *Enarrationes in psalmos* (1–50)
Clm 17053 Augustine, *Enarrationes in psalmos* (51–100)
Clm 17054 Augustine, *Homiliae super psalmos*
Clm 17087 *Homiliae in Epistolas et in Evangelia in circulum anni*
Clm 17116 Rupert of Deutz, *De divinis officiis*

| | |
|---|---|
| Clm 17161 | Gratian, *Decretum* |
| Clm 17174 | Praemonstratensian Statutes |
| Clm 17190 | Bernard of Clairvaux, *De consideratione* |
| Clm 17207 | Solinus, *Collectanea rerum memorabilium* |
| Clm 22002 | Homiliary |
| Clm 22003 | Homiliary |
| Clm 22004 | Flavius Josephus, *De bello iudaico* |
| Clm 22005 | Bible |
| Clm 22006 | Bible |
| Clm 22007 | Augustine, *Enarrationes in psalmos* |
| Clm 22008 | Gregory the Great, *Homiliae in Hiezechielem.* |
| Clm 22009 | Gregory the Great, *Moralia in Job* (6–10) |
| Clm 22010 | Gregory the Great, *Moralia in Job* (17–22) |
| Clm 22011 | Gregory the Great, *Moralia in Job* (23–27) |
| Clm 22012 | Gregory the Great, *Moralia in Job* (28–35) |
| Clm 22014 | Eusebius, *Historia ecclesiastica* |
| Clm 22015 | Cassiodorus, *Historia ecclesiastica tripartita* |
| Clm 22016 | Theological Collection |
| Clm 22030 | Hugh of St. Victor, *De sacramentis christianae fidei* |
| Clm 22034 | Jerome, *De viris inlustribus* |
| Clm 22040 | Ritual |
| Clm 22044 | Gospels |

### VORAU, STIFTSBIBLIOTHEK

| | |
|---|---|
| MS 193 | Irimbert, Commentaries |
| | Anonymous, Commentaries |

### WÜRZBURG, UNIVERSITÄTSBIBLIOTHEK

| | |
|---|---|
| M.p.th.f. 13 | Defensor, *Liber scintillarum* |
| M.p.th.f. 17 | Augustine, *Enarrationes in psalmos* |
| M.p.th.f. 28a | Isidore of Seville, *Synonyma* |
| | *Vita sanctae Eugeniae* |
| | *Vita sancti Potiti* |
| M.p.th.f. 45 | Gregory the Great, *Homiliae in Evangelia* |
| M.p.th.f. 69 | Pauline Epistles |
| M.p.th.f. 78 | *Passiones apostolorum* |


## PRINTED PRIMARY SOURCES


*Acta Murensia*, ed. P. Martin Keim. Quellen zur Schweizer Geschichte 3. Basel, 1883.

*Agii Vita et obitus Hathumodae*, ed. Georg Pertz. MGH, Scriptores 4, pp. 165–189.

Aldhelm, *De virginitate: Prosa*, ed. Rudolph Ehwald. MGH, Auctores antiquissimi 15, pp. 209–323.

Aldhelm, *The Prose Works*, ed. and trans. Michael Lapidge and Michael Herren. Totowa, NJ, 1979.

*Annales Admuntenses*, ed. Wilhelm Wattenbach. MGH, Scriptores 9, pp. 574–582.

*Annales Quedlinburgenses*, ed. Georg Pertz. MGH, Scriptores 3, pp. 22–69 and 72–90.

*Annales Scheftlarienses maiores*, ed. Philipp Jaffé. MGH, Scriptores 17, pp. 334–343.

Aurelian of Arles, *Regula ad virgines*. PL 68, cols. 399–406.

Bede, *Ecclesiastical History of the English People*, ed. and trans. Bertram Colgrave and R. A. B. Mynors. Oxford, 1969.

Benedict, Saint, *The Rule of Saint Benedict in Latin and English with Notes*, ed. Timothy Fry. Collegeville, MN, 1981. [RB 1980].

Boniface, *S. Bonifatii et Lulli epistolae*, ed. E. Dümmler. MGH, Epistolae 3, pp. 215–433.

Boniface, Saint, *The Letters of Saint Boniface*, ed. and trans. Ephraim Emerton. New York, 1940.

Boniface, *Briefe des Bonifatius, Willibalds Leben des Bonifatius*, ed. M. Tangl, Ph. H. Kälb, and Reinhold Rau. Darmstadt, 1968.

Caesarius of Arles, *The Rule for Nuns of St. Caesarius of Arles: A Translation with a Critical Introduction*, ed. and trans. Mother Maria Caritas McCarthy. Studies in Mediaeval History 16. Washington, DC, 1960.

*Casus monasterii Petrishusensis*, ed. Otto Feger, pp. 624–683. Schwäbische Chroniken der Stauferzeit 3. Lindau and Konstanz, 1956.

*Catalogus praepositorum Scheftlariensium*, ed. Philipp Jaffé. MGH, Scriptores 17, pp. 347–350.

*Collectio Reinheresbrunnensis*, ed. Friedel Peeck, MGH, Epistolae Selectae 5. Munich, 1978.

*Consuetudines Germaniae, Redactio sancti Emmerammi dicta Einsidlensis*, ed. D. Maria Wegener and D. Candida Elvert, pp. 187–256. Corpus Consuetudinum Monasticarum 7/3, ed. Kassius Hallinger. Siegburg, 1984.

*Constitutiones Hirsaugienses*. PL 150, cols. 927–1146.

Glauche, Günther and Hermann Knaus, eds., *Mittelalterliche Bibliothekskataloge Deutschlands und der Schweiz*, vol. IV/2. Munich, 1979. [$MBK_g$].

Grimlaic, *Regula solitariorum*. PL 103, cols. 575–664.

Hallinger, Kassius, ed., *Corpus Consuetudinum Monasticarum* 7/3. Siegburg, 1984.

Herman of Tournai, *De miraculis s. Mariae Laudunensis*. PL 156, cols. 961–1018.

Herrad von Landsberg, *Hortus Deliciarum*, ed. Rosalie Green. 2 vols. Studies of the Warburg Institute 36, ed. J. B. Trapp, Leiden, 1979.

*Historiae et Annales Windbergenses*, ed. Philipp Jaffé. MGH, Scriptores 17, pp. 559–566.

Hödl, Günther and Peter Classen, eds., *Die Admonter Briefsammlung*. MGH, Die Briefe der deutschen Kaiserzeit 6. Munich, 1983.

Höppl, Reinhard, ed., *Die Traditionen des Klosters Wessobrunn*. Quellen und Erörterungen zur bayerischen Geschichte, NS 32/1. Munich, 1982.

Hrotsvit von Gandersheim, *Opera*. Nuremberg, 1501.

Hugeburc of Heidenheim, *Vita Willibaldi episcopi Eichstetensis et Vita Wynnebaldi abbatis Heidenheimensis auctore sanctimoniali Heidenheimensi*, ed. O. Holder-Egger. MGH, Scriptores 15, pp. 80–117.

Hugo, Charles-Louis, ed., *Sacri et canonici Ordinis Praemonstratensis annales*. Sacrae antiquitatis monumenta historica, dogmatica, diplomatica, notis illustrata 1. Nancy, 1725.

Huygens, R. B. C., *Le moine Idung et ses deux ouvrages, "Argumentum super quatuor questionibus," et "Dialogus duorum monachorum."* Studi Medievali 13. Spoleto, 1972.

*Institutio sanctimonialium Aquisgranensis*, ed. A. Werminghoff. MGH, Concilia 2, pp. 421–456.
Jerome, Saint, *Select Letters of Saint Jerome*, ed. and trans. F. A. Wright. London, 1933.
Kraemer, Ross S., ed., *Maenads, Martyrs, Matrons, Monastics: A Sourcebook on Women's Religions in the Greco-Roman World.* Philadelphia, 1988.
*Kronkjken van Emo en Menko*. Werken Vitgegeven door het Historisch Genootschap NS 4. Utrecht, 1866.
Le Paige, Jean, *Bibliotheca Praemonstratensis ordinis*. Paris, 1633.
McNamara, Jo Ann, trans., *The Ordeal of Community*. Toronto, 1990.
ed. and trans., *Sainted Women of the Dark Ages*. Durham, NC, 1992.
Mairold, Maria, *Die datierten Handschriften in der Steiermark ausserhalb der Universitätsbibliothek Graz bis zum Jahre 1600*. 2 vols. Katalog der datierten Handschriften in Lateinscher Schrift in Österreich 7. Vienna, 1988.
*Monumenta Mallerstorfensia*. Monumenta Boica 15 (Munich, 1786), pp. 247–434.
Möser-Mersky, Gerlinde, ed., *Mittelalterliche Bibliothekskataloge Österreichs*. Vol. III. Graz, Vienna, Cologne, 1961. [ÖMBK].
*Necrologium Admuntense*, ed. Sigismund Herzberg-Fränkel. MGH, Necrologia Germaniae 2, pp. 287–309.
*Necrologium Scheftlariense*, ed. Franciscus Ludovicus Baumann. MGH, Necrologia Germaniae 3, pp. 116–133.
*Necrologium Wessobrunnense*, ed. Franciscus Ludovicus Baumann. MGH, Necrologia Germaniae 1, pp. 42–52.
O'Sullivan, Jeremiah F., Joseph Lehey, and Grace Perrigo, trans., *Cistercians and Cluniacs: The Case for Cîteaux. A Dialogue between Two Monks and an Argument on Four Questions by Idung of Prüfening*. Cistercian Fathers Series 33. Kalamazoo, MI, 1977.
Otloh, *Vita Sancti Wolfkangi*, ed. Georg Waitz. MGH, Scriptores 4, pp. 521–542.
Pez, Bernard, ed., *Thesaurus anecdotorum novissimus: seu Veterum monumentorum, praecipue ecclesiasticorum, ex germanicis potissimum bibliothecis adornata collectio recentissima*. 6 vols. Augsburg, 1721–1729.
ed., *Bibliotheca ascetica antiquo-nova*. 12 vols. Regensburg, 1723–1725.
Robinson, P. R., *Catalogue of Dated and Datable Manuscripts c. 737–1600 in Cambridge Libraries*. Cambridge, 1988.
Rudolph of Fulda, *Vita Leobae abbatissae biscofesheimensis auctore Rudolpho*, ed. Georg Waitz. MGH, Scriptores 15, pp. 118–131.
Ruf, Paul, ed., *Mittelalterliche Bibliothekskataloge Deutschlands und der Schweiz* vol. III/1. Munich, 1932. [MBKr].
*Salzburger Urkundenbuch*, ed. Willibald Hauthaler and Franz Martin. 4 vols. Salzburg, 1910.
*Sancti Caesarii vita*. Sancti Caesarii Episcopi Arelatensis Opera Omnia 2, ed. D. Germanus Morin. Maretioli, 1942.
Talbot, C. H., ed. and trans., *The Anglo-Saxon Missionaries in Germany*. London, 1954.
Van Waefelghem, Raphael, "Les premiers statuts de l'Ordre de Prémontré." *Les Analectes de l'Ordre de Prémontré* 11 (1913): 3–74.
*Vita Beatae Herlucae*. AASS, 2 April, pp. 549–554.
*Vita Bertilae abbatissae calensis*, ed. W. Levison. MGH, Script. rer. mer. 6, pp. 95–109.
*Vita Edigna von Puch*. AASS, 3 February, p. 668.
*Vita Gebehardi, Thiemonis, Chunradi, Eberhardi, Chunradi II Archiepiscoporum cum chronico Admuntensi*, ed. Philipp Jaffé. MGH, Scriptores 9, pp. 34–51.

*Vita Joannis abbatis Gorzienzis auctore Iohanne abbate s. Arnulfi.* MGH, Scriptores 4, pp. 335–377.
*Vita Mathildis reginae (posterior)*, ed. Georg Pertz. MGH, Scriptores 4, pp. 282–302.
*Vita Mathildis reginae antiquior*, ed. Rudolf Koepke. MGH, Scriptores 10, pp. 573–582.
*Vita sanctae Judith et Salomae.* AASS, 5 June, pp. 492–498.
*Vita sanctae Liutbirgae*, ed. Georg Pertz. MGH, Scriptores 4, p. 159.
*Vita, ut videtur, cuiusdam Magistrae Monialum Admuntensium in Styria saeculo XII.* Analecta Bollandiana 12 (1893), pp. 356–366.
von Gandersheim, Hrotsvita, *Opera.* Nuremberg, 1501.
Watson, Andrew G., *Catalogue of Dated and Datable Manuscripts c. 435–1600 in Oxford Libraries.* Oxford, 1984.
Webber, Teresa and Andrew G. Watson, eds., *The Libraries of the Augustinian Canons.* Corpus of British Medieval Library Catalogues 6. London, 1998.
Weissthanner, Alois, ed., *Die Traditionen des Klosters Schäftlarn, 760–1305.* Quellen und Erörterungen zur bayerischen Geschichte, NS 10/1. Munich, 1953.
Wichner, Jakob, *Catalogus codicum manu scriptorum Admontensis.* Admont, 1888. (*Catalog of Manuscripts in Stift Admont, Austria.* Ann Arbor, 1982.)

## SECONDARY SOURCES

Abstreiter, Leo, *Geschichte der Abtei Schäftlarn.* Schäftlarn, 1916.
Alexander, Jonathan J. G., *Medieval Illuminators and their Methods of Work.* New Haven, 1992.
Anson, Peter F., *The Call of the Desert: The Solitary Life in the Christian Church.* London, 1964.
Ardura, Bernard, *Abbayes, prieurés et monastères de l'ordre de Prémontré en France des origines à nos jours.* Nancy, 1993.
Arnold, Klaus, "Admont und die monastische Reform des 12. Jahrhunderts." *Zeitschrift der Savigny-Stiftung für Rechtsgeschichte* 89, Kanonistische Abteilung 58 (1972): 350–369.
Autenrieth, Johanne, *Datierte Handschriften in Bibliotheken der Bundesrepublik Deutschland.* Stuttgart, 1984.
Backmund, Norbert, *Monasticon Praemonstratense.* 3 vols. Staubing, 1956.
*Die Kollegiat und Kanonissenstifte in Bayern.* Kloster Windberg, 1973.
*Geschichte des Prämonstratenserordens.* Grafenau, 1986.
Bader, Karl Sigfried, *Das Benediktinerinnenkloster Friedenweiler und die Erschließung des südöstlichen Schwarzwaldes.* Veröffentlichungen aus dem fürstlich Fürstenbergischen Archiv 2 (1938).
Baker, Derek, *Medieval Women.* Oxford, 1978.
Baltrusch-Schneider, Dagmar Beate, "Klosterleben als Alternative Lebensform zur Ehe?" In *Weibliche Lebensgestaltung im frühen Mittelalter*, ed. Hans-Werner Goetz, pp. 45–64. Cologne, 1991.
Bange, E. F., *Eine bayerische Malerschule des XI. und XII. Jahrhunderts.* Munich, 1923.
Barraclough, Geoffrey, ed. and trans., *Medieval Germany, 911–1250.* Vol. II. Oxford, 1938.
Barrow, Julia, "Education and the Recruitment of Cathedral Canons in England and Germany 1100–1225." *Viator* 20 (1989): 117–137.
Basedow, Armin, *Die Inclusen in Deutschland vornehmlich in der Gegend des Niederrheins um die Wende des 12. und 13. Jahrhunderts.* Heidelberg, 1896.

Bateson, Mary, "Origin and Early History of Double Monasteries." *Transactions of the Royal Historical Society* 13 (1899): 137–198.

Bauerreiss, Romuald, "St. Georgen im Schwarzwald, ein Reformmittelpunkt Südostdeutschlands im beginnenden 12. Jahrhundert." *StM* 51–2 (April 1933): 196–201 (vol. 51); 47–56 (vol. 52).

*Kirchengeschichte Bayerns*. 7 vols. Munich, 1947–1970.

Bäuml, Franz H., "Varieties and Consequences of Medieval Literacy and Illiteracy." *Speculum* 55 (1980): 237–265.

Beach, Alison I., "Claustration and Collaboration between the Sexes in the Twelfth-Century Scriptorium." In *Monks and Nuns, Saints and Outcasts: Religion in Medieval Society*, ed. Sharon Farmer and Barbara Rosenwein, pp. 57–75. Ithaca, 2000.

"Voices from a Distant Land: Fragments of a Twelfth-Century Nuns' Letter Collection." *Speculum* 77 (2002): 34–54.

"Listening for the Voices of Admont's Twelfth-Century Women." In *Voices in Dialogue: New Approaches to Women's Cultural History*, ed. Linda Olsen and Kathryn Kerby-Fulton. Notre Dame, IN, forthcoming.

Bell, David N., *What Nuns Read: Books and Libraries in Medieval English Nunneries*. Cistercian Studies Series 158. Kalamazoo, MI, 1995.

Bénédictins du Bouveret, *Colophons de manuscrits occidentaux des origines au XVIe siècle*. Spicilegii Friburgensis Subsidia 2–7. Fribourg, 1979.

Bennet, Judith M., Elisabeth A. Clark, Jean F. O'Bar, B. Anne Vilen, and Sarah Westphal-Wihl, eds., *Sisters and Workers in the Middle Ages*. Chicago, 1989.

Benson, Robert L. and Giles Constable, eds., *Renaissance and Renewal in the Twelfth Century*. Cambridge, MA, 1982.

Bériou, Nicole, *La prédication de Ranulphe de la Houblonnière: sermons aux clercs et aux simples gens à Paris au XIIIe siècle*. 2 vols. Paris, 1987.

Berman, Constance, "Men's Houses, Women's Houses: The Relationship Between the Sexes in Twelfth-Century Monasticism." In *Medieval Studies at Minnesota* 2, ed. Andrew MacLeish, pp. 43–52. St. Cloud, MN, 1988.

"The Economic Practices of Cistercian Women's Communities: A Preliminary Look." In *Studiosorum Speculum: Studies in Honor of Louis J. Lekai, O. Cist*, pp. 15–32. Cistercian Studies Series 141. Kalamazoo, MI, 1993.

Bernhard, Marianne, *Stifts- und Klosterbibliotheken*. Munich, 1983.

Berschin, Walter, "Konrad Weiss über Hrotsvit von Gandersheim." *Literaturwissenschaftliches Jahrbuch*, NS 24 (1983): 235–243.

Bischoff, Bernhard, "Wer ist die Nonne von Heidenheim?" *StM* 49 (1931): 387–388.

"Die liturgische Musik und das Bildungswesen im frühmittelalterlichen Stift Essen." *Annalen des historischen Vereins für den Niederrhein* 157 (1955): 191–194.

"Die Kölner Nonnenhandschriften und das Skriptorium von Chelles." *Mittelalterliche Studien* 1 (Stuttgart, 1966): 16–34.

*Kalligraphie in Bayerns: achtes bis zwölftes Jahrhundert*. Wiesbaden, 1981.

*Latin Palaeography: Antiquity and the Middle Ages*, trans. Dáibhí Ó Cróinín and David Ganz. Cambridge, 1990.

Bischoff, Bernhard and Josef Hofmann, *Libri Sancti Kyliani. Die Würzburger Schreibschule und die Dombibliothek im 8. und 9. Jahrhundert*. Quellen und Forschungen zur Geschichte des Bistums und Hochstifts Würzburg 6. Würzburg, 1952.

Bishop, T. A. M., "The Prototype of the Liber glossarum." In *Medieval Scribes, Manuscripts and Libraries: Essays Presented to N.R. Ker*, ed. M. B. Parkes and Andrew G. Watson, pp. 69–86. London, 1978.

"The Scribes of the Corbie a-b." In *Charlemagne's Heir: New Perspectives on the Reign of Louis the Pious*, ed. Peter Godman and Roger Collins, pp. 523–535. Oxford, 1990.

Blumenthal, Uta-Renate, *The Investiture Controversy: Church and Monarchy from the Ninth to the Twelfth Century*. Philadelphia, 1988.

Bodarwé, Katrinette, "Sanctimoniales litteratae – Schriftlichkeit und Bildung in den ottonischen Frauenstiften Gandersheim, Essen und Quedlinburg." Ph.D. diss., University of Bonn, 2001.

Borgehammar, Stephan, "Who Wrote the Admont Sermon Corpus – Gottfried the Abbot, his Brother Irimbert, or the Nuns?" In *De l'homélie au sermon: Histoire de la prédication médiévale*, ed. Jacqueline Hamesse and Xavier Hermand, pp. 47–51. Louvain, 1993.

Borst, Arno, *Medieval Worlds: Barbarians, Heretics and Artists in the Middle Ages*. Trans. Eric Hansen. Cambridge, 1991.

Boyle, Leonard E., *Medieval Latin Paleography. A Bibliographical Introduction*. Toronto Medieval Bibliographies. Toronto, 1984.

Bradley, John W., *A Dictionary of Miniaturists, Illuminators, Calligraphers and Copyists, with References to their works, and Notices of their Patrons, from the Establishment of Christianity to the Eighteenth century*. 3 vols. London, 1887.

Brasington, Bruce. "The Prologue of Ivo of Chartres: A Fresh Consideration from the Manuscripts." In *Proceedings of the Eighth International Congress of Medieval Canon Law*, ed. Stanley Chodorow, pp. 3–22. Monumenta Iuris Canonici. Series C: Subsidia 9. Vatican City, 1992.

Braun, Johann Wilhelm, "Die Überlieferung der Schriften Gottfrieds und Irimberts von Admont mit einem Lebensabriß Irimberts." Ph.D. diss., University of Giessen, 1967.

"Irimbert von Admont." *Frühmittelalterliche Studien* 7 (1973): 266–323.

Brown, Michelle, *A Guide to Western Historical Scripts: From Antiquity to 1600*. London, 1993.

Buberl, Paul, *Die illuminierten Handschriften in Steiermark*. Beschreibendes Verzeichnis der illuminierten Handschriften in Österreich, ed. Franz Wickhoff. Vol. IV. Leipzig, 1911.

Bühler, Irma, "Forschungen über Benediktiner-Doppelklöster im heutigen Bayern." *Zeitschrift für bayerische Kirchengeschichte* 3–5 (1930): 197–207 (vol. 3); 1–13 and 199–229 (vol. 4); 17–33, 229–251 (vol. 5).

Bühler, Johannes, *Klosterleben im deutschen Mittelalter*. Leipzig, 1921.

Buzas, L., *Deutsche Bibliotheksgeschichte des Mittelalters*. Elemente des Buch- und Bibliothekswesens 1. Wiesbaden, 1975.

Cames, G., "Les grands ateliers d'enluminure religieuse en Alsace à l'époque romane." *Cahiers de l'Art Médiéval* 5 (1967): 5.

Carr, Annemarie Weyl. "Women as Artists in the Middle Ages." *The Feminist Art Journal* 5 (1976): 5–10.

Chenu, Marie Dominique, *Nature, Man, and Society in the Twelfth Century*, ed. and trans. Jerome Taylor and Lester K. Little. Chicago, 1968.

Christ, Karl, "Mittelalterliche Bibliotheksordnungen für Frauenklöster." *Zentralblatt für Bibliothekswesen* 59, nos. 1/2 (January 1942): 1–29.

"Bibliotheksgeschichte des Mittelalters." *Zentralblatt für Bibliothekswesen* 61, nos. 1/2 (1947): 233–253.

Clanchy, M. T., *From Memory to Written Record: England 1066–1307*. Second edition. Oxford, 1993.

Clark, John W., *The Care of Books*. Cambridge, 1901.

Classen, Peter, "Gottfried von Admont." *Neue deutsche Biographie* 6. Berlin, 1953–.

*Gerhoch von Reichersberg. Eine Biographie*. Wiesbaden, 1960.

Cohen, Adam, "The Art of Reform in a Bavarian Nunnery around 1000." *Speculum* 74 (1999): 990–1020.

*The Uta Codex: Art, Philosophy, and Reform in Eleventh-Century Germany*. University Park, PA, 2000.

Condello, Emma and Giuseppe de Gregoria, eds., *Scribi e colofoni: le sottoscrizioni di copisti dalle origini all'avvento della stampa*. Atti del seminario de Erice 10, Colloquio del Comité international de paléographie latine. Spoleto, 1995.

Constable, Giles, *Letters and Letter-Collections*. Typologie des sources du moyen âge occidental 17. Turnhout, 1976.

"Aelred of Rievaulx and the Nun of Watton." In *Medieval Women*, ed. Derek Baker, pp. 205–226. Oxford, 1978.

*Three Studies in Medieval Religious and Social Thought*. Cambridge, 1995.

*The Reformation of the Twelfth Century*. Cambridge, 1996.

Contreni, John J., "The Tenth Century: The Perspective from the Schools." In *Haut moyen-âge culture, éducation et société: études offertes à Pierre Riché*, pp. 379–387. La Garenne-Colombes, 1991.

Crusius, Irene, ed., *Studien zum Kanonissenstift*. Veröffentlichungen des Max-Planck-Instituts für Geschichte 167. Göttingen, 2001.

Curschmann, Michael, "Texte – Bilder – Strukturen. Der *Hortus deliciarum* und die frühmittelhochdeutsche Geistlichendichtung." *Deutsche Vierteljahrsschrift für Literaturwissenschaft und Geistesgeschichte* 55 (1981): 379–418.

Darlington, R. R., "The Anglo-Saxon Period." In *The English Church and the Continent*, pp. 9–24. London, 1959.

de Fontette, Micheline, *Les religieuses à l'âge classique du droit canon*. Paris, 1967.

de Hamel, Christopher, *Scribes and Illuminators*. Toronto, 1992.

de Jong, Mayke, "Growing up in a Carolingian Monastery: Magister Hildemar and his Oblates." *Journal of Medieval History* 9 (1983): 99–128.

de Meulemeester, Maur, "Les soeurs norbertines de Tusschenbeek." *Analecta Praemonstratensia* 4 (1928): 30–44.

Dengler-Schreiber, Karin, *Scriptorium und Bibliothek des Klosters Michelsberg in Bamberg*. Studien zur Bibliotheksgeschichte. Second edition. Graz, 1979.

Dereine, Charles, "Le premier ordo de Prémontré." *Revue Bénédictine* 58, no. 1 (1949): 84–92.

Derolez, Albert, *Les catalogues de bibliothèques*. Typologie des sources du moyen âge occidental 31, ed. L. Genicot. Turnhout, 1979.

"Pourquoi les copistes signaient-ils leurs manuscrits?" In *Scribi e colofoni*, ed. Condello and de Gregonia, pp. 37–56. Spoleto, 1995.

Diringer, David, *The Illuminated Book*. London, 1958.

*The Book Before Printing: Ancient, Medieval & Oriental*. New York, 1982.

Doerr, Ottmar, *Das Institüt der Inclusen in Suddeutschland*. Münster, 1934.

Donat, Lin, "Vie et coutume monastique dans la Vita de Jean de Gorze." In *L'Abbaye de Gorze au Xe siècle*, ed. Michel Parisse and Otto Gerhard Oexle, pp. 159–182. Nancy, 1993.

Dopsch, Heinz, ed., *Geschichte Salzburgs: Stadt und Land.* 7 vols. Salzburg, 1981.

Dronke, Peter, *Women Writers of the Middle Ages.* Cambridge, 1984.

Dunbar, Agnes B. C., *A Dictionary of Saintly Women.* 2 vols. London, 1904.

Eberl, Immo, *Geschichte des Benediktinerinnenklosters Urspring bei Schelklingen, 1127–1806: Außenbeziehungen, Konventsleben, Grundbesitz.* Schriften zur südwestdeutschen Landeskunde 13. Tübingen, 1978.

Eckenstein, Lina, *Woman Under Monasticism: Chapters on Saint-Lore and Convent Life between A.D. 500 and A.D. 1500.* Cambridge, 1896.

Eder, Christine, *Die Schule des Klosters Tegernsee in frühen Mittelalter im Spiegel der Tegernseer Handschriften.* Münchener Beiträge zur Mediävistik und Renaissance-Forschung. Munich, 1972.

Elkins, Sharon, *Holy Women of Twelfth-Century England.* Chapel Hill, 1988.

Ennen, Edith, *The Medieval Woman*, trans. Edmund Jephcott. Oxford, 1989.

Erens, A., "Les soeurs dans l'Ordre de Prémontré." *Analecta Praemonstratensia* 5 (1929): 5–26.

Fassler, Margot E., "The Office of the Cantor in Early Western Monastic Rules and Customaries: A Preliminary Investigation." *Early Medieval Music* 5 (1985): 29–51.

Faust, Ulrich, "Gottfried von Admont: ein monastischer Autor des 12. Jahrhunderts." *StM* 75 (1964): 272–359.

Felten, Franz J., "Wie adelig waren Kanonissenstifte (und andere weibliche Konvente) im (frühen und hohen) Mittelalter?" In *Studien zum Kanonissenstift*, ed. Irene Crusius, pp. 39–128. Veroffentlichungen des Max-Planck-Instituts für Geschichte 167. Göttingen, 2001.

Ferrante, Joan M., "The Education of Women in the Middle Ages in Theory, Fact, and Fantasy." In *Beyond Their Sex: Learned Women of the European Past*, ed. Patricia H. Labalme, pp. 9–42. New York, 1980.

Foot, Sarah, *Veiled Women.* 2 vols. Aldershot, 2000.

Freed, John B., *Noble Bondsmen: Ministerial Marriages in the Archdiocese of Salzburg, 1100–1343.* Ithaca, NY, 1995.

"German Source Collections: The Archdiocese of Salzburg as a Case Study." In *Medieval Women and the Sources of Medieval History*, ed. Joel T. Rosenthal, pp. 80–121. Athens, GA, 1990.

Fuhrmann, Horst, "Zur handschriftlichen Verbreitung der Vita B. Herlucae des Paul von Bernried." *Analecta Bollandiana* 74 (1956): 362–369.

*Germany in the High Middle Ages c. 1050–1200.* Cambridge, 1986.

Funk, Ph., *Jakob de Vitry, Leben und Werke.* Beiträge zur Kulturgeschichte des Mittelalters und der Renaissance 3. Berlin, 1909.

Gampl, Inge, *Adelige Damenstifte. Untersuchungen zur Entstehung adeliger Damenstifte in Österreich unter besonderer Berücksichtigung der alten Kanonissenstifte Deutschlands und Lothringens.* Wiener rechtsgeschichte Arbeiten 5. Vienna and Munich, 1960.

Ganz, David, "The Preconditions for Caroline Minuscule." *Viator* 18 (1987): 23–43.

Ganz, Peter, ed., *The Role of the Book in Medieval Culture.* Bibliologia: Elementa ad Librorum Studia Pertinentia 3–4. Turnhout, 1986.

Garand, Monique-Cécile, "Manuscrits monastiques et scriptoria aux XIe et XIIe siècles." *Codicologica* 3, ed. A. Gruys and J. P. Gumbert, pp. 9–33. Leiden, 1980.

Geary, Patrick J., *Phantoms of Remembrance: Memory and Oblivion at the End of the First Millennium.* Princeton, 1994.

Glare, P. G. W., ed., *Oxford Latin Dictionary*. Oxford, 1982.
Glenisson, Jean, *Le livre au Moyen Age*. Paris, 1988.
Goetz, Hans-Werner, *Das Geschichtsbild Ottos von Freising*. Beihefte zum Archiv für Kulturgeschichte 19. Cologne and Vienna, 1984.
ed., *Weibliche Lebensgestaltung im frühen Mittelalter*. Cologne, 1991.
Goetz, Walter, "Die Frauen und die Literatur im Mittelalter." *Archiv für Kulturgeschichte* 26, no. 2 (1935): 129–161.
Gold, Penny Schine, *The Lady and the Virgin: Image, Attitude and Experience in Twelfth-Century France*. Chicago, 1985.
Golding, Brian, *Gilbert of Sempringham and the Gilbertine Order c. 1130–1300*. Oxford, 1995.
Goldschmidt, E. Ph., "Austrian Monastic Libraries." *Transactions of the Bibliographical Society* 24, no. 1 (1944): 46–65.
Gonsa, Gerhard, "Einige paläographische Beiträge zur Erforschung der Admonter Schreibschule des 12. Jahrhunderts." MA thesis, University of Vienna, 1989.
Gottschaller, Eva, "Hugeburc von Heidenheim: philologische Untersuchungen zu den Heiligenbiographien einer Nonne des achten Jahrhunderts." *Münchener Beiträge zur Mediävistic und Renaissance-Forschung* 12 (1973): 9–115.
Graves, Frank Pierrepont, *History of Education during the Middle Ages and the Transition to Modern Times*. New York, 1919.
Green, Rosalie B., ed., *Hortus deliciarum*. London, 1979.
Griesser, Bruno, "Fragmente einer Diemuthandschrift aus dem Kloster Stams mit Hieronymus- und Augustinusbriefen." *StM* 53 (1935): 241–256.
Grundmann, Herbert, "Die Frauen und die Literatur im Mittelalter. Ein Beitrag zur Frage nach der Entstehung des Schrifttums in der Volkssprache." *Archiv für Kulturgeschichte* 26 (1936): 129–161.
"Litteratus – illiteratus. Der Wandel einer Bildungsnorm vom Altertum zum Mittelalter." *Archiv für Kulturgeschichte* 40 (1958): 1–65.
*Religious Movements in the Middle Ages*. Trans. Steven Rowan. Notre Dame, IN, 1995.
Hager, G., "Die Bautätigkeit und Kunst im Kloster Wessobrunn." *Oberbayerisches Archiv* 48 (1892): 195–521.
Haight, Anne Lyon, ed., *Hroswitha of Gandersheim: Her Life, Times, and a Comprehensive Bibliography*. New York, 1965.
Hallinger, Kassius, *Gorze-Kluny: Studien zu den monastischen Lebensformen und Gegensätzen im Hochmittelalter*. Studia Anselmiana 22–25. Rome, 1950.
Hamburger, Jeffrey F., "Art, Enclosure and the *Cura Monialium*: Prolegomena in the Guise of a Postscript." *Gesta* 31 (1992): 108–134.
Härdelin, Alf, "God's Visiting. A Basic Theme in the Homilies Ascribed to Godfrey of Admont." In *Munkarnas och mystikernas medeltid. Tjugofyra kapitel om teologi, spiritualitet och kultur*, pp. 201–218. Opuscula Selecta 1. Skellefteå, 1996.
Harrsen, Meta, "The Manuscripts." In *Hroswitha of Gandersheim: Her Life, Times, and Works, and a Comprehensive Bibliography*, ed. Anne Lyon Haight. New York, 1965.
Hartmann, W., "Review of Walter Steinbock's Erzbischof Gebhard von Salzburg." *Deutsches Archiv* 29 (1973): 628–629.
Hashagen, Justus, *Otto von Freising als Geschichtsphilosoph und Kirchenpolitiker*. Leipzig, 1900.
Haskins, Charles Homer, *The Renaissance of the Twelfth Century*. Cambridge, MA, 1927.
Hauck, Albert, *Kirchengeschichte Deutschlands*. 5 vols. Berlin, 1954.

Haverkamp, Alfred, *Medieval Germany, 1056–1273*. Second edition, trans. Helga Braun and Richard Mortimer. Oxford, 1992.

Heimbucher, Max, *Die Orden und Kongregationen der katholischen Kirche*. 2 vols. Third edition. Paderborn, 1933.

Heinrich, Mary Pia, *The Canonesses and Education in the Early Middle Ages*. Washington, DC, 1924.

Hemmerle, Josef, *Die Benediktinerklöster in Bayern*. Bayerische Heimatforschung 4. Munich, 1951.

Herlihy, David, "Land, Family, and Women in Continental Europe, 701–1200." In *Women in Medieval Society*, ed. Susan Mosher Stuard, pp. 13–45. Philadelphia, 1976.

Hilpisch, Stephen, *Die Doppelklöster: Entstehung und Organisation*. Beiträge zur Geschichte des alten Mönchtums und des Benediktinerordens 15 (1928): 1–95.

*Benedictinism through Changing Centuries*. trans. Leonard J. Doyle. Collegeville, MN, 1958.

Historical Commission of the Bavarian Academy of Science. *Neue deutsche Biographie* 1. Berlin, 1953.

Hochstetler, Donald, *A Conflict of Traditions: Women in Religion in the Early Middle Ages, 500–840*. Lanham, MD, 1992.

Hoffmann, Hartmut, "Zur Geschichte Ottos des Grossen." *Deutsches Archiv* 28 (1972): 42–73.

*Buchkunst und Königtum im ottonischen und frühsalischen Reich*. 2 vols. MGH, Schriften 30–31. Stuttgart, 1986.

"Das Skriptorium von Essen in ottonischer und frühsalischer Zeit." In *Kunst im Zeitalter der Kaiserin Theophanu*, pp. 113–153, Akten des Internationalen Colloquiums veranstaltet vom Schnütgen-Museum Köln. 13.–15. Juni 1991, ed. Anton von Euw and Peter Schreiner. Cologne, 1993.

*Bamberger Handschriften des 10. und 11. Jahrhunderts*. Hanover, 1995.

Hofmeister, Adolf, "Studien über Otto von Friesing." *Neues Archiv* 37 (1912): 99–161.

Hofmeister, Philipp, "Von den Nonnenklöstern." *Archiv für katholisches Kirchenrecht* 114 (1934): 3–96; 353–437.

Hollis, Stephanie, *Anglo-Saxon Women and the Church*. Woodbridge, 1992.

Howell, Martha, "A Documented Presence: Medieval Women in Germanic Historiography." In *Women in Medieval History and Historiography*, ed. Susan Mosher Stuard, pp. 101–131. Philadelphia, 1987.

Hunt, Noreen, ed., *Cluniac Monasticism in the Central Middle Ages*. London, 1971.

Huygens, R. B. C., "Zu Idung von Prüfening und seinen Schriften 'Argumentum super quatuor questionibus' und 'Dialogus duorum monachorum'." *Deutsches Archiv für Erforschung des Mittelalters* 27 (1971): 544–555.

Huyghebaert, N., *Les documents nécrologiques*. Typologie des sources du moyen âge occidental 4, ed. L. Genicot, Turnhout, 1972.

Irtenkauf, Wolfgang, *Hirsau: Geschichte und Kultur*. Sigmaringen, 1978.

Jakobs, Hermann, *Die Hirsauer: ihre Ausbreitung und Rechtsstellung im Zeitalter des Investiturstreites*. Kölner historische Abhandlungen 4. Cologne, 1961.

*Der Adel in der Klosterreform von St. Blasien*. Kölner historische Abhandlungen 16. Cologne and Graz, 1968.

Johanek, Peter, "Klosterstudien im 12. Jahrhundert," In *Schulen und Studium in sozialen Wandel des hohen und späten Mittelalters*, ed. Johannes Fried, pp. 35–68. Sigmaringen, 1986.

John, James J., "The Named (and Namable) Scribes in *Codices Latini Antiquiores*." In *Scribi e colofoni*, ed. Condello and de Gregoria, pp. 107–121. Spoleto. 1995.

Johnson, Penelope D., *Equal in Monastic Profession: Religious Women in Medieval France*. Chicago, 1991.

Junkelmann, Marcus, *Napoleon und Bayern: von den Anfängen des Königreiches*. Regensburg, 1985.

Karpp, Gerhard, "Bemerkungen zum Bücherbesitz des Essener Damenstifts um 900." In *Octogenario: Dankesgabe für Heinrich Karpp*. ed. Jurgen Honscheid and Gerhard Karpp, pp. 51–115. Düsseldorf, 1988.

"Bemerkungen zu den mittelalterlichen Handschriften des adeligen Damenstifts in Essen (9.–19. Jahrhundert)." *Scriptorium* 45 (1991): 163–204.

Kirchner-Feyerabend, Cornelia, *Otto von Freising als Diözesan- und Reichsbischof*. Frankfurt-am-Main, 1990.

Klemm, Elisabeth, *Die romanischen Handschriften der Bayerischen Staatsbibliothek*. 3 vols. Wiesbaden, 1980–1988.

Knapp, Fritz Peter, *Die Literatur des Früh- und Hochmittelalters in dem Bistümern Passau, Salzburg, Brixen, und Trient von den Anfängen bis zum Jahre 1273*. Geschichte der Literatur in Österreich 1. Graz, 1994.

Kottje, Raymund, "Klosterbibliotheken und monastische Kultur in der zweiten Hälfte des 11. Jahrhunderts." *Zeitschrift für Kirchengeschichte* 80 (1969): 145–162.

Kraus, Andreas, *Geschichte Bayerns: von den anfängen bis zur Gegenwart*. Munich, 1983.

Krause, Adalbert, "Eigentumsvermerke, Ex libris und Supralibros aus der Stiftsbibliothek Admont." *Biblos* 2 (1953): 14–25.

*Die Stiftsbibliothek in Admont*. Linz, 1969.

Kristeller, Paul Oskar, *Latin Manuscript Books Before 1600: A Bibliography of the Printed Catalogues and Unpublished Inventories of Extant Collections*. Third edition. New York, 1965.

Kronenberg, Kurt, *Roswitha von Gandersheim: Leben und Werk*. Bad Gandersheim, 1962.

Küsters, Urban, *Der verschlossene Garten: volkssprachliche Hohelied-Auslegung und monastische Lebensform im 12. Jahrhundert*. Studia Humaniora 2. Düsseldorf, 1985.

Lamy, Hugues, *L'Abbaye de Tongerloo depuis sa fondation jusqu'en 1263*. Recueil de travaux publiés par les membres des conférences d'histoire et de philologie 44. Louvain and Paris, 1914.

Lawless, George, ed., *Augustine of Hippo and his Monastic Rule*. Oxford, 1987.

Lawrence, C. H., *Medieval Monasticism: Forms of Religious Life in Western Europe in the Middle Ages*. Second edition. London and New York, 1989.

Leclercq, Jean, *The Love of Learning and the Desire for God: A Study of Monastic Culture*. New York, 1961.

"*Otium Monasticum* as a Context for Artistic Creativity." In *Monasticism and the Arts*, ed. Timothy Gregory Verdon, pp. 63–80. Syracuse, NY, 1984.

"Conversion to the Monastic Life in the Twelfth Century: Who, Why, and How?" In *Studiosorum Speculum: Studies in Honor of Louis J. Lekai, O. Cist*, pp. 201–231. Cistercian Studies Series. 141. Kalamazoo, MI, 1993.

Lefèvre, Pl., "Le problème des soeurs aux origines de l'abbaye d'Averbode." *Analecta Praemonstratensia* 52 (1976): 38–43.

Leistle, David, "Ueber Klosterbibliotheken des Mittelalters." *StM* 36 (1915): 197–228.
Lemaire, Jacques, *Introduction à la codicologie*. Publications de l'Institut d'Études Médiévales – Textes, Études, Congrès 9. Louvain, 1989.
Lesne, Émile, *Les livres, scriptoria et bibliothèques du commencement du VIIIe à la fin du XIe siècle*. Histoire de la propriété ecclésiastique en France 4. Lille, 1938.
Leuttner, Cölestin, *Historia monasterii Wessofontani*. 4 vols. Augsburg and Freiburg, 1753.
Levison, Wilhelm, "Review of K. Heinrich Schäfer, Die Kanonissenstifter im deutschen Mittelalter." *Westdeutsche Zeitschrift* 27 (1908): 491–512.
*England and the Continent in the Eighth Century*. Oxford, 1946.
Leyser, Henrietta, *Hermits and the New Monasticism: A Study of Religious Communities in Western Europe, 1000–1150*. London, 1984.
Leyser, Karl J., *Rule and Conflict in an Early Medieval Society: Ottonian Saxony*. Oxford, 1979.
*Medieval Germany and its Neighbors: 900–1250*. London, 1982.
Lifshitz, Felice, "Gender and Exemplarity East of the Rhine: Jesus, Mary, and the Saints in Manuscript Context." *Early Medieval Europe* 9 (2000): 325–343.
Lindner, Pirmin, *Monasticon Episcopatus Augustani antiqui. Verzeichnisse der Aebte, Pröpste und Aebtissinnen der Klöster der alten Diözese Augsburg*. Bregenz, 1913.
ed., *Germania Benedictina*. Augsburg, 1970–. vol. II.
Lingard, John, *The History and Antiquities of the Anglo-Saxon Church*. London, 1845.
Lintzel, Martin, "Die Mathilden-Viten und das Wahrheitsproblem in der Überlieferung der Ottonenzeit." *Archiv für Kulturgeschichte* 38 (1956): 152–166.
List, Rudolf, *Stift Admont. 1074–1974. Festschrift zur 900- Jahrfeier*. Reid im Innkreis, 1974.
Loeffler, K., *Deutsche Klosterbibliotheken*. Bücherei der Kultur und Geschichte 27. Bonn and Leipzig, 1922.
Lortz, Joseph, *Bonifatius und die Grundlegung des Abendlandes*. Wiesbaden, 1954.
Lowe, Elias Avery, *Codices Latini Antiquiores*. 11 vols. and supplement. Oxford, 1934–1971.
Löwe, Heinz, "Bonifatius und die bayerisch-frankische Spannung." *Jahrbuch für Fränkische Landesforschung* 15 (1955): 85–127.
Mabillon, Jean, *Iter Germanicum*. Hamburg, 1717.
McKitterick, Rosamond, "Knowledge of Canon Law in the Frankish Kingdoms before 789: Manuscript Evidence." *Journal of Theological Studies* NS 36 (1985): 97–117.
"The Diffusion of Insular Culture in Neustria between 650 and 850: the Implications of the Manuscript Evidence." In *La Neustrie. Les pays au nord de la Loire de 650 à 850*, pp. 395–492. Sigmaringen, 1989.
*The Carolingians and the Written Word*. Cambridge, 1989.
"Frauen und Schriftlichkeit im Frühmittelalter." In *Weibliche Lebensgestaltung im frühen Mittelalter*, pp. 67–118. Cologne and Vienna, 1991.
"Nuns' Scriptoria in England and Francia in the Eighth Century." *Francia* 19 (1992): 1–35; reprinted in eadem, *Books, Scribes and Learning*, article VII, pp. 1–35.
"Continuity and Innovation in Tenth-Century Ottonian Culture." In *Intellectual Life in the Middle Ages*, ed. Lesley Smith and Benedicta Ward, pp. 15–24. London, 1992.
*Books, Scribes and Learning in the Frankish Kingdoms, 6th–9th Centuries* (Aldershot, 1994).
ed., *The Uses of Literacy in Early Mediaeval Europe*. Cambridge, 1990.

McNamara, Jo Ann, "The Need to Give: Suffering and Female Sanctity in the Middle Ages." In *Images of Sainthood in Medieval Europe*, ed. Renate Blumenfeld-Kosinski and Timea Szell, pp. 199–221. Ithaca, NY, 1991.

*The Ordeal of Community*. Toronto, 1993.

ed. and trans., *Sainted Women of the Dark Ages*. Durham, NC, 1992.

Maitland, Samuel R. *The Dark Ages: A Series of Essays Intended to Illustrate the State of Religion and Literature in the Ninth, Tenth, Eleventh, and Twelfth Centuries*. London, 1853.

Mälzer, Gottfried and Hans Thurn, eds., *Die Bibliothek des Würzburger Domstifts, 742–1803*. Würzburg, 1988.

Mayo, Hope, "Three Merovingian Rules for Women." Ph.D. diss., Harvard University, 1974.

Mazal, Otto, *Buchkunst der Romantik*. Buchkunst im Wander der Zeiten 2. Graz, 1978.

McGuire, Thérèse B., "Monastic Artists and Educators of the Middle Ages." *Woman's Art Journal* 9, no. 2 (September 1988): 3–9.

Mews, Constant, "Monastic Educational Culture Revisited: The Witness of Zwiefalten and the Hirsau Reform." In *Medieval Monastic Education*, ed. George Ferzoco and Carolyn Muessig, pp. 182–200. London, 2000.

Mezler-Andelberg, Helmut J., "Admont und die Klosterreform zu Beginn des 12. Jahrhunderts." *Zeitschrift des historischen Vereines für Steiermark* 47 (1956): 28–42.

Millett, Bella, "Women in No Man's Land: English Recluses and the Development of Vernacular Literature in the Twelfth and Thirteenth Centuries." In *Women and Literature in Britain, c. 1150–1500*, ed. Carole M. Meale, pp. 86–103. Cambridge, 1993.

Miner, Dorothy, *Anastasie and Her Sisters*. Baltimore, 1974.

Mitterer, Sigisbert, ed., *1200 Jahre Kloster Schäftlarn*. Schäftlarn, 1962.

Montalembert, Charles Forbes, comte de, *The Monks of the West from Saint Benedict to Saint Bernard*. 7 vols. Edinburgh and London, 1879.

Morrison, Karl F., *Tradition and Authority in the Western Church, 300–1140*. Princeton, 1969.

Mundo, A., " 'Bibliotheca'. Bible et lecture du carême d'après saint Benoît." *Revue Bénédictine* 60 (1950): 65–92.

Muchar, A., "Handschriften des Stiftes Admont in Steiermark." *Neue Jahrbücher für Philologie und Pädagogik*. Supplement-Band 6 (1840): 421–444.

Mütherich, F., "The Library of Otto III." In *The Role of the Book in Medieval Culture*, ed. Peter Ganz, pp. 11–26. Bibliologia 4. Turnhout, 1986.

Naumann, H., "Glossen aus Admont." *Zeitschrift für deutsches Altertum und deutsche Litteratur* 64, no. 1 (1927): 77–79.

Nichols, John A. and Lillian Thomas Shank, eds., *Distant Echoes*. Medieval Religious Women. Vol. I. Kalamazoo, MI, 1984.

eds., *Peace Weavers*. Medieval Religious Women. Vol. II. Kalamazoo, MI, 1987.

Nightingale, John, *Monasteries and Patrons in the Gorze Reform: Lotharingia c. 850–1000*. Oxford, 2001.

Norman, Gertrude, *A Brief History of Bavaria*. Munich, 1906.

Ohly, Friedrich, "Ein admonter Liebesgruß." *Zeitschrift für deutsches Altertum und deutsches Literatur* 87 (1956): 13–23.

*Hohelied-Studien. Grundzüge einer Geschichte der Hohelied-Auslegung des Abendlandes bis um 1200*. Wiesbaden, 1958.

Ong, Walter, "Orality, Literacy, and Medieval Textualization." *New Literary History* 16 (1984): 1–12.

Parisse, Michel, "Les chanoinesses dans l'empire germanique (IXe–XIe siècles)." *Francia* 6 (1978): 107–126.

"Les femmes au monastère dans le Nord de l'Allemagne du IXe au XIe siècle." In *Frauen in Spätantike und Frühmittelalter*, ed. Werner Affeldt, pp. 311–324. Sigmaringen, 1990.

Parisse, Michel and Otto Gerhard Oexle, eds., *L'Abbaye de Gorze au Xe siècle.* Nancy, 1993.

Parkes, Malcolm. "Tachygraphy in the Middle Ages: Writing Techniques Employed for *Reportationes* of Lectures and Sermons." In idem *Scribes, Scripts and Readers. Studies in the Communication, Presentation and Dissemination of Medieval Texts*, pp. 19–33. London, 1991. Originally published in *Medioevo e rinascimento* 3 (1989): 159–169.

Petit, Françoise, *La spiritualité des Prémontrés aux XIIe et XIIIe siècles: études de théologie et d'histoire de la spiritualité.* Paris, 1947.

Petroff, Elizabeth Alvilda, ed., *Medieval Women's Visionary Literature.* New York and Oxford, 1986.

Petzolt, Helmut, "Abtei Kitzingen: Gründung und Rechtslage." *Jahrbuch für Fränkische Landesforschung* 15 (1955): 69–83.

Peyroux, Catherine, *The Governance of Women: Double Monasteries in the Early Medieval West.* Ithaca, NY, forthcoming.

Piper, A. J., "The Libraries of the Monks of Durham." In *Medieval Scribes, Manuscripts and Libraries: Essays Presented to N.R. Ker*, ed. M. B. Parkes and Andrew Watson, pp. 213–249. London, 1978.

Powitz, G. and H. Buck, *Die Handschriften des Bartholomaeusstifts und des Karmeliterklosters in Frankfurt-am-Main.* Frankfurt, 1974.

Putnam, George Haven, *Books and their Makers in the Middle Ages.* New York, 1962.

Radspieler, Hans, "Regilind aus Admont, Äbtissin von Bergen und Hohenburg. Reformerin – Lehrerin – Dichterin." *Neuburger Kollektaneenblatt* 115 (1962): 33–48.

Reed, Ronald, *The Nature and Making of Parchment.* Leeds, 1975.

Reuter, Timothy, "The 'Imperial Church System' of the Ottonian and Salian Rulers: A Reconsideration." *Journal of Ecclesiastical History* 33, no. 3 (1982): 347–374.

*Germany in the Early Middle Ages, 800–1056.* New York, 1991.

ed. and trans., *The Medieval Nobility: Studies on the Ruling Classes of France and Germany from the Sixth to the Twelfth Century.* Amsterdam, 1978.

Reynolds, L. G. and N. D. Wilson, *Scribes and Scholars: A Guide to the Transmission of Greek and Latin Literature.* Third edition. Oxford, 1991.

Riché, Pierre, *Education and Culture in the Barbarian West.* Trans. John J. Contreni. Columbia, SC, 1976.

*Les écoles et l'enseignement dans l'Occident chrétien de la fin du Ve siècle au milieu du XIe siècle.* Paris, 1979.

Rinnerthaler, Reinhard, ed., *St Peter in Salzburg: das älteste Kloster im deutschen Sprachraum.* Salzburg, 1986.

Robinson, P. R., "The 'Booklet': A Self-Contained Unit in Composite Manuscripts." *Codicologica* 2, pp. 46–60. Leiden, 1978.

"A Twelfth-Century *Scriptrix* from Nunnaminster." In *Of the Making of Books: Medieval Manuscripts, their Scribes and Readers. Essays Presented to M. B. Parkes*, ed. P. R. Robinson and Rivkah Zim, pp. 77–93. Aldershot, 1997.

Rouse, Richard A. and Mary A. Rouse, "Wax Tablets." *Language and Communication* 9 (1989): 175–191.

Rück, P., ed., *Pergament. Geschichte, Struktur, Restaurierung, Herstellung.* Sigmaringen, 1991.

Ruf, Paul, "Die Handschriften des Klosters Schäftlarn." In *1200 Jahre Kloster Schäftlarn 762–1962*, ed. Sigisbert Mitterer, pp. 21–122. Schäftlarn, 1962.

Schäfer, Karl Heinrich, *Die Kanonissenstifter im deutschen Mittelalter: ihre Entwicklung und innere Einrichtung im Zusammenhang mit dem altchristlichen Sanktimonialentum.* Kirchenrechtliche Abhandlungen 43–44. Stuttgart, 1907.

Schauwecker, Helga, *Otloh von St. Emmeram, Ein Beitrag zur Bildungs und Frömmigkeitsgeschichte des II. Jahrhunderts. StM* 74 (1963): 3–240.

Scheichl, Andrea, "Studien zu Handschriften des 12. Jahrhunderts aus der Stiftsbibliothek Admont." MA thesis, University of Vienna, 1989.

Schieffer, Theodor, *Winfrid-Bonifatius und die christliche Grundlegung Europas.* Freiburg, 1954.

Schilp, Thomas, *Norm und Wirklichkeit religiöser Frauengemeinschaften im Frühmittelalter: die Institutio sanctimonialium Aquisgranensis des Jahres 816 und die Problematik der Verfassung von Frauenkommunitäten.* Veröffentlichungen des Max-Planck-Instituts für Geschichte 137. Göttingen, 1998.

Schmitz, Philibert, *Histoire de l'ordre de Saint-Benoît.* 7 vols. Paris, 1942–1956.

Schneider, Karin, *Gotische Schriften in deutscher Sprache.* 2 vols. Wiesbaden, 1987.

Schreiner, Klaus ed. *Hirsau St. Peter und St. Paul 1091–1991.* Forschungen und Berichte der Archäologie des Mittelalters in Baden-Württemburg 10. 3 vols. Stuttgart, 1991.

Schroll, Mary Alfred, *Benedictine Monasticism as Reflected in the Warnefrid-Hildemar Commentaries on the Rule.* New York, 1941.

Schulenburg, Jane, "Strict Active Enclosure and its Effects on the Female Monastic Experience (ca. 500–1100)." In *Distant Echoes*, ed. John A. Nichols and Lillian Thomas Shank, pp. 51–86. Medieval Religious Women. Vol. I. Kalamazoo, 1984.

Seeberg, Stefanie, *Die Illustrationen im Admonter Nonnenbrevier von 1180. Marienkrönung und Nonnenfrömmigkeit – Die Rolle der Brevierillustration in der Entwicklung von Bildthemen im 12. Jahrhundert.* Imagines Medii Aevi. Interdisziplinäre Beiträge zur Mittelalterforschung 8. Wiesbaden, 2002.

Semmler, Josef, *Die Klosterreform von Siegburg.* Bonn, 1959.

Shailor, Barbara A., *The Medieval Book.* Medieval Academy Reprints for Teaching 28. Toronto, 1991.

Siegwart, Josef, *Die Chorherren- und Chorfrauengemeinschaften in der deutschsprachigen Schweiz vom 6. Jarhundert bis 1160 mit einem Überblick über die deutsche Kanonikerreform des 10. und 11. Jahrhundert.* Freiburg, 1962.

Sims-Williams, Patrick, "Cuthswith, Seventh-Century Abbess of Inkberrow, near Worcester, and the Würzburg Manuscript of Jerome on Ecclesiastes." *Anglo-Saxon England* 5 (1976): 1–21.

"An Unpublished Seventh- or Eighth-Century Anglo-Latin Letter in Boulogne-sur-Mer MS 74 (82)." *Medium Ævum* 48 (1979): 1–22.

*Religion and Literature in Western England, 600–800.* Cambridge, 1990.

Smalley, Beryl, *The Study of the Bible in the Middle Ages.* Notre Dame, IN, 1964.

Smith, Lesley, "Lending Books: The Growth of a Medieval Question from Langton to Bonaventure." In *Intellectual Life in the Middle Ages*, ed. Lesley Smith and Benedicta Ward, pp. 265–279. London, 1992.

Southern, R. W., *The Making of the Middle Ages.* New Haven, 1953.

*Western Society and the Church in the Middle Ages.* New York, 1970.

Spilling, Herrad, "Reinhard von Munderkingen als Schreiber und Lehrer." In *900 Jahre Benediktinerabtei Zwiefalten*, ed. Josef Pretsch, pp. 73–100. Ulm, 1989.

Spindler, Max, *Handbuch der bayerischen Geschichte*. Vols. I and II. Munich, 1967.

Spitz, Hans-Jörg, "Zur Lokalisierung des St. Trudperter Hohenliedes im Frauenkloster Admont." *Zeitschrift für deutsches Altertum und deutsches Literatur* 121 (1992): 174–177.

Spunar, Pavel, "Paleographical Difficulties in Defining an Individual Script." In *Miniatures, Scripts, Collections: Essays Presented to G.I. Lieftinck* 4, pp. 62–68. Amsterdam, 1976.

Stegmüller, Friedrich, *Repertorium biblicum medii aevi*. 11 vols. Madrid, 1950.

Stein, Mark Frederick, "The Religious Women of Cologne: 1120–1320." Ph.D. diss., Yale University, 1977.

Steinböck, Walter, "Die Gründung des benediktinischen Reformklosters Admont." *StM* 84, no. 1 (1973): 52–81.

*Erzbischof Gebhard von Salzburg (1060–1088). Ein Beitrag zur Geschichte Salzburgs im Investiturstreit*. Veröffentlichungen des Historischen Instituts der Universität Salzburg 4. Vienna and Salzburg, 1975.

Stelzer, Winfried, *Gelehrtes Recht in Österreich: von den Anfängen bis zum frühen 14. Jahrhundert*. Mitteilungen des Instituts für Österreichische Geschichtsforschung. Ergänzungsband 26. Vienna, 1982.

Stock, Brian, *The Implications of Literacy: Written Language and Models of Interpretation in the Eleventh and Twelfth Centuries*. Princeton, 1983.

Swarzenski, Georg, *Regensburger Buchmalerei der X. und XI*. Leipzig, 1901.

Talbot, C. H., "St. Boniface and the German Mission." In *The Mission of the Church and the Propagation of the Faith*, ed. G. J. Cuming, pp. 45–57. Cambridge, 1970.

Tellenbach, Gerd, *Church, State and Christian Society at the Time of the Investiture Contest*. Trans. R. F. Bennett. Toronto, 1991.

*The Church in Western Europe from the Tenth to the Early Twelfth Century*. Trans. Timothy Reuter. Cambridge, 1993.

Thompson, James Westfall, *The Medieval Library*. Chicago, 1939.

Tomek, Ernst, "Die Reform der deutschen Klöster vom 10.–12. Jahrhundert." *StM* 32 (1911): 65–84.

Trost, Vera, *Skriptorium: die Buchherstellung im Mittelalter*. Heidelberg, 1986.

Tyroller, S., "Zu den Säkularisationen des Herzog Arnulf." *StM* 65 (1953): 303–312.

Van den Eynde, Damien, *L'oeuvre littéraire de Gérhoch de Reichersberg*. Spicilegium Pontificii Athenaei Antoniani 11. Rome, 1957.

Van Engen, John. *Rupert of Deutz*. Berkeley, 1983.

"The 'Crisis of Cenobitism' Reconsidered: Benedictine Monasticism in the Years 1050–1150." *Speculum* 61 (1986): 269–304.

"The Voices of Women in Twelfth-Century Europe." In *Voices in Dialogue: New Approaches to Women's Cultural History*, ed. Linda Olsen and Kathryn Kerby-Fulton, Notre Dome, IN, forthcoming.

Van Houts, Elisabeth, "Women and the Writing of History in the Early Middle Ages: The Case of Abbess Matilda of Essen and Aethelweard." *Early Medieval Europe* 1 (1992): 53–68.

Verheijen, Luc, *La règle de saint Augustin*. 2 vols. Paris, 1967.

Victor, Benjamin, "Aux origines de la bibliothèque monastique: la distribution du carême." *Scriptorium* 50 (1996): 247–253.

von Borries-Schulten, Sigrid, *Provenienz Zwiefalten. Katalog der illuminierten Handschriften der Württembergischen Landesbibliothek Stuttgart.* Vol. I. Stuttgart, 1987.

von Büren, Veronika, "Le grand catalogue de la bibliothèque de Cluny." In *Le gouvernement d'Hugues de Semur à Cluny. Actes du colloque scientifique international. Cluny, September 1988*, pp. 246–261. Cluny, 1990.

von Hefner, Joseph, "Ueber die Nonne Diemud von Wessobrunn und ihr literarisches Wirken mit einem Facsimile ihrer Handschrift." *Oberbayerische Archiv* 1 (1839): 355–373.

Walter, Joseph, "Les miniatures du codex Guta-Sintram de Marbach- Schwarzenthann (1154)." *Archives Alsaciennes d'Histoire de l'Art* 4 (1925): 1–40.

Warren, Ann K., *Anchorites and their Patrons in Medieval England.* Berkeley, 1985.

Watteck, Nora, *Einsiedler. Inklusen, Eremiten, Klausner und Waldbrüder im Salzburgischen.* Salzburg, 1972.

Wattenbach, Wilhelm, *Das Schriftwesen im Mittelalter.* Third edition. Leipzig, 1896.

Webber, Teresa, *Scribes and Scholars at Salisbury Cathedral, c. 1075–c. 1125.* Oxford, 1992.

"The Patristic Content of English Book Collections in the Eleventh Century: Towards a Continental Perspective." In *Of the Making of Books: Medieval Manuscripts, their Scribes and Readers. Essays Presented to M.B. Parkes*, ed. P. R. Robinson and Rivkah Zim, pp. 191–205. Aldershot, 1997.

Weinfurter, Stephan, *Salzburger Bistumsreform und Bischofspolitik im 12. Jahrhundert.* Kölner historische Abhandlungen 24. Cologne, 1975.

Weinstein, Donald and Rudolph Bell, *Saints and Society: The Two Worlds of Western Christendom: 1000–1700.* Chicago, 1982.

Wemple, Suzanne Fonay, *Women in Frankish Society: Marriage and the Cloister, 500–900.* Philadelphia, 1985.

"Female Monasticism in Italy and its Comparison with France and Germany from the Ninth through the Eleventh Century." In *Frauen in Spätantike und Frühmittelalter*, ed. Werner Affeldt, pp. 291–310. Sigmaringen, 1990.

Werminghoff, Albert, *Geschichte der Kirchenverfassung Deutschlands im Mittelalter.* Hanover and Leipzig, 1905.

Wichner, Jakob, *Geschichte des Benediktiner-Stiftes Admont.* 4 vols. Graz, 1874–1880.

"Das ehemalige Nonnenkloster O.S.B. zu Admont." *StM* 2 (1881): 75–84 (part one) and 288–319 (part two).

*Kloster Admont und seine Beziehungen zur Wissenschaft und zum Unterricht.* Graz, 1892.

Widemann, Josef, "Die Traditionen der bayerischen Klöster." *Zeitschrift für bayerische Landesgeschichte* 1 (1928): 225–243.

Will, Robert, "Les origines de l'abesse Relinde de Hohenbourg." *Archives de l'Église d'Alsace* 37 (1974): 1–12.

Wilson, Katharina M., *Medieval Women Writers.* Athens, GA, 1984.

"The Saxon Canoness: Hrostvit of Gandersheim." In *Medieval Women Writers*, ed. Katharina M. Wilson, pp. 30–63. Athens, GA, 1984.

Wind, Peter, "Zur Lokalisierung und Datierung des Millstätter Psalters." *Codices manuscripti: Zeitschrift für Handschriftenkunde* 8 (1982): 115–134.

Winhard, Wolfgang, *Die Benediktinerabtei Wessobrunn im 18. Jahrhundert.* Munich, 1988.

Wisplinghoff, E., *Die Benediktinerabtei Siegburg.* Germania Sacra 9. Berlin and New York, 1975.

Wolf, Gunther, ed., *Kaiserin Theophanu: Prinzessin aus der Fremde – des Westreichs Große Kaiserin.* Cologne, 1991.

Wolff, C., "Die Gorzer Reform in den Verhältnis zu deutschen Klöstern." *Elsass-lothringisches Jahrbuch* 9 (1930): 95–111.

Wollasch, Hans-Josef, *Die Anfänge des Klosters St. Georgen im Schwarzwald.* Forschungen zur oberrheinischen Landesgeschichte 14. Freiburg im Breisgau, 1967.

Wollasch, Joachim, "Monasticism: The First Wave." In *The New Cambridge Medieval History.* Vol. III, ed. Timothy Reuter, pp. 163–185. Cambridge, 1999.

Zarnecki, George, *The Monastic Achievement.* New York, 1972.

Zeller, Joseph, "Das Prämonstratenserstift Adelberg, das letzte schwäbische Doppelkloster, 1178 (1188) bis 1476. Ein Beitrag zur Geschichte der Doppelklöster, besonders im Prämonstratenserorden." *Württembergische Vierteljahrshefte für Landesgeschichte* 25 (1916): 107–162.

Ziegelbauer, Magnoald, *Historia rei literariae ordinis S. Benedicti.* 4. vols. Augsburg, 1754.

# *Index*

The following abbreviations are used in the index: ab. = abbess, abp. = archbishop, abt. = abbot, bp. = bishop, dk. = duke, emp. = emperor, k = king, St. = saint, pr. = prior. In some cases, supplementary information is included to assist in identification.

Lightning Source UK Ltd.
Milton Keynes UK
UKHW030758210721
387509UK00008B/619

9 780521 792431